PLAYING FOR ENGLAND

The author returns to the pavilion at Hastings after completing
his record-breaking seventeenth century in the 1947 season.

Playing for England

by

DENIS COMPTON

*The Middlesex and England Cricketer
and Arsenal–England Footballer*

SAMPSON LOW, MARSTON & CO., LTD.
25 GILBERT STREET, LONDON, W.1.

First published May 1948
Second impression May 1948
Third impression July 1948
Fourth impression September 1948
Second edition May 1949
Second impression second edition June 1949
Third impression second edition March 1950

*This book is produced in complete conformity
with the Authorised Economy Standards*

MADE AND PRINTED IN GREAT BRITAIN BY PURNELL AND SONS, LTD.
PAULTON (SOMERSET) AND LONDON

To

" YOUNG ENGLAND ",

from whom our future international
cricketers and footballers will be drawn

Contents

CHAPTER I

Contents

Contents

Contents

List of Illustrations

*Captain of School at 12—Jack Hobbs' Influence—
Soccer Trial for England—114 at Lord's—Spotted
by Sir Pelham Warner—Offer to Join Lord's Staff—
I get Hobbs' Autograph—Farewell School.*

MR. MARK MITCHELL, master in charge of the top
form at Bell Lane Elementary School, Hendon,
looked up from the examination papers he had been
marking, stroked his chin, pushed up his glasses until they
rested upon his forehead. His deep brown eyes swept
around the class of thirty boys, in the manner, I thought,
of a hunter looking for game.

Then his eyes met mine!

"I've just been looking at your papers, Compton," he
said in a tone that did not suggest I was altogether in his
favour. "No, I'm not going to be angry with you," he
added quickly, no doubt noticing the alarmed look that
must have shown itself on my face, "but I'm convinced,
after looking through your papers, that you're more interested in sport than schooling. As a matter of fact, lad, I've
been of the opinion that you will one day earn your living
in sport."

One or two of my class-mates chuckled when I burst out
with: "I've already decided to do so, sir!"

Mr. Mitchell, a man of ripe experience, knew boys pretty
well, but, as he later told me, that statement coming from
a twelve-year-old lad standing little higher than a pound's-
worth of coppers took him by surprise, and for a minute
or so he did not reply. Then he gulped: "Good luck,
sonny."

I do not suppose, when he later thought over what I had
said, that Mark Mitchell was altogether surprised. You
see, he had done everything possible to encourage me to

develop my sporting skill, and, by the time I had reached the age of twelve, he had entrusted the captaincy of the cricket and football teams to me. Shortly afterwards, the school paid me the honour of electing me captain.

At the moment, thanks to the exercise demanded by a sporting life, I stand 5 ft. 11 ins. *and weigh* 13 *stone*. When Bell Lane School appointed me their captain I was only 5 ft. 4 ins. tall and tipped the scales at 9 stone.

"It's what's in your frame that counts, not the size of it," Mr. Mark Mitchell said to me when I took over the captaincy of the cricket team, and I have never forgotten those words when playing with, or against, men whose size makes them appear either giants or minnows. Such advice prevents you over-rating or under-estimating your opponents; a most important thing.

Cricket, of course, was my great love in those days, just as it is at the moment. I enjoy football, but cricket is my first and greatest love. I suppose this enthusiasm can be traced to my father, for he had been a cricket enthusiast ever since I can remember, and always found me keen to talk, or argue cricket and go to matches with him.

On Saturday afternoons, after he had finished work for the day, and I had completed Mother's errands (after playing for the school) and after the dinner crocks had been washed, Father and I, sometimes with brother Leslie, used to take the bus to Lord's and watch Middlesex in action. Dad, of course, was an ardent Middlesex supporter, but for me the great enjoyment was studying the great cricketers of 1928–29–30 in action.

My hero? Jack Hobbs, of course! To me there has never been a batsman with the touch of the "Surrey Master". Call it schoolboy idolatry if you like, but with the passing of the years I have never lost my admiration for one of the grandest men it has ever been my pleasure to shake by the hand.

Sometimes, as a special treat, father would take me to Kennington Oval to see Hobbs in action. "When Jack Hobbs is at the wicket, Denis is so quiet you'd never recognise your youngest son," he once said to Mother. Her

2

response was short, and very much to the point. "We could do with him here, then, when Denis is in one of his chatty moods and we want to be quiet!"

Jack Hobbs, of course, was more than just a charmer so far as I was concerned. By watching very carefully, sometimes with the aid of Dad's field glasses, I was able to study the wonderful stroke play of the Surrey batsman. Hobbs, it quickly struck me, had a stroke for every occasion; was rarely, if ever, caught off his guard.

Often, when we arrived home, and it was time for me to go to bed, I would think over the strokes I had seen made by Hobbs. Many a time have I risen after a short time, switched on the light, got hold of a bat, stood in front of the wardrobe mirror, and attempted to emulate Hobbs!

The encouragement of Mr. Mitchell, coupled with the valuable and knowledgeable advice of my father, helped me considerably. I read many books on cricket, too, and in due course found my play considerably improving. I batted right-handed, but for some unaccountable reason, bowled left-handed spinners. As batsman and bowler I opened for the school.

It was in 1930 that I received my first cricketing honour, being selected to play for North London Schools against our great rivals from the South. Etherington, now one of my Middlesex colleagues, was in the North's team with me, while McIntyre, the Surrey batsman–wicketkeeper, was the South's star bowler.

Never shall I forget the proud feeling that came over me when I went out to bat on the Lord's wicket. The pitch, by the way, had been laid out close to the boundary, near the Tavern, and not on a "star wicket", but to me it was everything that Denis Compton had been chosen for this important match!

For longer than I expected, considering their reputation, the South bowlers allowed me to stay at the crease, and when my wicket was finally flattened, 88 runs were credited to my name—on the scoreboard that I was going to help manipulate in years to come.

Playing for England

Later that same season, in another inter-school match—this time played at Leyton, then one of the Essex county grounds—I scored 90, but, so it seemed to me, lacked the stamina to achieve the century that was my great aim.

"Never mind, lad," sympathised Mr. Mark Mitchell, as we made our way home, "it will come. It will come. . . ."

With the conclusion of the cricket season I at once turned my attention towards football. In those days—I suppose it applies even now—I did not count time by months, holidays, and the other normal ways, but in terms of football, and cricket matches . . . who was playing at Lord's or Highbury . . . when the fifth Test was due to be fought out at Kennington Oval. . . .

Well, as I said earlier, football had a place in my heart, even if it was not quite so beloved as cricket, and although only a little fellow, I quickly developed into something of a terrier at left-half-back. My brother, Leslie, had by this time signed professional forms for Arsenal, and, knowing what my mother might say when I eventually announced to her my plans about turning professional sportsman, I kept football "up my sleeve" as a trump card to play at the opportune moment.

Once again good fortune smiled upon me, for after playing for Middlesex Boys, selection for an England Schools team followed. It should be made clear, that although we played against a team bearing the title "Wales" it was not a full international. If anything, the match, played at Bristol, was used by both countries to size up possible players. Anyway, we defeated the Welshmen, 1—0, and I must have done well enough to satisfy the Selectors, for when the teams for the International Trial at Chesterfield were announced, my name was again in the England side.

During the course of the Bristol match I had developed quite an understanding with a tall, well-built left-back from Leeds named Leslie Goldberg—who now plays for Reading. He was a truly fine defender; with him behind me I felt that I must get the coveted cap.

4

Playing for England

Fate, which had hitherto been kind, on this occasion turned against me. Leslie Goldberg had to drop out of the team because of injury and a substitute brought in. Never let it be said that I blame another for a bad game played by myself, but at Chesterfield, as complete strangers, the substitute defender and I understood little of each other's play and before the referee blew his whistle for half-time my heart was heavy, my legs ached, and my head was in a whirl.

Two little fellows who composed "The Rest's" right wing, were responsible for my sorry state. Rarely in the history of schoolboy football has there, in my opinion, been a better wing than that composed by these two small boys from the North-East. At outside-right was Jackie Spuhler, now of Middlesbrough, while his partner was Jimmy Hagan, to-day famous as the England and Sheffield United inside-left, and, strange as it may seem, on ten occasions my team-mate in war-time England international teams.

At Chesterfield, apart from getting three of the four goals "The Rest" scored against our one, Spuhler and Hagan gave as perfect an exhibition of football as I've ever seen. While Spuhler, with his great speed, dashed down the touch-line and then sent in either snorting shots or "goal-asking centres", Hagan, with deft flicks, neat footwork and beautifully-judged passes, made more than one of us opposing him wish we'd stayed at home, sat in front of a roaring fire, and read a book!

The brilliant showing of Hagan and Spuhler, won those two fine sportsmen the international cap they deserved.

What of Denis Compton? That match put the north-country boys in the England team; it resulted in me becoming 12th man against Scotland and Wales!

A disappointment? Yes, it was, but I had not proved myself good enough. At least, that was how I consoled myself, at the same time thinking that being 12th man for England's schoolboy team might be a good reference when the moment arrived for me to think about football as a career during the winter months.

Playing for England

In 1930–31 I played more games of football than ever before, or since, in my life. The effect—at least, I put it down to football—was to add three inches to my height, and when the cricket season commenced in May, 1931, I no longer found myself dwarfed by my opponents. Mind you, I was by no means a giant, but the extra inches I soon discovered of infinite use when it came to making shots that had hitherto proved difficult to accomplish on account of my lack of height.

As a result of some good performances for Hendon, the London Schools Sports Association invited me to play for London Elementary Schools, against the Public Schools, at Lord's. It was an honour I fully appreciated, and I was still more delighted when I was made captain of the side.

Lord's, by now, had become something of a second home to me. Often, as a treat, I would travel together with other boys from Hendon, to have a spell of net-practice at the famous ground. Some of the Middlesex professionals, including Jack Young, now one of my colleagues, frequently stayed behind in their own time to give us hints that later proved of great value. Whenever Middlesex were at home, too, I used to pay my sixpence to watch such giants as Pat Hendren, Jack Hearne and Jack Durston demonstrating their skill. In short, I was well acquainted with Headquarters.

When the morning of the great match arrived I found myself, for the first time in my life, well and truly scared. It was not the kind of nervousness that makes you tremble, but there seemed to be nothing in my stomach; an empty feeling that was not exactly pleasant.

"You'll feel better when you meet Mr. Mitchell," said my mother, as she wished me good-bye, adding with a smile, "and I hope you're pleased with the trousers."

For this match Mother had bought me my first pair of long white flannels.

Father, a short time before, had made me a present of a new pair of white boots, studded them, and in general done everything to help give me the right "cricket atmosphere".

They say that a boy's mother is usually right when it comes to giving her son a piece of advice. Mother was right that day about my nervousness—for when I linked up with schoolmaster Mark Mitchell, all my fears departed and once again a feeling of "I'll show them" formed an important part of my psychological make-up.

When we reached the Grace Gate at Lord's I tried to put on an air of easiness, but inside me my heart was thumping like mad. For the first time in my life I was about to pass through one of the most famous entrances in the world and—what was to me just as important—without having to pay!

"Well?" asked the gateman, as Mr. Mitchell and I made to enter.

"This boy's playing in the match," said Mr. Mitchell, and as the gateman, I thought, looked suspiciously at me, I held my cricket bag in such a way that he could not but help see it, and wriggled through the gap which he grudgingly opened for us.

Hundreds of boys, many of them given a holiday for the occasion, had crowded into Lord's for this match. I remember, as we entered the dressing-room, feeling awed by the surroundings. During the long winter evenings I had read dozens of books about the great men of cricket. Many of them had used the dressing-room in which we changed, and as we prepared for the game I said to some of the lads: "You know, fellows, this room has a great history. We are honoured in being allowed to change here."

No one said anything, for I was the skipper, but on reflection I guess they must have thought their captain was a queer fellow, talking about history. What they wanted to do was to set foot on the Lord's turf to get runs and wickets!

The captain of the Public Schools team was a tall, good-looking young man named E. D. R. Eagar—he is now captain and secretary of Hampshire—we inspected the

7

Playing for England

wicket together, and tossed in true county-style. I said "Heads", guessed correctly, and, as the wicket was first-class, decided to bat.

It's a wonderful feeling to walk from the pavilion out to the middle at Lord's for the first time. In recent years I have been on some of the biggest barrack squares in the country, but they have nothing on Lord's for vastness and when it comes to feeling "lost". As you walk on the well-kept, closely-cut grass, the wicket appears miles away; you wonder whether or not you are taking it too easy or striding so fast that it does not look dignified!

The atmosphere, however, is so friendly, that it does not take one long—and I am now speaking from personal experience—to settle down, and when I faced the Public Schools the awe that was with me when I stepped out of the pavilion quickly departed.

Those young fellows representing the Public Schools, although older than our Elementary School lads, found the London boys a much tougher proposition than they possibly at first anticipated. Many of my team-mates had never owned a cricket bat of their own. On no occasion received any coaching. But what cricketers many of them were! As is the case to-day, the elementary schools all over the country have first-class cricketers if someone only took the trouble to find them.

Anyway, against the Public Schools, I was fortunate enough to score my first century, and when finally the opposing fast bowler got through my defence and knocked back my off-stump, 114 runs stood to my credit.

The return journey to the pavilion was most pleasant. I had accomplished something I never dreamt I would do— score a century at Lord's!

Shortly afterwards, however, when the remaining London batsmen had gone the way of most "tail-enders", it was our turn to field. As I said just now, the Elementary Schools produce fine cricketers. Against the Public Schools they again demonstrated this fact, and we ended the day fairly easy winners.

It so happened that Sir Pelham Warner (then plain "Mr.") chanced to be at Lord's when I made my first century. Sir Pelham, as all the cricket world knows, is a great encourager of young people, and the fact that I was able to get 114 at the age of thirteen, he has since told me, impressed him a great deal. Without my being aware of the fact, Sir Pelham began to make inquiries as to my name, address, background, and plans for the day when I left school. The outcome of this was a meeting with my father and an offer, through him, of a job on the Lord's ground-staff, when I left my lessons.

Only a short time before my brother, Leslie, the Arsenal full-back, had mentioned my soccer ambitions to Mr. Herbert Chapman, the great Arsenal manager. Once again my father had discussed my future with a world-famous sporting figure, received an invitation for me to join the ground-staff at Arsenal Stadium, and decided to talk the matter over with my mother and I.

"Well, Denis," Father said one evening, after he, Mother, and I, had finished tea. "I want to have a talk with you. It won't be so very long now before you leave school and plans for your future must be drawn up. I suppose you have made up your mind what you want to do? Is it still to be sport?"

"Yes," I replied. "Football and cricket are going to be my business with any luck."

Mother was not a bit keen on me developing into a professional sportsman. As a matter of fact if I had not received an offer from Lord's, in addition to Highbury, it is doubtful whether I should have entered the world of sport. Mother, quite wisely, wanted me to have security and favoured a job as a clerk in the local town hall, but Father, with an all-the-year-round position being offered, decided, if I were wise, I should accept the offers from Lord's and Arsenal Stadium.

It was left to me to make the decision, and I needed no urging to sign on the dotted line.

That was in the summer of 1931, and with another nine

9

months' schooling ahead of me I took every opportunity of polishing up my—cricket and football!

Father, as usual, did everything in his power to encourage me. Soon after my 114 at Lord's I received from *The Star*, a well-known London evening newspaper, a beautiful bat signed by Jack Hobbs, as a reward for my innings. In those days *The Star* presented bats to the London schoolboys who performed the best feat of the week. My knock for London Elementary Schools, apparently, was adjudged to have merited the award.

"Having got a Jack Hobbs bat you'll have to try and play like him," said my father. "He'll be batting against Notts at the Oval on August Monday. Let's go down and see him."

A huge crowd had gathered outside the entrance to the famous ground by the time we had crossed London and we found ourselves on the end of a long snake-like queue that stretched for about 200 yards. Father said: "We'll be lucky if we get a good seat. Still, Denis, I've brought my field glasses, so that's one thing in our favour." As fortune would have it, we managed to get quite a fairly good view, and when Jack Hobbs, with his brilliant partner, Andy Sandham, made their way to the wicket, I followed him closely through the field glasses.

That easy walk, kindly face, hawk-like eyes, and elastic-like wrists, will never be forgotten by me and millions of others who admired "The Master".

As fate would have it, Jack Hobbs did not make a century. He was bowled by Barret for 22, but Sandham remained to delight us all with a wonderful assortment of strokes. There have been few batsmen to equal Andy Sandham so far as late-cutting is concerned, and when stumps were drawn for the day, and Father and I commenced to talk over the play, I felt, in my heart, that my cricket education had been considerably enriched.

What is more, I had secured the autograph of Jack Hobbs!

The great batsman was about to enter the pavilion when I stepped into his path, rather timidly, I must admit, and asked him to sign my autograph book. "Of course," said Jack. As he was penning his name the batsman, noting the many other players' signatures, said: "Got quite a lot, haven't you son?" Then, when he had finished, "All right?"

I was too overawed to even say "Thank You!"

Little did I realise that Jack Hobbs, within six or seven years, would be one of my friends. . . .

Quite frequently, at this time, I played at week-ends for Bell Lane Old Boys, a team captained by my father, and during one of my earliest matches I was concerned in a rather unusual incident. As I told you earlier, so tiny was I for my age that quite a number of folk would not believe I could play either football or cricket. "He's too small," they would smile.

On this memorable occasion we were playing at West Hendon, and when the time arrived for me to put on my pads, grip my bat, and go to the wicket, our opponents appeared very surprised when I put in an appearance.

"We cannot play against such a small lad," the opposing skipper said to my father, who was batting at the other end. "It's not fair to our bowlers."

My dad smiled knowingly. "Don't you worry about his lack of inches," he replied. "Carry on and bowl normally."

It was obvious that our opponents were not going to heed Father's words, but after I had knocked four boundaries off their fast bowler, who had reverted to slow spinners when he faced me, they realised that Father knew what he was talking about, and tried hard to get my wicket. In this manner I was able to get in some first-class practice, and, at the same time, collect 40 runs, which helped us win an exciting match.

The season ended with me batting at number four for Bell Lane Old Boys, opening for the school, and in general doing everything possible to prepare myself for the big job ahead: *the job of making good in a profession that has little time for sympathy but heeds only results.*

Playing for England

A football season followed that was not out of the ordinary run of things, then, at Easter, 1932, the moment arrived for me to bid everyone at Bell Lane School farewell.

"I'm glad you've made up your mind what career you plan to follow," said Mr. R. Burgess, my headmaster. "We've been happy to have you here. I know, for your part, you have enjoyed yourself. Best of luck in sport, Denis."

As I had my last walk round the old school I felt a lump in my throat and tears well up in my eyes. I had enjoyed every minute of my school-days; had probably spent more time at cricket and football than at my lessons. They were happy, carefree days.

Then, as I made my way sadly out of the school gate for the last time, something inside of me seemed to say: "You've been waiting for this chance. Set your eye on your goal. Put everything into your efforts."

I have. . . .

*I Become A "Professional"—There's Money in
Selling Score-cards—"Found" by G. O. Allen—
Selected for M.C.C. And Forgot My Kit—A Night
of Worry.*

"WELL, sonny boy, and what do you want? Autographs? You'll have to come back later, there's no match to-day."

The speaker? A big red-faced man wearing a thick blue serge suit, despite a warm sun. The place? The Main Gate at Lord's.

As he looked down at me, big blue eyes twinkling beneath the thickest pair of eyebrows I had seen since George Robey appeared at Golders Green Hippodrome, his giant frame barred my entrance into the famous cricket ground. I pulled myself up to the full of my 5 ft. 7 in., tried very hard to look important, and said: "I have just been given a job on the ground-staff; I wish to see Mr. Phil Edwards."

Once again the big blue eyes twinkled. The body barring my entrance moved slightly aside, and, as I passed, the gateman said: "I don't know why you didn't say earlier you'd come to work here!"

I felt like reminding him he had so dominated the conversation that I had had little chance of saying anything. As a "new boy", however, I thought it better to forget the whole affair and concentrate upon the task of finding Mr. Phil Edwards.

It was the second week in May, 1932. Two weeks before I had said good-bye to my schooldays. Now, following the talk my father had with Sir Pelham Warner after my century at Lord's the previous summer, I had arrived at the great cricket arena to "Report For Duty", as a ground-boy.

Playing for England

As many of you know, Lord's is a vast ground and for some time I found it difficult to locate Mr. Edwards. Eventually one of the ground-staff, after eyeing me up and down after hearing my request, pointed to a building and said: "You'll find Phil Edwards in there." The building, I later learnt, was known as the ground-boys' room, and when I entered it struck me that there were quite a number of lads on similar missions to mine.

After queueing up for a time I eventually found myself facing Phil Edwards. Instantly I took a liking to him. A tiny little fellow only a few inches over 5 ft. with his round, cheery face, long tapering fingers, and rolling walk, he looked more like a jockey than a cricketer. Phil, experience taught me, was known as "Number One Boy". His duty it was to issue the orders received from Groundsman Harry White. Anyway, after taking down particulars regarding my age, address, and the usual answers to stock questions, he introduced me to other ground-boys.

"Remember," said Phil, as he took me around the ground and explained the various jobs that would have to be undertaken, "you have a wonderful opportunity of learning what is, after all, a great science. It will not be easy at first. I'll warn you right now. Pulling a heavy roller, as you will find, is harder than it looks when you're sitting in the crowd. But, lad," and here he patted me on the head, "if you want to become a great cricketer you'll learn more on the ground-staff in six months than you would under a coach in six years."

After Phil Edwards had left me to have my lunch I sat down and took stock of the position in which I now found myself. I had been engaged for sixteen weeks during the summer months at a wage of thirty shillings a week, plus extra for selling match cards. I was to do the hundred-and-one jobs that always need attention on a ground the size of Lord's. During the winter months I had signed up to follow a similar occupation with Arsenal F.C.

At first the life at Lord's appeared to be very hard. I had to report for duty at eight o'clock in the morning and almost at once commence hauling the heavy roller. For just over an hour we ground-lads would tug, moan, grouse, and talk of quitting as we tramped backwards and forwards across the Lord's wicket.

After our fifteen-minute break for a cup of tea, however, we were like men refreshed, and, as we resumed our "pull", we dreamt of the day when we would watch others do this and ourselves knock centuries, or take wickets, on the pitch we were helping to make.

Do not run away with the idea that we were driven about like slaves at Lord's. On the contrary, everyone was thoughtful, kind, and understanding. In addition, too, as one settled down the easy and more pleasant jobs were discovered. For example, a special " treat " meant helping in the score-box. I shall never forget, when first this "honour" went my way, thinking what a wonderful view scorer Bill Mavins had from his lofty perch just beneath "Father Time", and how fortunate I was to land such a good job. It was not until I had to start work in earnest—my jobs included putting up figures denoting bowling changes, the man who made the last catch, the number of wickets that had fallen, and, of course, getting the scorer's tea!—that I realised working in the score-box, although pleasant, was *work*.

On one occasion eight wickets fell in one hour and, believe me, I was probably among the most tired people at Lord's when two "tail-enders" made a stand and so provided me with the opportunity of sitting down and recovering my breath! Running up and down stairs, carrying numbers, and then, almost immediately, repeating the performance, was, believe me, hard work. Still, when I look back, I think what fun it could be.

At this stage, we lads on the ground-staff had been issued with made-to-measure grey-flannel suits and, as we went about our jobs, looked quite smart. As a matter of fact, when I started selling score-cards quite a number of people commented on our "turn-out".

Oh, yes, like so many distinguished cricketers before me,

Playing for England

I have sold score-cards at Lord's! This, you will be interested to know, proved quite a lucrative side-line for the ground-boys. Score-cards are sold at 2*d*. each. For every card sold we used to receive ½*d*., and, as some parts of the ground favoured the sellers, we arranged to pool our profits and share them. The Main Gate was the busiest spot, for spectators, on entering, at once wanted a card. The members' stand was recognised as the "quiet spot".

In 1934, when the Australians played England at Lord's, and Jack Young, Jack Robertson, and Sydney Brown, now my colleagues in the Middlesex team, together with me, helped pull the heavy roller, we often went without our lunch so that we could sell the maximum number of score-cards to the crowd who, even in those "queueless days", were prepared to line up for the valuable pieces of cardboard.

At the end of that Test, as a result of pooling our profits, we ground-lads pocketed £14 6s. 1½*d*. each from selling score-cards.

I might mention that every penny I made out of score-cards went into the bank. Even in those days I was afraid that I might not make the grade as a cricketer and wanted to have something behind me in case I had to try and find another job.

The opportunity of making this extra cash to take home with my thirty shillings a week, was warmly welcomed, but when Walter Hammond batted at Lord's my takings, I'm afraid, fell rather sharply. Yes, you've guessed it, I was a great Hammond fan and willing to sacrifice valuable shillings for the opportunity of watching the master in action.

"How I'd like to bat with him!" I remember saying to Archie Fowler, the Lord's coach, and his reply rather took me off my guard: "You will, if you practise hard," he said.

At this stage Archie Fowler, who had taken over from George Fenner, entered my life as a kind of fairy godfather, and when twice a week we boys were given the opportunity of bowling against each other in the nets, Archie took considerable pains to show me how I should make a certain stroke or improve my technique.

16

Fowler, who has the reputation of being one of the finest coaches in the world, really looks the part. He is stocky, broad-shouldered, grey-haired, kindly-faced, and possessor of a quiet voice that simply oozes authority. When Archie, who is now fifty-two years old, says the stroke you made was bad he says it in such a way that you cannot help but agree with him! He had also mastered that most difficult art of being able to pass on the knowledge he has accumulated over many years in such a manner that even the most slow-witted lad can understand and appreciate.

Like Sir Pelham Warner, who has kept his word and given me every opportunity to make good, Archie Fowler from the first has made it clear that he believed in me. It was he who first mentioned me as a promising lad to G. O. Allen, the famous Test captain, who one afternoon came with Sir Pelham and Archie Fowler and watched me at practice in the nets. Not a word was said, but, as the group moved on, turned, watched me for a few more minutes, I sensed that they were talking about Denis Compton!

A few days later, when I was again in the nets, G. O. Allen came and stood behind me. I must confess that a feeling of self-consciousness came over me, and twice I was nearly bowled!

"Don't worry about me, son," said G. O. Allen, "play your natural game."

The friendly tone of his voice, plus the knowledge I knew he possessed, gave me confidence, and for the remainder of the afternoon I tried hard to follow the advice given by the Test cricketer standing behind the stumps.

Soon after this incident the famous amateur decided to try his hand at bowling against me. Within a very short time I realised how much I had to learn, but G. O. Allen, a great encourager of young cricketers, went out of his way to explain where I went wrong; how I should play a certain shot.

When first I joined the Lord's ground-staff I went into what was known as the "Fourth Class" for ground-boys. Next season I rose to the "Third Class". The following year

Playing for England

I missed the second class and went into the "First Class". This meant, for the most part, I had few other duties but playing cricket, mostly for M.C.C. teams when they had away fixtures, and bowling to M.C.C. members in the nets.

Early in 1935, three years after "joining up" at Lord's, I had the rare opportunity—and honour for me as a youngster—to meet P. G. H. Fender. For years, long before I can even remember, the Surrey amateur has been known as one of the wiliest bowlers in cricket. When, one afternoon, he arrived at Lord's and asked Archie Fowler if he could find someone to bat against him, the Lord's coach at once suggested me. After Fowler had introduced me to P. G. H. Fender the former Surrey captain said: "You don't mind me bowling a few balls to you?"

I fear the great all-rounder's reputation rather overawed me, for I mumbled something that should have been "Yes, sir," donned my pads, and walked over to the nets with "P.G.H." Two or three years ago I had lined up for hours to watch him bat and bowl. Had waited patiently for his autograph. Been among his greatest admirers.

Now I found myself facing him in the nets!

It did not take me long to appreciate that Fender was a bowler in a class well above that I have ever met before. As he gripped the ball with his long tapering fingers, shuffled up to the wicket, swung his arms, and made his wrist turn like a cartwheel, you could never be sure what was going to happen. Since that May afternoon I have faced many great bowlers. Fender still ranks among the best.

Leg-breaks and "googlies" were his specialities that afternoon and twice he hit my stumps; on more occasions than I can remember he beat me all ends up when, according to the rules as I knew them at the time, the ball should have met the middle of my bat!

"Well played, lad," "P.G.H." said, after he had put in a good spell of bowling. "Keep up the good work."

After that experience Coach Archie Fowler was very pleased, but was quick to stress that I should not think I knew it all. "You've still a great deal to learn, Denis," he said. "Don't be afraid to ask, either, if you're not sure of anything."

I took advantage of that offer which, to this day, remains in force! As a point of interest, Archie Fowler used to bring along to face me all the good bowlers he could find. The result of this was that I found myself getting experience of top-class bowling without even appearing in top-class cricket, although I did not need convincing that net practice and the real things were miles apart.

The training and experience gained in the nets at Lord's, however, paid me in good stead when I began to play in their bigger games for the various teams I assisted.

"Just go on the way you are and your big chance will not be so far off," Archie Fowler said to me, early in 1935. "Practice, remember, is your biggest friend."

I remembered all right. Even when I was not at Lord's but in my own little room at home, I read, talked, and dreamt cricket. I used to practise strokes in front of the mirror, read all the books I could buy on the great players and study carefully press photographs of the leading batsmen.

I have learnt much more than most people would believe from photographs!

Well, a short time after Archie Fowler had made his forecast—maybe he knew something at the time, but he has never told me this was so—I found myself selected to play for the M.C.C. against Suffolk at Felixstowe.

I have always tried hard to keep cool, but, as soon as the news was given me I rushed home to mother, banged hard at the front door, stamped about impatiently as I waited for it to be opened, and when finally she could leave the jam-tarts she was cooking to open the door, I burst out with "It's happened, mother, I've been selected to play for the M.C.C.!"

She patted me on the back, her flour-tipped fingers leaving a mark on my sports coat, and said: "Well done, Denis. Be sure, though, that you take everything with you."

Playing for England

That remark, although well-meant, made me wince. You see, it happened to be true. I was always forgetting things and my family's hope that I might grow out of this unfortunate habit as I grew older was real and anxious.

For this particular match at Felixstowe the M.C.C. included three professionals, the others, apart from myself, being George Brown, the former Hampshire and England batsman, and Jim Powell of Middlesex.

Mother, as usual, took great delight in making sure that my shirt was as white as the proverbial lily; that my flannels were cleaned. Father looked over my boots, whitened them until they looked almost new. Then, watched by my parents, I packed away my kit in an almost ritual-like manner. First into the bag loaned me by my old schoolmaster went the Pat Hendren bat, which had cost me thirty shillings, and had been autographed by the little England master. Pads, which had cost me a similar sum followed, together with shirt, gloves, flannels, socks and boots.

This ceremony complete, I shouldered the bag, somewhat proudly, climbed aboard the bus that took me to Lord's, and then left my bag at headquarters.

"I'll be back for it," I told them in the office.

A few hours later I was aboard the train bound for Felixstowe and the match that was for me the most important in my life. George Brown, a man of ripe experience, one of the biggest humourists in cricket, but very human, was one of my travelling companions. Like so many other professional sportsmen of long experience, he had acquired that wonderful ability to " father " and advise a youngster. In my case he did this by mixing a little sound advice with a great deal of good humour. Although I frequently laughed at his sallies and jokes there was something at the back of my mind that kept me worried. What it was I could not for the life of me discover. But when I endeavoured to convince myself that everything was as it should be, something inside me disagreed.

As the train was running into Felixstowe, and my teammates rose from the seats and grabbed their bags from the

Photo : Central Press

An aerial view of Lord's.

Photo : Central Press

George Brown, Hampshire and England cricketer.

racks, it suddenly dawned on me what was at the back of my mind and proving so worrying.

I had forgotten to collect my cricket bag! While I was in Suffolk, about to play in a match that meant more to me than anything else, my bag was where I had left it—in the office at Lord's!

I must confess I thought it would have been brought along with the rest of the kit but, although this may not have sounded a very strong argument at the time, our skipper was prepared to accept it, and I wired Lord's asking them to forward my bag.

Back came the reply: "Bag on the way. You'll leave your head behind one day."

They obviously knew their man!

The cricket ground at Felixstowe is one of the prettiest in the country. It is oval in shape, fringed by trees that are among the greenest I have ever seen, has a perfect wicket, and one of the friendliest crowds I have met.

As fate would have it, the M.C.C. wickets fell quickly and the one man on either side without a bat, shirt, trousers, or boots, found that he was due to take his place at the wicket. Remember, I was only seventeen years old at the time, a boy among men who knew how to play cricket, and to say that I was embarrassed as a result of my thoughtlessness is an understatement.

All I wanted to do was hide from my team-mates whom I thought must have looked upon me as a woolly-headed young fool.

It was big-hearted George Brown, however, who came to the rescue.

Standing 6 ft. 3 ins., with shoulders nearly as broad, and feet that must rival Maurice Tate's for size and distinction, George Brown, although I felt rather depressed, made me smile when he suggested that I should wear his kit.

"But George," I explained, "it's like Oliver Hardy offering his suit to Stan Laurel. It just won't fit."

Brown looked at me seriously, then replied: "Put them on, Denis. Make a go of it until your own kit comes." This said, he walked from the dressing-room, leaving behind a neatly folded pair of trousers, clean shirt and cricket boots.

George, as I said earlier, stood 6 ft. 3 ins. I was by now 5 ft. 8 ins. Brown's boots were a size 10½, mine were "8s." As I "clambered" into the shirt it felt as if a circus tent had collapsed and draped itself around me. To see my hands I rolled up the sleeves what might have been yards; to find the feet that disappeared from view when I donned Brown's trousers, I turned the pants up about twelve inches. Then, on to my feet I placed the boots that were two sizes too large for me. They had, it is true, been literally packed in the toes with paper, but I did not feel exactly comfortable with my toes threatening to poke their way through the point where the tongue links with the boot!

Still, I thought, beggars cannot be choosers, and after struggling into George Brown's pads—which appeared a little tight under my arms!—and taking a grip upon a bat he loaned me, I prepared to take my place at the wicket.

Quite a number of people smiled, not unkindly, mind you, when I went to the wicket. I must have appeared almost Heath Robinson-like with my shirt sleeves rolled up and the rest of the garments looking as if a parachute had suddenly settled upon my shoulders. As for the bat, it was so heavy that I almost needed both hands to lift it, let alone swing it.

"Well, Denis," I said to myself, as I took centre, "you asked for punishment, forgetting your bag, and you're certainly getting it."

What happened next? No, I did not surprise everyone by scoring a century. On the contrary, the first ball I received flashed by the tree-trunk George Brown wielded so effectively, and knocked back my middle-stump with a thwack!

"Better luck next time, lad," said George Brown, as he entered the dressing-room, bitterly disappointed. "You'll do better when your kit arrives."

In my heart I knew that it was imperative that I should get runs at the second time of asking, and, when my kit arrived, and I realised we would have to bat again, I made sure everything was perfect before again going to the crease.

Well, to my delight, and to George Brown's satisfaction, I managed to score 110, but, if I felt delighted I was pulled up with a jerk when, in extracting my handkerchief from a pocket the telegram from Lord's came out with it, and once again I read: "You'll leave your head behind one day!"

My absent-mindedness, on reflection, might well have seriously interfered with my cricket career.

By now the Middlesex C.C.C. officials were beginning to take notice of me, and early in the 1935 season I found myself being invited to assist the County's second eleven in Minor Counties matches. Among my colleagues were Jack Young, Jack Robertson, Len Muncer, and Bill Watkins, all former ground-boys and later to become County players, and with them I had quite a lot of fun, at the same time taking another step forward in learning my business of being a good cricketer. As a matter of fact, although hoping it would not be so long, I was quite prepared to wait another four years before being given an opportunity in the County side.

Then, one morning, after reporting for duty at Lord's, I found myself confronted by Archie Fowler, the coach. He was all smiles, looked very pleased with himself, and the very least I thought could have happened to Archie was that he had been left a small fortune.

"Denis," he said, still smiling, "G. O. Allen has asked me to tell you that you're going with the 12 to Maidstone to-morrow. Best of luck, lad!"

I know I muttered my thanks, but, for the moment, I could not say anything more. When I fully realised the significance of his remark I packed my bag, said farewell to the lads, and hurried home.

"Well, what's happened now?" asked Mother, as I bustled into the kitchen, where she was cooking our tea. "Forgotten something else?"

"No," I replied, "but I'm to go with the team to play against Kent to-morrow. Is Dad likely to be long?"

Playing for England

"No," replied Mother, "but he'll be pleased to hear what you've got to tell him."

Sure enough my father, who had coached me from my earliest days, felt as proud as if he'd been awarded his county cap when I told him the news, and, over tea, and late into the evening, we discussed "Tich" Freeman, Wally Ashdown, Leslie Ames, Brian Valentine, and other mighty men of Kent who would be facing me the following day. "Don't be overawed, Denis," said Father, "you can do it."

That night, as I lay in my bed, sleep did not come easily. I dozed off occasionally, only to wake up with a start and wonder just how "Tich" Freeman might be played, and so start up a chain of thought that usually ended in a short bout of uneasy slumber.

When the morning dawned, however, I felt as fresh as a young daisy, made sure I had my bag carefully packed, and, with Father by my side, went to our meeting-place. Within an hour we were on the train and bound for Maidstone.

The previous night there had been a heavy fall of rain, but, after our skipper had inspected the wicket, I was not altogether prepared for what would happen. Then someone broke the news to me.

"As the wicket will suit Jack Young's bowling you'll be twelfth man," they said.

To say that I was bitterly disappointed is putting it mildly, but when Jack Young began to get among the wickets I realised that the right thing had been done.

At the same time I wondered just how long it would be before once again I would have the honour of being considered for a place in the Middlesex County side, and the thought made me worry a little.

Had I but known what the future held for me my fears would never have developed as they did. . . .

3

*My first chance in County Cricket—These Yorkshire-
men are Great Players—I get a Duck—and a
Century—How Kent "Robbed" Me of Two Hundreds—Cricket Becomes a Strain—Travelling
Through the Night.*

I DO NOT know why I should have felt this way, but
when reporting at Lord's for duty in May, 1936, something inside of me seemed to say: "This is to be your
big chance. Take it with both hands."

By now I was on the first-class ground staff—on an
M.C.C. contract—and this meant, when I assisted Middlesex
C.C.C. I received match money but lost the fee paid me
by the M.C.C. As things worked out quite well financially,
however, I was not perturbed, and when the great moment
did arrive for me to make my County début, I was simply
bubbling over with enthusiasm.

There was something dramatic about my first appearance
in county cricket; something that will always make me
remember the occasion and date of the match. It happened
like this.

On Whit-Saturday, when Middlesex were due to meet
Sussex, I walked into the players' dressing-room to have a
talk with some of the men who were now my friends to be
greeted by Jack Durston, the well-known fast bowler, with:
"Denis, you're playing to-day for Middlesex. The very best
of luck."

If I stood looking at him with open-mouthed amazement
I hand it to Jack Durston for not making any comment.
The fact of the matter was that I had experienced one of the
greatest shocks in my young life. I was to play for my County.

Then Archie Fowler, with Jack Robertson and Jack
Young, two particular friends of mine, came up to wish me

luck, a gesture I deeply appreciated. After this, and as soon as I could get away from the dressing-room for a moment, I went to the nearest telephone, got through to my parents, and told them the news. Naturally they were elated, promised to get ready and rush to Lord's. This task completed, I left word at the gate that they were to be cared for, and then returned to the Middlesex dressing-room.

During the past few weeks I had been batting quite well, and assumed that the Middlesex folk were going to try me out because of my run-getting possibilities. Imagine my surprise, then, when the batting list came in and it was noted that I was at number 11.

In other words I had been selected on account of my slow left-arm bowling!

There is always a huge crowd at Lord's during the holidays, and this Whit-Saturday was no exception. Fortunately for me, because of my football experience, the size of a crowd did not put my nerves on edge, and in next to no time I had forgotten its existence in the excitement of my first County match.

I looked around me at the experienced cricketers who were my colleagues. There was R. W. V. Robins, our skipper, a great leader for discipline, a truly grand cricketer, and a man who when I was young, and perhaps a little impetuous, taught me things that have since proved invaluable. G. O. Allen, another former England captain, was to become one of my leading mentors; he was kindness itself. Then, of course, there was Pat Hendren, high on the list of my schoolboy idols, who was always anxious to give me a valuable hint; Joe Hulme, great Arsenal and England footballer, an all-round cricketer of considerable skill; Fred Price, the stumper, who would frequently give me a word of advice when I was fielding in the slips, and Big Jim Smith, the fast bowler, a fine man who never got upset when a catch was dropped off him. These gentlemen, among others, were the cricketers with whom I was to grow up, and, as you will gather, they all went out of the way to try to help me, a seventeen-year-old product of the ground-staff.

Sussex, at this time, were a strong side, and when R. W. V. Robins tossed me the ball as first change bowler, I accepted this as something of a compliment and got to work with enthusiasm.

From the first one thing impressed itself upon me—the scientific placing of the field in county cricket. Our skipper, after a talk with me, put the fielders in the position he thought would best suit the style of bowling to which I was committed, and, in next to no time, I realised that if a man does bowl to the field set for him, that the opposing batsman, no matter how brilliant he might be, does not find runs come easily.

Without bowling sensationally, I plugged away and eventually, to my delight, got the wicket of Harry Parks, that very steady Sussex batsman, after he had scored 50. I was naturally elated at this success, but the skipper, wisely I think on reflection, shortly afterwards gave me a rest, and before the end of the day had dismissed Sussex and seen our own men go to the crease.

On Whit-Monday the "House Full" notices were outside Lord's and inside the headquarters of cricket the great crowd were having as thrilling an exhibition as it is possible to get. It was thrust and counter-thrust between batsmen and bowlers. Nothing was being given away on either side, and when the time for me arrived to join G. O. Allen at the wicket, we still required 20 runs to pass the Sussex total.

I could feel thousands of eyes turned in my direction as I made for the players' gate. I have no doubt that a large number of the spectators felt sorry for me, a seventeen-year-old having to face such an ordeal in my first County game, but, strange as it may seem, considering my youth, I felt very cool once I stepped on to the ground.

On my way through the pavilion, though, my heart bumped, and it seemed to me as if my legs might buckle at any moment!

Playing for England

G. O. Allen, who was to prove a very great friend, walked forward from the crease to meet me half-way from the pavilion. He smiled a greeting, then said: "You'll be all right, Denis, it's not so very difficult, but here is a word of advice you'll find useful. Play forward to Maurice Tate. Good luck."

As I walked by Tate, the great Sussex and England bowler grinned, then said: "Good luck, Denis, but don't forget I'm going to try and get you out."

After I had taken guard, and prepared for action, one thing caught my eyes and held them. It was Tate's boots! From my earliest days I had read, and heard, much about Tate's huge boots. Now, for the first time, I was getting a close-up of them!

My thoughts in this direction were shaken when I suddenly saw Tate commence to bowl. The ball swished through the air, it passed my bat as I played BACK, and zipped over the top of the stumps. The second ball did the same thing, and again I played BACK. Glancing up-wicket I saw G. O. Allen, a smile on his face, going through the action of playing forward, so wisely, when Tate hurled down one of his "specials", I went forward to it, and felt the ball meet the middle of my bat.

It was a wonderful feeling, to hit the ball for the first time in a top-class match, gave me confidence, and next delivery I sent the ball to third man for a single.

Slowly but surely, G. O. Allen and I, by means of singles and an occasional couple, crept up towards the Sussex total. Once, too, I managed to crack one of Jim Parks' very rare inaccurate deliveries to the boundary, and when finally we did manage to pass the Sussex total, a cheer went up that might have been heard across London at Kennington Oval. Eventually, with my score at 14, I "walked into" a straight one from Jim Parks and was justly given out, lbw. Altogether G. O. Allen and I had put on 36 for that last-wicket, giving us a lead of 13, and as I passed Maurice Tate, on my way back to the pavilion, the great bowler gave me a broad grin and said, "Well played, boy!"

Those few words, I can assure you, meant a great deal to me.

But then, no young cricketer could have received more encouragement than I did. G. O. Allen, Pat Hendren, and Archie Fowler, all gave me a pat on the back. Sir Pelham Warner, the man chiefly responsible for me making cricket my career, sent to me the first of many telegrams of congratulations.

Naturally I hoped that my first appearance in the Middlesex side would result in a win, but in this direction I was doomed to disappointment, for although I managed to get another wicket in Sussex second innings—this time that of Alan Melville, destined to captain South Africa in Test cricket—Sussex forced a draw.

At home in the evening, with my first County match completed, father, a keen club cricketer, ran through the game with me. We talked for a long time, discussing every aspect of the match: the mistakes made by me as a bowler and batsman; tactics adopted by opposing bowlers. In general, finding out as much as possible, in the light of my experience, that would prove of use in the future.

Apparently I must have satisfied the Middlesex selectors, for when the team to meet Nottinghamshire, in the next match, was announced, I was once again included.

Never forget I was still a youngster, and the thought that I was to meet such great bowlers as Harold Larwood and Bill Voce—men whom I had but a short time before sought for their autographs—as opponents, gave me a kick it is impossible to put into print. I was terrifically elated—until I realised that these two Nottingham men were ranked among the greatest of all bowlers. Then, for one lingering moment, I wondered, after all, if I had taken on more than I could handle.

The Middlesex batting list, though, gave me heart, for I had been promoted to number eight, and this gesture struck me that certain folk must have confidence in my ability. When, therefore, the time arrived for me to go to the wicket and face the distinguished "Nottingham Twins"

Playing for England

—as Larwood and Voce were known—it was by no means with an inferiority complex.

To play against Larwood and Voce was an experience I would not have missed for worlds. Without argument they are the most accurate pair of pace-bowlers I have ever faced, and Larwood, the fastest. The man who made headlines so often, and is claimed by many to be the speediest bowler of all time, hurled down his "thunder-bolts" with an accuracy that made me nippier on my feet than Alex James. I soon realised that the only way to cope with Harold Larwood is to "stand up" to him.

A batsman who hesitated to do this invariably fell to the great king of speed.

Voce, too, was the left-handed counterpart of Larwood, and between them they made up an opening attack that had no equal in the country.

Both, also were humorous fellows in their way, and on this occasion, when I stood up to Harold Larwood, and then hooked him for three fours, the Notts man gave me such an old-fashioned look I nearly burst out laughing.

Having heard balls whistle past my head so quickly I feared ear-ache from the draught!—and yet carried my bat for 26—I felt quite satisfied with myself. On account of this knock, too, I was promoted to number three in the batting order, but this time things did not work out quite so well, Larwood getting me lbw after I had scored fourteen.

Middlesex, to my delight, won this match, but, from my point of view, I had learnt something that I have never forgotten, and which had since become such a dominant feature on my cricket outlook. It was this: Never, if you can avoid it, give the bowlers an opportunity to think they are on top. Stand up to them, and whenever possible, hit them hard. It is a sound policy and invariably pays good dividends.

In my first two matches for Middlesex, although I had done nothing sensational, the steadiness in which I had gone about things made me feel confident I would in due course make the grade. Anyway, I told myself, I haven't yet made a "duck". But this doubtful honour was not so very far away, for in the next match, against Northamptonshire, after being promoted to number 7, Partridge snapped me up off a fast ball from "Nobby" Clark—for 0.

Back in the dressing-room I felt rather crestfallen, but it was then that experienced colleagues such as Pat Hendren, Joe Hulme and Jim Smith, proved how valuable it is to have such men among youngsters. They pointed out that there was no disgrace in getting a "duck", that everyone had that experience at some time or another. In fact, they were so kind and helpful that I began to feel that I had really done well!

In the second innings, Austin Matthews and "Nobby" Clark bowled magnificently for Northamptonshire, and we had lost five wickets for 21 runs when I joined R. W. V. Robins at the wicket, and quickly, to my delight, I got off the mark, and with the skipper encouraging me, as only he can, began to find my club cricket form. Matthews, especially, bowled like a champion, but by following my belief that the best way to play a really good bowler is to stand up to him, I found the runs began to come. With my score at 87 I felt well on the road towards getting my first century.

But not yet, for once again I cocked up a catch off Clark, and this time Timms took it without difficulty. For the fifth wicket, however, I had put on 129 runs with the skipper, and we won by 283 runs, but how I wished that I had made that century.

All the time, however, I was learning the art of playing cricket. Every match was an education in itself, and when we met Yorkshire, at Lord's, it was to prove by far my best lesson.

These men from the north take their cricket far more seriously than most people in the south. It is a game to be won—and the Yorkshiremen, from the moment they set foot on the field, are all out to defeat their opponents. This is as it should be. From the moment I first met them, it struck me that they must be just about the keenest cricketers in the world. There was a "zip" about their fielding that stamped them as being above the ordinary; nothing was given away; and the slightest chance was promptly seized.

In short, the Yorkshiremen were the perfect cricket machine.

What of their bowlers? Let us first examine Hedley Verity, that grand gentleman who lost his life while fighting in Italy. Verity, one of the best left-handed spin-bowlers of the century, kept a wonderful length for long periods, and the power of concentration needed to play him was, to say the least, most tiring. In fact, Verity eventually made some batsmen so fed-up by tying them down that they decided to "have a go", and promptly found themselves back in the pavilion.

Hedley Verity's greatness was his ability to appreciate when a batsman such as this was on the point of "blowing up". Then he sent down a ball, wrapped up in guile, that made the batsman destroy himself.

Bill Bowes was of a different type. He may not look so very fast from the ring. As a matter of fact I had often wondered why Bowes had been described as among our quickest bowlers—until I faced him at Lord's. The secret of Bowes' success is that he can make the ball come off the pitch at terrific speed. This, allied with his immaculate length, made him one of England's greatest bowlers for many seasons.

I know, when I met Verity for the first time, it did not take me long to understand that here was a bowler with a difference. All the time you faced him you had the feeling he was "sizing you up" just as one boxer does another. Then—wham!—when least you expected it he sent down a ball that got your wicket. That is what happened to me, when I had scored 26. Maybe I was feeling a little confident when I opened my shoulders at a ball that seemingly asked to be clouted to the boundary, and came a dull click behind me.

I had been bowled!

For ever after that, whenever Hedley Verity and I were

to cross bat and ball, the Yorkshireman, so far as I was concerned, was treated with the greatest possible respect!

Experience against such teams as Yorkshire, if a cricketer does wish to make progress—and I most certainly did!—is worth more than years of coaching in the nets. After this match, I felt a little better cricketer, and against Gloucester, who followed Yorkshire to Lord's, I scored 35 and 81. In fact, the young chap who entered the Middlesex side as a bowling "hope", like so many cricketers before him, was finding most success as a run-getter instead of taker of wickets!

Wisely, as I now appreciate, the Middlesex club were not putting me in early every match. They realised that a series of low scores might well upset such a young cricketer, so, after a spell among the top batsmen, I was once more sent in among the "tail-enders". Against Northamptonshire, whom we next visited at Northampton, this tactical move on our skipper's part was to prove a great success, for after we had dismissed Northampton for 298, they set about our batsmen and had sent the stars back to the pavilion for a small score by the time I went in at number "eight".

It was a good hard wicket and Austin Matthews—yes, the same fellow who later bowled so magnificently for Glamorgan—made the ball come off the pitch at great speed. It was not until Jim Sims, who was number "ten", joined me at the wicket that we were able to make any progress. Altogether Jim Sims, who supported me like a guardian angel, helped me put on 76, and when he went, after scoring 31 valuable runs, Ian Peebles took his place at the crease.

Now Ian Peebles, a Test match bowler, had never claimed to be a batsman, but that June afternoon, when he went to the wicket, and noted how well-set I was, I know he felt what a pity it would be if, because of him, I did not get the century I so badly wanted. So, while I attacked the bowling, Ian Peebles, apart from scoring an occasional run, was content to keep an end up. How well he succeeded. In fact, when my score stood at 96, and most folk felt that

Playing for England

I would probably take things easy, I was so excited at our stand against such good bowling that I stepped out to the next ball and sent it through the covers for four.

A century was now beside my name on the score-board. As I watched Ian Peebles applauding my effort, I could not but help say to myself—"Thanks a lot, Mr. Peebles, for proving such a great colleague."

Two balls later Ian Peebles was bowled for 11. Together we had made a stand of 74, no mean effort for the last wicket, and the Northamptonshire players, grand sportsmen, were the first to congratulate us. Vallence Jupp, who was then the Northants skipper, presented me with the ball, specially mounted, and inscribed:

"To Denis Compton on scoring his first century in first-class cricket."

That ball, I might add, holds pride of place, along with my other souvenirs, on a sideboard in the dining-room of my Kenton home.

At the same time Sir Pelham Warner, who had become my "Fairy Godfather" in cricket, sent me another wire. "Hearty congratulations on the first," he said.

I liked "the first" passage best. It at least proved that someone thought I was capable of doing it again!

That first century, of course, ranks among my great moments in cricket. I well remember, as soon as the match was over, rushing home, booking seats at the local theatre, and taking my mother as a celebration treat. It was a great thrill this; so was the greeting I received from Archie Fowler, the coach, when I next went into Lord's. "I knew you could do it," he said. "Well done!"

This was praise indeed, for Archie Fowler, a great coach, knew well enough that if you commenced praising a youthful cricketer too much it would not help him improve. I was not different to any other. The praise, therefore, came, as I said earlier, in the nature of a special treat.

Although I had by now begun to settle down in County cricket, I quite realised that there was much I had to learn. As a matter of fact, in the years that have passed, it has impressed itself upon me that you can never know all there is to learn about the science of cricket. To try to prepare myself for the future, and improve my style for the present, I still spent hours in the nets when the opportunity presented itself.

Sometimes Archie Fowler would stand behind me and give me a word of advice. Often, in the nicest possible manner, he would explain some fault I had developed. But Archie, ever observant, could see that I was willing to learn and had not got a "big head" because of my Middlesex appearances.

That was one thing, above everything else, I was determined to avoid. Once any youngster allows himself to develop false ideas as to his own worth he is finished—and, believe me, it was not my intention to end up in that manner.

My colleagues, too, never allowed me to forget that I was a young man making my way in the game, and I think I am a better chap for it. Without a doubt, too, it helped my game, and made me look upon my cricket as one of the greatest joys of my life.

It remains that way.

A happy frame of mind, especially if you happen to be a cricketer, is half the battle. Largely because of the kindness of everyone in my first season in County Cricket, I could not have felt better towards the world. This outlook, I know, began to show itself in my play, and when we met Kent at Maidstone—where the previous season I nearly made my debut—I felt like a million dollars and fit to score a thousand!

The fact that I had to face "Tich" Freeman, the little "giant of spin" did not unduly worry me, for I had, as a youngster, spent hours watching him in action and like so many much better batsmen than myself, had a theory that he was not so difficult as he looked providing you attacked him. At this stage, as you will notice, I had "attack mania", and when the time came for me to have a crack I went to the wicket determined to try out my luck. What is more,

35

it "came off", and I rattled up 87 before Wally Ashdown, who had been watching me, went up to his skipper and said: "Give me the ball, skipper, he's going to be my rabbit."

And this was no idle boast on Wally Ashdown's part, the Kent all-rounder DID get me out.

In the second innings, when I was again dreaming of a century, it was "Tich" Freeman, the little fellow who could almost make a ball apologise to you for knocking out your middle-stump, who brought to an end my dream of another century. I was well-set, and 96 runs stood against my name when "Tich" sent down an innocent-looking delivery. Like Hedley Verity, the Kent man was a great "kidder", and this time he completely outpointed me, for in trying to glide the ball down the leg side I was magnificently caught behind the wicket by Howard Levett.

By now, with the football season not so very far off, I was beginning to feel the strain of County Cricket. When, at the beginning of June, some of the more experienced players told me that I would feel tired inside two months I was amused, but they were correct. Professional cricket can be most tiring, for it asks much of a man, six days a week, and, if you are scoring runs, and spending long hours at the wicket, taxes your stamina to the utmost.

The long hours of travel, if you are not used to it, can also make a man weary, and this experience of near-exhaustion first came my way after we had played Somerset at Taunton. The following morning, believe it or not, Middlesex were due to meet Yorkshire at Scarborough, so we had to travel through the night.

That journey will for ever remain among the worst travel experiences of my life—and don't forget I've served in India with the Army!—and to while away the time we talked, read, played cards, dozed, in due course arriving at five o'clock on Saturday morning.

It was a red-eyed, tired set of cricketers who went to the Scarborough ground on the morning of the match, all of them hoping that Middlesex would win the toss and so give us the chance of batting, and, at the same time, an opportunity to catch up with the sleep of which we had lost so much the previous night.

But Yorkshire won the toss, and into the field we had to go. It was like leading sheep to the slaughter, and Herbert Sutcliffe, one of the players I had idolised from my earliest days, scored a brilliant 202. It was a wonderful knock, but we could not fully appreciate it, after our long night journey.

On reflection, that was one of the most disappointing moments of my career, for I had been looking forward with the utmost enthusiasm to studying the great Herbert Sutcliffe in action. A train journey robbed me of something, I feel sure would have ranked among my cherished memories.

That first season in County Cricket, however, had been fairly successful. I had scored 1,004 runs—the thirty I secured against Lancashire with my last knock of the season assuring me of this, and had an average, for 31 innings—three times not-out—of 34.62.

But, as I packed away my gear for the season, and prepared to resume my football career with Arsenal, one thought was in my mind: to do even better next summer.

In 1936 I had got my big chance, had taken it with both hands, and, slowly but surely, gained vital experience. Now, in my heart, I had a feeling that I was on the road that might well lead to success, and maybe Test Cricket.

Had I known just what was ahead, however, I doubt very much if I would have been so concerned with my football career.

4

*Cricket and Football Do Mix—Will Lack of Stamina
Beat Me?—We Defeat the Men of Yorkshire—
Walter Hammond's "Well Done"—I'm Picked
for England—And Lose Wicket Through a Freak.*

"CRICKET and football don't mix," has for years been
a much-used maxim, but I, for one, have never paid
much heed to it. Why? Because I have always held
the view that a professional sportsman, such as myself,
could follow two careers. As Middlesex C.C.C. and Arsenal
F.C. were both most considerate, an understanding was
quickly developed between them which made it possible
for me to resume my activities on either side when the new
season opened.

Thus, in April 1937, when the Middlesex players reported
for practice at Lord's, I was with them, although the soccer
season had not yet drawn to a close.

My natural desire was to continue where I had left off
in the previous season, but early I found that things were
not quite working out for me. I was either falling to good
balls, or smart catches, or, if this was not the case, getting
myself out in ways that annoyed me. Against the New
Zealanders, for example, when Middlesex met them, I was
out for seven when I felt that it was my day for runs; soon
after when we met Northampton, after four times being
missed in the slips, I struggled through to make 57; Essex
got my wicket for only eight runs.

When things began to go wrong I tried hard not to panic
and let it depress me to such an extent that I might lose my
confidence. I reasoned with myself that this state of things
could not go on; spent every spare moment in the nets. I
am convinced that net practice, if you're passing through
a phase in which nothing will go right, is one of the surest

38

"cures". In my case it worked, too, for after one or two more reverses I began to feel an improvement in my batting. The ball was being caught in the "middle" instead of on the edge.

I began to wonder, when I found that I tired quickly, if my stamina might not be suspect. There was only one solution to this, I thought, so, before I went to Lord's for a day's cricket, I made it my business to go down to Arsenal Stadium, don sweater, and put in an hour or so of lapping the track, and exercises. Often it was not possible to get to Arsenal Stadium, so in the evening, after I had finished cricket, I used to go for a trot round the streets of Hendon. Again, this extra trouble paid dividends. My stamina improved, and before I knew what had happened, the runs were coming once more.

My county, Middlesex, were experiencing a good season, and when you are a member of a winning side it gives you, especially if you are a young player, terrific confidence. When, for example, we met Yorkshire, the champions, I did not shirk this match but looked forward to again facing the wily Hedley Verity. What is more, when Yorkshire went into bat I had the satisfaction of catching the great Herbert Sutcliffe before he had scored. Apart from the fact that we defeated Yorkshire by an innings—first time this had happened since 1935—the match will always be remembered because of the brilliance of our stumper, Fred Price. He took seven catches in the Yorkshire first innings, a wonderful feat, and it was his smartness, in addition to the keen fielding of our side as a whole, that gave us such a victory.

I mention fielding. One of the first things that was impressed upon me, when I entered first-class cricket, was that stopping runs is just as important as scoring them, and with the ambition to make myself proficient in this direction, I spent many hours practising, often alone. I have seen the great R. W. V. Robins running around the field at Lord's, tossing the ball in the air, running after it, and bringing off a catch. I did likewise. What is more, I often used to erect a stump, take up a position some thirty yards from it, and spend hours aiming to knock it down. It was disappointing work at first, but the old saying that practice makes perfect is true, for in due course I was able to get a high percentage of hits and feel, if nothing else, that I was making headway in a branch of cricket that is essential if you wish to make your way to the top of the tree.

As a schoolboy one of my pet hobbies was throwing a cricket ball. In the local park, along with numerous friends, we spent dozens of evenings throwing a ball to each other, and it helped me in developing a long throw. This, too, resulted in my being put into the outfield, for a long throw, allied to my speed, developed as a footballer, was just "the thing the doctor ordered" for a man fielding on the boundary.

During my period of non-success with the bat I often felt that it might be worth while altering my natural style, and instead of attacking the bowling, assuming the role of a "waiter for loose balls". It was quite appreciated by me, I might add, that loose balls are not frequent in first-class cricket, and that I might have a good deal of waiting, but I was most anxious to get out of my bad spell.

Then, against Gloucestershire, I once more "got off the mark".

The Gloucester team have never been an easy side to defeat, and when Tom Goddard, that great spin bowler, is on form—which is quite often—the batsman is inclined to think more of defending his wicket than scoring centuries!

Tom Goddard is a good-natured giant with the biggest pair of hands on which I have set eyes. The ball, when he wraps his long fingers around it prior to sending down a "twister", looks like a pill. Down at Lord's, where he was a frequent visitor, I often watched Goddard very carefully. I had ambitions, in those days, to follow in his footsteps, and fancied I knew quite a few of his tricks. Anyway, when the time came for me to pick up my bat, and go to the crease to face him, I felt, to some extent, that I knew what to expect.

Playing for England

It is no use, when an intelligent bowler such as Tom Goddard is bowling at you, to sit on your bat and think the only thing to do is defend your wicket. Tom's too wily a player to allow you to do that. He'll find a way of piercing your guard. That is why my policy, when opposing him, was to attack and try and contact the ball before it landed on the pitch and commenced its tricks.

As I sallied up the wicket, clouted the ball on the volley, and saw it go flying to the boundary, I carefully watched Goddard. He just grinned back at me—until I was nearly at my century. Then, when he sent down a ball that might well have taken out my middle peg had it been allowed to land, and I walked up the pitch to crack it for four, Tom looked at me and said: "One of these days, Denis, it'll be a one-way journey for you."

"Maybe you're right, Tom," I grinned back, and sure enough he was right. For next season he "trapped" me— but that is jumping ahead. . . .

The fact that I was getting runs against Gloucester spurred me on, and when, with a quick single, I scored a century, the Western County men were quick to pat me on the back. "Well played," said Walter Hammond, when I'd got my hundred and those few words—from him— meant more to me than the actual scoring of the runs.

It was the first occasion that the great cricket personality, under whose captaincy I was destined to play against Australia, had spoken to me. . . .

On reflection, I consider that as a young cricketer, I was very fortunate to play in the same team as Pat Hendren. The great little Middlesex and England batsman, without any outward show of taking an out-of-the-ordinary interest in me, did help a very great deal in helping shape my cricket future. A word here and there, a tip about a certain bowler, and other little points that he knew would help me, came frequently from Pat Hendren, and when it was my good fortune to partner him at the wicket, I can truthfully say that I learnt more by watching him than if I had spent a whole year in the nets.

Playing for England

As a schoolboy Pat Hendren was one of my idols, and it was his beautiful style, coupled with free hitting, that made me determined, to some extent, to try and mould myself on Hendren. For his part, I'm sure, Pat was delighted to see another former Lord's ground-boy, like himself, joining the Middlesex county side, and together he and I enjoyed several profitable partnerships.

Against Essex, for example, we put on 109, and, I must admit, it was Pat who did most of the scoring. He was like a jack-in-the-box at the wicket, danced around like a fairy, watching the ball right on to his bat.

Often Pat, when I was batting in the nets, would stand behind me and pass on hints. Never, I must stress, did Pat Hendren try to do the work of the coach. All he did was pass on hints he knew would help me. Right here I would like to say how deeply his kindness was appreciated. All the time, though, like Archie Fowler, our coach, he must have realised that the best way of allowing a young cricketer to improve his play is not to curtail strokes, no matter how bad they might be according to the copybook, if they produce runs. Even to-day, after some years in first-class company, I frequently produce strokes that would not win me first prize in any competition—but never forget that *runs* count in cricket.

You cannot win matches by stroke play alone!

Without a doubt my biggest honour, until chosen for a Test Match, was my selection for the Gents. *v.* Players match in 1937. Two years previously as a ground-boy, when I helped prepare the pitch at Lord's for this historic fixture, it had been my great ambition to appear against the Gentlemen.

At the age of eighteen my wish was granted.

No, I did not make the sensational appearance desired. My name did not figure in the headlines. As a matter of fact, in the first innings I was stumped by Maxwell, off one of F. R. Brown's googlies, for a "duck", and the walk back from the wicket to the pavilion seemed endless.

Playing for England

Never was I more pleased to seek the "comfort" of the dressing-room than after that "blob".

In the second innings I was more fortunate, being unbeaten with 34, but, runs apart, the "education" of playing against such fine bowlers as Ken Farnes, Freddie Brown, and Owen-Smith, was worth much.

Kenneth Farnes, who was unfortunately killed in an air-crash, ranks as one of the best fast bowlers I've ever faced. The Essex schoolmaster, whose tragic death was such a blow to everyone, had the happy knack of keeping a good length. For long periods—a blessing in a fast bowler —he could keep plugging along without giving away many runs, and his wonderful temperament was one of the reasons Ken proved so successful.

Being hit to the boundary did not upset Ken Farnes. Next ball he tried hard not to make the same mistake!

Yes, to bat against such a fine pace bowler was a grand experience, and altogether, during 1937, I felt that I was being handed wages for getting a cricket background many young men would have been willing to pay a big fee to secure.

At the commencement of the season, if anyone had suggested to me that I might soon gain the English Test Team, I would have looked hard at them and wondered if they were pulling my leg. Towards the end of the season, however, following a good run on my part, when things seemed to go right for me no matter what else happened, some of the critics kindly suggested that I might be considered for a place. I remember how bucked I was over this suggestion, and it holds a prominent place in my collection of newspaper cuttings. At the time I thought they were being maybe a little premature, but one evening, at about 6.45, my father, usually such a quiet man, rushed in full of excitement, waving the evening paper. "Look at that," he said, pointing to the sports page, "you've been selected for England, Denis."

He was right. Included in the side to meet New Zealand in the last Test at Kennington Oval was "D. Compton".

Playing for England

I do not think there would have been more excitement in our house if father had won the Irish Sweep, and far past our normal bed-time, we sat round the table discussing the forthcoming Test. Dad, a good cricketer himself, talked to me about keeping cool. Mother was anxious that I should take the field looking my smartest. In fact, every conceivable angle, so far as my Test debut was concerned, was examined during our "round the supper-table" conference!

Next morning, when the excitement had diminished a little, the postman called and left for me an envelope which had the M.C.C. crest in one corner. Full of excitement, I opened it, pulled out the letter and read:

"Dear Compton,
    You have been selected to play for England v. New Zealand at Kennington Oval on August 14, 16 and 17. Do you require accommodation? If so let me know. Also let me know by reply if you are available."

The letter was signed by the M.C.C. Secretary.

That was a great moment for me, to hold in my hand the first official invitation I had received to play for my country, and when I went into the office at Lord's, to say that I was available, I sensed that everyone, who had watched me grow up from a small lad on the ground-staff, was pleased to see good fortune had gone my way.

So were my colleagues in the Middlesex team.

Our skipper, however, who was leading the England team, has never been one to throw praise around unless it has been earned—a great thing this, for you appreciate it all the more when it does come!—and when he saw me, R. W. V. Robins said: "Well, you've got your big chance. Now make full use of it."

It was not necessary for me to tell the English captain that I would be on my toes. He knew me well enough to take that for granted.

For the Oval Test my mother went to a great deal of trouble to make sure that my white flannels, and shirt, were

44

just right for such an important occasion. Father, too, apart from whitening my cricket boots, re-studded them carefully, and when, on the Saturday morning, we said good-bye to Mother, I was feeling rather good.

At that time I owned a little second-hand car—it cost me £35!—and it was the pride of my life. In this by no means up-to-date model Father and I travelled to Kennington Oval.

On arriving I was at once surrounded by autograph hunters—some of them young fellows older than myself!—and I could not resist thinking, at the time, how better it would have been had they tried to improve their own cricket by playing. Still, I suppose the Test was a special treat. Anyway, after seeing my father to his seat, I reported at the dressing-room. Because I looked so young, the attendant on the door stared hard at me; maybe he wondered if I was an autograph hunter trying to get into the dressing-room. Whatever his views, he allowed me to pass, and in the "room of a hundred secrets" I met my colleagues.

There was Len Hutton, Cyril Washbrook, Charlie Barnett, Walter Hammond, Joe Hardstaff, Leslie Ames, all players I had once idolised and gone miles to see. Now—I could hardly believe it!—I was to play in the same England Test team.

I must confess I did pinch myself to make sure I was not dreaming, but those fine cricketers were friendliness itself. With Walter Robins, one of the greatest of all captains to lead us, we were a most happy team.

As the "baby"—in years—of the team, every member of the side, without making too much of a show about it, came up to wish me well, and before the match I was presented with my England cap—size $7\frac{1}{8}$.

In the years that have since passed I have successfully kept to this size!

Was I a little overawed when New Zealand made us field? To some extent I did have an empty feeling in my stomach. Maybe I would have felt a little better if the match had been played at Lord's, for Kennington Oval has never been one of my favourite grounds. Once the first over was bowled, however, I forgot everything but the game, and largely as a result of the skipper's bowling—he took four wickets for 40 runs—we dismissed the New Zealanders for 249.

As I sat on the Oval balcony looking down at the scene far below, I wondered how I would fare as a batsman. Many thoughts came into my mind: Would I settle down quickly or lose my nerve? Would the wicket play tricks? Was the bowling first-class?

Such thoughts were knocked out of my mind—by the New Zealand bowlers! Within a very short time, with Hutton and Barnett out, and only 31 runs on the scoreboard, I was called upon to play my first Test innings—and it was a very subdued young chap who walked out of the players' gate at the Oval.

When I sat on the balcony I felt, as I said just now, scared. Once at the wicket, though, that fear left me—just as Jack Hobbs said it did him on his Test début—and, believe it or not, I was anxious to get on with the game.

My first over in Test cricket was sent down to me by H. G. Vivian. I survived, and got off with a single. But my partnership with Cyril Washbrook was not to last for long, for with only six runs added, the Lancashire batsman became another of Vivian's victims.

This meant that Joe Hardstaff, the blond Nottingham stroke-artist, joined me at the wicket.

Although, to some extent, there is a similarity in our style of play, on one point Joe and I had a great difference of opinion—the weight of a cricket bat. I prefer a light one of 2 lb. 3 ozs. because I can wield it easily, while Hardstaff carries one of the heaviest in the game. It weighs 2 lb. 7 ozs. His reason for preferring such a hefty "weapon"? Because, says Joe, he can get more power behind his shots. When you come to think of it, Joe probably has a great deal in this, for he "punches" the ball really hard, as I know from fielding against him.

Anyway, at the Oval, when we joined forces, it did not

take us long to settle down and runs began to come quickly. As I watched Hardstaff batting, one thing immediately struck me—he holds the bat higher on the handle than any other batsman I have seen; so high, in fact, I thought that a really fast ball might well knock it out of Joe's hands. But the Nottingham man's grip is deceiving, and the illusion that he did not hold it tightly was—an illusion!

The New Zealanders, who relied upon four bowlers in Vivian, Cowie, Dunning and Roberts, frequently made changes in an effort to break the resistance of Joe and myself. Often, I must admit, Vivian, a young player like myself, did get me in difficulties, but, as time progressed, our rate of scoring increased.

Instead of feeling nervous, as I thought I should when I went to the wicket, time proved a great ally to me and I really did sense that I was on my way to getting a century; once past 60 I thought my normal game would assure me of this honour.

But with my score at 65 I was dismissed through no fault of my own. Vivian was bowling to Joe Hardstaff, and the merry man from Nottingham, in one of his hard-hitting moods, stepped out to a short one and hit it hard up the wicket. The bowler tried to get his hand to the ball, could not make a catch, but accidentally deflected it on to my wicket.

It so happened that I was out of my crease, backing up Joe Hardstaff. . . .

Yes, by one chance in a million I was run out.

Poor Joe Hardstaff! He was terribly upset to think that he had, by sheer accident, helped rob me of a possible century in my first Test, but I pointed out that it was just "one of those things" that occur in cricket. I happened to be unlucky to have it happen to me in a Test. . . .

Altogether Joe Hardstaff and I had put on 125 for the fourth wicket, and, if for nothing else, we felt rather pleased. Our skipper, with only seven wickets down, and rain in the air, declared the England innings closed with the score at 254.

Playing for England

When New Zealand batted again we dismissed them for 187 and I was fortunate to take a couple of cheap wickets in my first Test.

"Well, Denis," said my father, when I got home after the match, which rain made into a draw, "how do you feel about playing in a Test match?"

"It is good—providing you forget that it is a Test match and take the angle that it is a game of cricket," I replied.

That is the attitude I have tried to adopt since first I took up cricket. Remember, as a small boy, I was playing for my father's side against grown men, and, if I were not to lose confidence, I had to assume a certain "perky" air. It certainly never allowed me to be overawed by the big occasion, and for that, when I played at Kennington Oval, I was most thankful.

What else had I learnt from this first Test match? One very important thing, thanks to R. W. V. Robins. I had developed a habit of putting my hands on my knees when fielding in the gully, and during the match our skipper came up to me.

"If you want to become a good cricketer," he said, "you'll always be ready to take a catch. At the present rate, however, you'll be caught unawares. Rid yourself of that habit."

I did, for R. W. V. Robins knows what he is talking about. . . .

As for the first England cap awarded me, I put it away, and even to-day, only my son, Brian, is allowed to wear it.

One day, I hope, he may win one of his own.

Apart from my first Test match, the 1937 season will always remain in my memory because of the great game against Nottingham at Trent Bridge. To become County Champions we had to win this match, and Nottinghamshire, we knew from past experience, were no mean foes. That is why we took everything carefully.

To commence with, we arrived at our hotel at six o'clock, and just over three hours later were tucked up in bed. If nothing else we intended to be fresh when we stepped on to Trent Bridge!

To cut a long story short, we scored 539—9, Fred Price, our stumper, scoring a solid 104. Our bowlers, who were doing well at the time, managed to get Notts out for 316, and they were forced to follow-on, 223 runs behind.

Two wickets quickly fell, and when Joe Hardstaff arrived at the crease one of our chaps remarked to the great batsman: "Well, Joe, what do you think of the new champs?"

Hardstaff never replied, but his actions did more than anything he could have said to show his opinion of this sally. Joe well and truly flogged our bowling. Hit it all over the field—and that goes for me as well!—and scored a faultless 243 not-out, an innings that forced a draw, and, at the same time, put paid to our championship aspirations.

Once again we were behind Yorkshire.

We were all bitterly disappointed at missing the honour, and when I returned home, and began to tell my father my tale of woe, he looked up at supper and said: "What are you worrying about? You've years of cricket ahead of you. Anyway, the Australians are here next season."

"I know that," I replied, "but do you think I'll be good enough to play against them?"

"It's up to you," came the reply.

I was determined to be good enough.

5

"I WONDER if I'll be lucky enough to get chosen to play in the first Test against the Australians?" I said to my father, as we sat down to breakfast one sunny morning in the June of 1938. "Maybe, after my showing against New Zealand, the selectors will give me another chance."

Father, who was reading the morning newspaper, looked up for a moment and said: "I sincerely hope you will get another chance, Denis. We shall know this afternoon, shan't we, when the team is officially announced."

"That's right, Dad," I replied, and, although I tried to appear at ease, I knew that until the side was announced, time was going to weigh heavy on my hands.

I had been given a rest from the Middlesex side, the County feeling that I should not be overworked, and, while waiting for the afternoon to roll around, I busied myself helping Mother around the house, and cleaning up my gear.

Then, about an hour before the man with the evening papers was due at the top of the Hendon road in which I lived, out I went to wait for him.

How slowly the minutes seemed to pass. Once, as I hung about at the top of the road a policeman, on patrol, looked at me so hard I felt guilty about nothing, and, for the moment at least, started a brisk walk to the corner of a nearby road!

Then, after what seemed hours, the newsvendor arrived on the scene.

"What you waiting for, Denis," he grinned. "Looking for the winner of the 2.30?"

I didn't answer that "joke", but, without waiting, grabbed a paper, looked down the stop-press column, and saw: "England team for the First Test: W. R. Hammond (Capt.), K. Farnes, Barnett, Hutton, Edrich, Paynter, Ames, Wright, Verity, Sinfield, and—COMPTON!"

My eyes nearly jumped from my head as the name "Compton" seemed to jump out of the newspaper, and with a shout of "I'll see you later", I sprinted up the road as if a policeman were chasing me, knocked at the door of my house, and, when Mother opened it, exclaimed: "I'm in against Australia, Ma!"

She smiled. "That's good, Denis. Now, lad, sit back and relax, otherwise you won't be able to enjoy the Test match."

As usual, Mother was right, for I was shaking with excitement and had I been called upon to go to the wicket at that moment there is no doubting my stay would have been short.

Two days later the official invitation arrived, and it was a very proud young man who called into the office at Lord's to report that he would be able to accept the M.C.C. invitation and take part in the Test match at Trent Bridge, Nottingham.

And, of course, Mother and Father took a great interest in helping me prepare for my biggest match to date. Mother washed my shirts and flannels. Father whitened and re-studded my boots. I spent a considerable time making sure that my pads were in perfect condition and my bats well oiled and cleaned.

As the match was due to start on a Friday, Bill Edrich, my Middlesex colleague and I arranged to travel to Nottingham together on the Thursday afternoon. Mother and Father saw me off at the station and four hours later Bill and I arrived in Nottingham. It so happened that the Australian players were staying at the same hotel as the Englishmen, and when we went down to dinner the first people we set eyes on were the men from "Down Under".

Playing for England

Don Bradman, Australia's great captain, was the first man to greet me. Coming up, hand extended, the small man with the big reputation said, with a smile: "I'm very glad to see you were selected, Denis. The very best of luck."

By the manner in which he said this I know "The Don" was sincere. He himself came into Test cricket as a young player and knew what a bit of encouragement, no matter how small, meant to me. For that I will always be thankful.

"Why don't you come up to my room and have a talk about cricket?" said Bill "Tiger" O'Reilly, Australia's star bowler. "You're coming, aren't you?" he said, turning to Fleetwood-Smith, his bowling comrade, and with these two ace trundlers to "talk me out", I accepted the invitation.

Over a glass of orangeade—"Of course, you're only a youngster," said Bill O'Reilly, when I ordered this soft drink—these two grand fellows talked with me about cricket in general, and Australia in particular.

"I guess you may go to Australia in the future," said Bill O'Reilly, "and I reckon you'll want to know something about our wickets."

And so, for over two and a half hours, he talked about wickets, cricketers, and cricket clubs "Down Under". It was a most interesting "lecture"—that is the only word for it—and during the time he talked I learnt a very great deal about cricket, and what to expect if, in due course, I was to visit the Dominion.

"Mind you," concluded Bill, with a smile, as I looked at my watch, saw it was getting on for ten o'clock, and decided it was time for bed, "Smithy and I have cooked up something special for you to-morrow. We're going to get you out cheaply, young Denis Compton. See if we're not right. There's going to be no long spell at the wicket for you.

"In the meantime, good night, lad—*and the best of luck!*"

I thought the latter remark most amusing, coming on top of the "threat", for O'Reilly, although he said this in a light-hearted manner, was deadly serious. These Australians, you see, are great fellows off the field, but, once you are at

Photo · Central Press

Tom Goddard, Gloucester and England bowler.

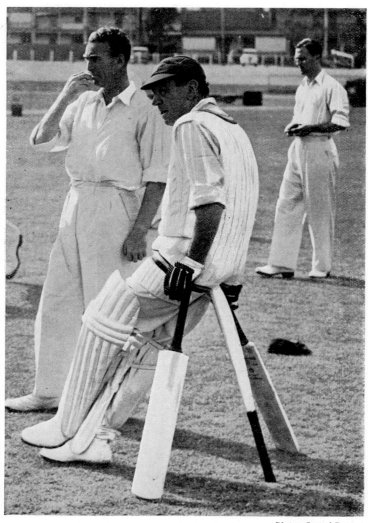

English Test cricketers in the nets. Walter Hammond sitting on a "seat" made of three bats.

the wicket, they do not allow sentiment to interfere with the job of getting you out!

By ten o'clock I was in bed and asleep, up sharp at 7.30, and down to breakfast with Bill Edrich by 8.30. What a breakfast we had in those non-austerity days! Bacon and eggs, hot rolls and lashings of butter. . . . It makes my mouth water to think of it. Then, our bags packed, we climbed aboard taxis and were away to the famous Trent Bridge ground.

A great crowd was waiting to cheer the arrival of the England team, and as we climbed the stairs to the dressing-room Bill Edrich turned to me and said: "Y'know, Denis, this is quite a moment for me."

"That goes for me, too," I replied, and, entering the dressing-room, was greeted with: "There's a pile of telegrams for you over there, Mr. Compton."

All my colleagues had their quota of wires. Altogether I received thirty-five. They ranged from my parents to the Arsenal football club. From Sir Pelham Warner to my old schoolmaster, Mark Mitchell, and, as I read them all carefully, I could feel a lump in my throat. Yes, if I was becoming hardened in the tough world of sport, I had my sentimental moments. . . .

"Well, Denis, how are you feeling?" asked wee Eddie Paynter, that wonderful little Lancastrian. "You look good for a century."

"I hope it works out that way," I replied, as Eddie, patting me on the back, passed on.

On reflection, I do not think I could have made my début for England, against Australia, in a finer batting side. Len Hutton and Charlie Barnett, who opened the England innings, were both in grand form, and no matter how well the Australians bowled—and they *did* bowl well —the man from Yorkshire and his partner from Gloucester played everything with confidence. They made an opening stand of 219 before Len Hutton, who had made a beautiful 100, was lbw to Fleetwood-Smith, and my friend and colleague, Bill Edrich, went to the wicket.

Playing for England

Now Edrich, at this time, could rarely get going in big matches. In county games he was terrific, against Australia nothing would go right for him in Tests, and after he had scored five, O'Reilly found a way through his defence and knocked back one of his stumps.

Charlie Barnett and Walter Hammond did not last long after this, and when the time came for me to join Eddie Paynter at the crease, the score stood at 281—4.

Once again, when I walked through the pavilion towards the players' gate, I felt nervous, but on the green turf the awed feeling departed. I felt as confident as if a century already stood by my name although, at tea-time, I had not felt like eating too much, being "full" of my forthcoming battle with the Australian bowlers.

As I passed Bill O'Reilly, on my way up the wicket, the giant looked at me and grinned: "Best of luck, Denis, but I'm going to try and send you back quickly."

"That's O.K. by me," I replied—and determined, for all that, to do my utmost to beat-up "Big Bill".

After taking guard, I looked up, took stock of the field, and decided, if nothing else, not to be rushed. I noted how O'Reilly had set an attacking field for me; obviously intending to try and get my wicket as quickly as possible.

He nearly succeeded!

I watched carefully as the "Tiger" bounded up to the wicket and sent down a good-length ball pitched on the middle stump. Suddenly it moved to the off, I snicked it, and the ball dropped just short of first slip.

O'Reilly threw his arms up into the air, as if he were about to start a war-dance, wicket-keeper Ben Barnett "encouraged" me by saying: "My heavens, that turned," and my inside did a somersault as I realised how near I'd been to going back to the pavilion.

Before sending down his second ball, Bill O'Reilly looked hard at me. I thought, for the moment, that he was trying to hypnotise me, but obviously the Australian was "sizing me up," for the next ball was entirely different to the first one, and I played it, in the middle of my bat, back to the bowler.

That "crack" as ball met bat was like music in my ears, and off the third ball I was able to take a single, and, as they say in the cricket world, "got away".

From that moment, until stumps were drawn for the day, at 6.30, I did not give a chance. All the bowling, mind you, was treated with wariness, but, as I have stressed already, experience had taught me that the way to success in cricket is to make the bowler respect the batsman, not go out of your way to encourage the man with the ball into thinking he has you worried.

That is why attack is the best way of defending your "castle".

Anyway, with Eddie Paynter as my colleague, I managed to get 65 before the close of play.

Sitting with my colleagues, discussing the match, I was very interested to hear the reactions of such an august company to the Australian bowlers. Their summing up of various men fitted into the impressions I had gained, most important being that Bill O'Reilly was, at that time, just about the greatest bowler in the world.

O'Reilly, first and foremost, was a student of cricket. He studied opposing batsmen with the same care a boxer does a prospective opponent, and if any man had a chink in his defensive armour you can be sure that O'Reilly would spot it and use the knowledge to the advantage of his side.

Another thing about O'Reilly, apart from his ability to make the ball turn a good deal, was his outlook on the game. From first to last he was an attacking bowler. Was willing to "bowl his heart out" rather than give opposing batsmen the impression that they were getting the better of him.

In short, the ideal bowler.

Supporting him, among others, in the Australian attack, was L. O'Brien Fleetwood-Smith, a left-arm spin bowler who bowled with his right until he was taken ill with influenza. While recuperating from this illness, Fleetwood-Smith, playing cricket with a friend in the garden of his home, experimented with bowling left-handed. To his surprise, the Australian found that he had a much better control of the ball with his left hand, decided to concentrate upon this type of bowling, and was later coached by the great Arthur Mailey. The result? The unknown right-arm bowler shot into the top flight as a left-handed "trundler", and ranks among the most difficult men I have had to face.

Just before I resumed my innings on the Saturday morning, when I knew Fleetwood-Smith and O'Reilly would be most anxious to send me back before I had really settled down, our skipper, Walter Hammond, called me on one side.

"When you get a hundred," Walter Hammond said, "I want you to get two hundred. Make sure of that. Don't take unnecessary chances and get out when you reach your century. Best of luck."

With this good wish—and warning!—still ringing in my ears, I went out with Eddie Paynter to resume the "battle".

As I anticipated, those Australian bowlers were in their most deadly mood, and the first ball I received from McCormick, the fast bowler, came off the wicket like a bullet. But Eddie and I, once we had got a sight of the ball, quickly settled down, and took the score steadily along. At 12.20, with my own score at 98, I glanced at the scoreboard, and, to this day, I remember the thought that flashed through my mind. It was: "Will I get my century, and so become the youngest Englishman to score a hundred, in a Test match, against the Australians?"

Once again the "ideal temperament" people told me I possessed pulled me through, for Fleetwood-Smith sent down a loose ball, and I cracked it good and hard. With Eddie Paynter flying between the wickets as if his very life depended upon me getting a couple, we got the necessary two, and Don Bradman, when I had got my breath, and taken stock of the situation, walked up to me and shook my hand.

"Well done, Denis," he said. "Congratulations!"

As they passed, too, the other Australian players said: "Well done," and this tribute, with the crowd also applauding, made me wonder if it were a dream and I should awake to find myself having a fight with the bedclothes. But it was true enough—as I was to find a few minutes later.

As a schoolboy I noticed that my idol, Jack Hobbs, when he had passed the hundred mark, began to hit out. I forgot, though, that the Surrey master did not do this in Test Matches, for in the middle of Fleetwood-Smith's next over I tried to sweep him to leg. Although I say this myself, it was a good shot, and should have been a certain boundary. Stan McCabe, however, had other ideas, and the grand Australian all-rounder, flashing round the boundary in a manner that would have done MacDonald Bailey credit, made a catch from a chance that did not exist—and I was out for 102.

Did I feel pleased when the Australians, and the crowd, gave me a cheer! I had set up a record by becoming the youngest player to score a century for England against Australia, and had taken part, with Eddie Paynter, in a new record stand for the fifth wicket. Altogether, between us, Paynter and I had added 206.

"Well played," said my colleagues, sitting on the balcony, as I walked in.

Then came the anti-climax—Walter Hammond came up to me, and the skipper looked anything but pleased.

"First I would like to say 'Well done'," said the skipper, "but I thought I told you to get 200?"

I coloured at this, for the skipper *had* given me those instructions.

"I'm sorry," I said, and Walter Hammond could obviously sense my feelings, for he quickly said: "Never mind, it's a great start."

In due course I began to appreciate why the skipper had been so careful to point out to me the wisdom of always playing carefully, and not throwing away your wicket, when opposed to the Australians. They are terrific fighters, never give away a wicket themselves, and make their opponents battle for every success. To stand a chance of defeating them you have to adopt their methods, and in the years that have passed I have never forgotten the "Trent Bridge

Playing for England

lesson", when Walter Hammond pointed out my error, in the middle of my greatest triumph.

Anyway, thanks to a wonderful 216 not-out by Eddie Paynter we were able to declare at 658—8, leaving our bowlers with a reasonable chance of getting the Australian wickets needed for the victory we visualised might now be ours.

But these Australians are great fighters, and on this occasion, at Trent Bridge, it was Stanley McCabe, one of the best all-rounders in the game, who came to Australia's rescue with a brilliant 232. Stan, quite one of the nicest chaps I've ever met in sport, was, apart from being a beautiful stroke player, a batsman who cracked the ball hard. When Stanley hit a ball he did hit it—and it was too bad for the fieldsman who got in the way of it.

I know, when we had six Australian wickets down for 194 runs, everyone had visions of us dismissing the visitors cheaply and then, putting them in again, ramming home our advantage. But when Ben Barnett, the Australian stumper, joined McCabe, we soon appreciated how much there was to be said for the old maxim that the Australians always find a man able to rise to the occasion. This time it was Barnett who, without making a great show about it, stayed with McCabe at the wicket while the man upon whom Australia relied so much really "went to town". Altogether this pair put on 69 most valuable runs, of which Barnett scored 22.

Eventually, when McCabe, although the "tail-enders" were in, was hitting our bowlers all over the field as a resnlt of some really glorious batsmanship, we had visions of him reaching 300. Then the late Hedley Verity bowled a ball that looked just the same as many others that had been sent up to McCabe, and Stanley, not realising that Verity had put down one of his "specials", tried to drive him to the boundary. Instead he cracked the ball into my hands —and for hours afterwards the sting told me that McCabe had put plenty of "beef" behind his stroke!

At last the Australian innings closed, with their score at

411, and, quite naturally, we felt very elated. This meant the men from "Down Under" had to follow on; that we stood an excellent chance of winning the first Test providing our bowlers could take full advantage of the strong position in which we found ourselves.

Earlier I said that the Australians rank among the most difficult of teams to beat. They will never admit defeat, and are so "well-knitted" that it is rare that one man, at least, does not rise to the occasion.

In the first innings it was Stan McCabe. At the second time of batting, Brown and Bradman well and truly stepped into the breach, Brown scoring a classic 133, and Don Bradman a not-out 144.

This was the first occasion I had been afforded the opportunity of a close-up of Don Bradman in action during a Test match. In the first innings he had scored 51, and looked very formidable. This time, however, he was the perfect run-getting machine; merciless with any loose balls. None escaped. So nimble was Don on his feet, too, that he made runs out of opportunities that few batsmen would have spotted.

They say that the spectator sees more of the game than the players themselves. In football, and boxing, this may be right, but, so far as cricket is concerned, nothing could be further from the truth. I understood this as I watched Don Bradman. From the ring he appears to be a cheerful man with a ready smile on his lips. On the field, however, you soon realise that the smile means nothing. Don rarely, if ever, says a word. His job is to concentrate upon "slaughtering" the bowling—and how well he concentrates.

When you bowl against Bradman, as I have done, you understand what an extraordinary cricketer he is. From an academic viewpoint he cannot be classed, in my opinion, with Jack Hobbs, or Frank Woolley, but as a run-getter, pure and simple, he is way out by himself.

Study Bradman when a bowler runs up to the crease. He watches that man's hand like a hawk, has a perfect sight of the ball from the moment it leaves his hand, and such is his cricket knowledge, and judgment, it is rare that Bradman is forced to change his mind.

Against England, at Nottingham, Bradman gave a display that was masterly. He set out to prevent us from winning; he did that, at the same time giving me a truly wonderful opportunity of seeing "how it was done".

Eventually, with six wickets down, and Bradman still undefeated at the wicket, the Australians had scored 427 in their second innings, and the match was drawn. A bitter disappointment to us. Still, we thought, there are four more Tests to play. . . .

The Second Test of the 1938 series, as usual, was played at Lord's, and being chosen for this game—for it is my "home ground"—naturally gave me a good deal of pleasure—but in the first innings little more than that, for after Walter Hammond had scored a grand 240, and Eddie Paynter, with his score at 99, had fallen to O'Reilly, an lbw victim, I, too, "walked into a straight 'un" from O'Reilly, after scoring only six, and went back to the dressing-room a bitterly disappointed young man, and for a very good reason.

A short time before I had been talking to "Tiger" Smith, the old England player, and he brought up the subject of how I kept trying to sweep O'Reilly to leg.

"Do go careful with that shot, Denis," he said to me. "Don't try and play the ball round the corner when it's on the leg stump."

I listened carefully to what the "Tiger" had to say, and determined to follow his advice. The result. First ball of this type I received from Bill O'Reilly sent me back, an lbw victim, and the umpire who gave me out was—"TIGER" SMITH!

"You're a silly little chap," he said to me, as I passed him, and I felt like agreeing with him. After all, I had been warned!

Leslie Ames, who followed me, rattled up a quick 83, and when the England innings closed we had scored 494. A good total, true, but, when you're playing the Australians . . .

Our visitors replied with a score of 422 of which Brown, who carried his bat, made 206. This knock ranks among the best I've ever seen, not so much because of the number of runs Brown secured, but the manner in which he accomplished his task. It was an innings both pleasing to watch, but, for all that, very solid.

The England second innings began with disaster, Hutton, Barnett, Edrich and Hammond all out and only 64 runs on the board. And when I joined Eddie Paynter out there in the middle at Lord's I fully understood just how much depended upon me this time.

By now I had built up quite an understanding with Paynter, for off the field we used to "talk cricket" a good deal, so when we "joined arms" together at Lord's I felt, in my heart, that it was with one of the best possible partners.

Slowly, but surely, we took the score along, O'Reilly, McCabe and McCormick making sure we had little chance to get runs quickly. Then, when we had added 21, Eddie Paynter hit a ball to fine leg and called for two. I responded only to see Jack Fingleton making a glorious return to the wicket and knock off the bails while Paynter was still out of his ground.

Naturally I felt very perturbed over this, but Eddie Paynter, as he walked towards the pavilion, came up to me and said: "It was not your fault, Denis, understand that."

Surely the action of a grand little gentleman and sportsman.

Things were now beginning to look grim, half the side being out for 76, and after first Ames, and then Verity, had departed, we still were only credited with 142.

Then in walked Arthur Wellard, the cheery big-hitter from Somerset. Although he played his natural game, and tried to knock the cover off the ball, Arthur, for all that, did not ignore defensive play when the occasion demanded it, and together we gradually took the score along towards the safety mark. Eventually Wellard, after making 38, was bowled, but only after we had added 74.

Playing for England

How was I playing? In my opinion it was the best knock I'd ever made in my life—and one of the grimmest struggles against any attack. The Australian bowlers, once they had "tasted blood", bowled like men inspired. So varied were the "trundlers" skipper Don Bradman could call upon that I was given an opportunity to study—and not at my leisure! —fast bowling, spin bowling, in fact, every known form of attack. It was tiring work, for you had to keep your wits about you all the time, and when, with 242—8 on the board, Walter Hammond declared, I was unbeaten with 76, and England were safe from defeat—we hoped!

Yes, the match, which started full of promise, ended in a draw, Australia scoring 204—6 in their second innings, the wonderful Don Bradman being not-out with 102.

My personal reaction, after this match, was that I had learnt my lesson after falling to O'Reilly in the first innings. On thinking things over I was ready to admit, O'Reilly did overawe me a little, but now, having played him so confidently once more, I did not intend to let him "get me" too often in the future.

Yet in the Fourth Test—after the Third, at Manchester, had to be abandoned, because of rain, without a ball being bowled—"Big Bill" got me in both innings at Leeds, we lost the match by five wickets, and I honestly began to wonder if, after all, O'Reilly was not something of a "Jonah" to me. Altogether, in the course of the tour, he got my wicket on five occasions, but, for all that, I fought against the feeling that he was my master.

If I had taken any other attitude I could no longer have been justly considered for Test honours. . . .

6

KENNINGTON OVAL has never been among my
favourite grounds although, as a small boy, I used
to make regular visits to the Surrey C.C.C. headquarters for the purpose of seeing Jack Hobbs, my idol, in
action. It is the flats surrounding the Oval, which to my
way of thinking interfere with the light, that makes it so
unpopular with me, but, when I was selected to play for
England, in the Fifth Test of the 1938 series, I never for a
moment gave a thought to my feelings in this direction.

This great match, which was one of the much-discussed
"Timeless Tests", commenced on August 20, 1938, and
when Walter Hammond won the toss he did not hesitate
before deciding to bat.

The wicket was perfect; "Bosser" Martin, head groundsman at the Oval, had made a wonderful job of it, and
everyone felt in their hearts that plenty of runs would be
scored.

Few, though, were prepared for the terrific score that was
to follow.

They would have been justified, for with only 12 runs on
the score-board Bill Edrich, who opened the innings with
Len Hutton, misjudged a delivery from "Tiger" O'Reilly,
and the big Australian bowler, in a manner that must have
been heard at Westminster, appealed when the ball rattled
Bill's pads.

Up went the umpire's finger—and back to the pavilion
went Edrich!

63

Playing for England

Maurice Leyland of the broad bat and ready wit followed Edrich, linking up with his Yorkshire colleague, Len Hutton. With only 28 runs on the board and the Australians on their toes, things did not exactly look rosy for us. That is, until Len and Maurice joined bats. Then those Yorkshiremen well and truly "went to town". They hit the Australian bowlers from here to Sydney and back!

Don Bradman, a cute captain, rang the bowling changes in a manner that might have bewildered most batsmen, but Hutton and Leyland are not "ordinary" batsmen, as they proved at Kennington Oval. By the end of the day 347 runs were credited to England—Hutton 160, and Leyland 156—and they still remained to bat another day.

The following morning, when the Australians resumed their attack, it was noticeable how well everyone fielded and backed up the bowlers. Hutton and Leyland, though, had that wonderful feeling of being on top, and it was not until they had put on 382 runs—a record stand for any England wicket in a Test—that the Australians managed to part them, Bradman collecting a return from Hassett, and running out Leyland at 187. The great left-hander, who had spent 6¼ hours at the wicket, and scored 17 boundaries, played grandly. When Walter Hammond, our skipper, succeeded Leyland, it did not take Hutton long to once more get cracking, for with 411 on the scoreboard, for the loss of only two wickets, we could afford to take a few liberties.

Walter Hammond, who played some great shots, fell an lbw victim to Fleetwood-Smith with his personal score at 59, and 546 on the scoreboard, which meant that Eddie Paynter, the wee Lancashire left-hander, had to go out to the crease.

Just before this wicket had fallen Paynter, who had been wearing his pads for a long time, had a small personal bet with me. It came about as a result of a conversation we were having. Eddie, a man of great experience, expressed the opinion that we would, because of the long hours spent in the semi-darkness of the dressing-room, be very fortunate to get ten between us.

"After this light you're going to notice the difference when you get out beneath that fierce sun," he said to me. When I said he was incorrect in his theory, the Lancastrian was prepared to back his judgment to the extent of £1. What is more, Paynter proved to be correct, for he was lbw to O'Reilly before he had scored, while Waite bowled me after I had scored a single!

"Well, Denis, wasn't I right?" was the greeting I received from Eddie Paynter when I returned, very disappointed, to the dressing-room.

I did not answer—just handed him the pound note!

Joe Hardstaff, with the score at 555—5, was the next batsman to join forces with Len Hutton, and by now the young Yorkshireman, who was batting in masterly fashion, must have felt the great strain of concentrating so hard. For patience, perseverance, and stamina, his innings is among the best I have ever seen, but when Stan McCabe, for example, had to have his leg massaged after stopping a hard drive, and play was held up, Len took the opportunity of throwing himself full-length on the damp turf.

How tired he must have felt, although, in his heart, there must have been a glowing pride, for he had but a few minutes earlier beaten "Tip" Foster's 287 made at Sydney 35 years previously, and so set up a new record for an Englishman in Tests against Australia.

Having "tasted" one record Len, to whom the ball must have now appeared as big as a football, continued to bat like a champion, and when play was halted for the day, because of bad light, Hutton had reached 300, and everyone went home asking each other: "Will he beat Bradman's Test record of 334?"

Meanwhile, in the dressing-room, Len Hutton, looking very weary, had a thorough massage from Sandy Tait, the Surrey masseur. It is really wonderful how refreshing a massage can be. Anyway, when the game was resumed the following day Len quickly got off the mark, and when he reached 331 everybody who had packed into the Oval hoped he would get the boundary needed to top "The Don's" record.

But the Australians, proud of their skipper's 334, were not going to allow Hutton to establish a new record against them without a fight; none so more than Bradman himself. Don fielded like a demon. Was here, there, and everywhere. A cordon of white-clad fieldsmen, too, appeared to be creeping in close, still closer, upon Hutton. For ten minutes, with the Australian bowlers sending down first-class, good-length deliveries, Hutton's score stood at 331. We all wondered if, under such obvious pressure, he might fail. But the serious-faced young Yorkshireman with the keen eyes and ice-cool brain refused to be worried by such tactics, and when Fleetwood-Smith sent down a ball just a little outside the off-stump Hutton, with a perfect late cut, made the historic stroke that put him at the head of the "Highest Ever" scorers in Test cricket.

Even then, with the record beneath his belt, Len Hutton was not finished with the Australian attack, and for some time afterwards he continued to punish them, to the tune of 29 runs, before finally giving Hassett a catch, off O'Reilly, with 364 runs standing to his credit.

For thirteen hours, seventeen minutes, Len Hutton had been concentrating all his energies upon dealing with the wiles and speed of the Australian attack. Bradman and Co. had "foxed" him, encouraged Hutton to hit out, and done everything possible to obtain his wicket, but the young chap for whom Herbert Sutcliffe forecast such a future as a boy was not to be beaten—at least, not until he had scored 364 runs!

What an ovation Len received when he strode into the pavilion at the Oval, and when he entered our dressing-room, everyone was anxious to shake his hand. This completed, Hutton plonked himself down on a bench, closed his eyes, and remained like this for some time. Then, feeling refreshed, he had a shower and climbed on the table for a massage.

Never did a cricketer more deserve the services of the masseur than Len Hutton. He must, that afternoon, have felt just about the most weary man in England.

In the meantime Arthur Wood, the cheery little Yorkshire wicket-keeper, who was playing in his first Test against the Australians, went out to join Joe Hardstaff, who had become yet another centurion.

"Woody," a plump little chap with an ever-smiling face, had been a last-minute selection for this Test and was not notified that he would be required at the Oval until the Friday evening prior to the match, which commenced on Saturday.

As the last train had left for London some time before Arthur Wood received the summons to play for England he wondered just how he was to reach London in time. Eventually the stumper decided that the only way to do so was by hiring a taxi.

So through the night drove Arthur Wood, and when London was finally reached there was £7 10s. on the clock, and a somewhat-tired wicket-keeper trying hard to snatch a little sleep behind the driver!

I may be wrong, but after that night dash I expect Arthur felt pleased that he did not immediately have to keep wicket against the Australians, but had a chance of resting in the pavilion.

Anyway, when the time came for him to have a crack at the Australian bowlers Arthur Wood fairly bounded out of the pavilion. What is more, his joyous spirit was to be seen in his play. The little Yorkshireman fairly darted up and down the wicket as he hit the Australian bowlers hard and often, and when finally Sydney Barnes caught and bowled Wood, our stumper had knocked up a most refreshing 53.

"Well, and what do you think of me, a mere stumper, being able to score runs?" he wisecracked at me. "But then," he added, trying to look serious, "maybe, after all, I'm being played for my batting."

At this everyone laughed, for Arthur Wood is a rare leg-puller.

Eventually, with 903 runs on the board, and only seven wickets down—Hardstaff being unbeaten with 169—Walter Hammond declared the innings closed, and our bowlers, on a wicket that still looked full of runs, wondered what the future held for them.

During the latter part of our innings there had been an unfortunate incident when Don Bradman, who had put himself on to bowl, had fallen in one of the holes made by Bill O'Reilly, twisted his ankle, and was carried off the field in great pain. We visited him in the dressing-room at the end of the day, and he looked white; was still in pain.

Although, naturally, we hoped that Don would be fit enough to take his place at the wicket, it was quite obvious to everyone that a miracle would have to be performed if Bradman were to play any further part in the match. This proved to be the case, and we managed to dismiss the Australians for 201 and 123, winning the Test by an innings and 579 runs.

Naturally we were elated at such a terrific victory, and the fact that our side had made the highest score in Test cricket, but, for all this, we had not won the "Ashes", Australia, by reason of her earlier victory, and the other two Tests being drawn—remember, not a ball was bowled in the Manchester Test—holding on to them.

Apart from the century I had scored against the Australians when making my Test début against them at Nottingham, and the not-out 76 knocked up at Lord's, I had not done so well against the visitors as many had hoped, finishing up with an average of 42.80 in Test matches.

Despite several disappointments, though, playing against the Australians had taught me many things that were to prove invaluable in the future, not the least being to never underestimate the opposition. The Australians, I was not slow to appreciate, are great "kidders", and quite early in my innings against them I learnt, behind a smile and a joke, they were carefully "sizing you up".

Bill O'Reilly was a typical example of what I mean. The wonderful Australian bowler, if he had not before played against a batsman with a big reputation, used to try various types of deliveries, watch the batsman's reaction to them all. Then, when he found one, or two types, that worried him, the "Tiger" would wait until he thought the moment was ripe. Then down flashed the ball, and, more often than not, that batsman was out.

I thought after this series of Tests—and remembered this following the 1946-7 series in Australia—that we can learn much from the Australians, for they look upon cricket as a game to be won, and go all out to win as a result of their careful study of the opposition.

In short, they are students of cricket, and because of this are, in my opinion, all the better players because of it.

Although many of these Australians—the first I was to meet in Test cricket—have to-day packed their bags for the last time, I think it is interesting to reflect upon some of them. Bill O'Reilly, for instance. Tall, bald, and possessing big hands and feet that were the cartoonist's delight, O'Reilly ranks among the truly great bowlers of my generation. As I said just now, he was a student of cricket and cricketers; was normally very good-tempered. I remember, however, on one occasion, during a Test at Leeds, that O'Reilly saw red. It was after Umpire Frank Chester had twice no-balled him, and Joe Hardstaff had cracked the Australian to the boundary. Grabbing the ball, which looked like a small pea in his huge hand, O'Really, livid in the face, stalked back to take his run-up, turned, flew up to the crease, and sent down a fast ball on the leg stump. Just how it happened I have never been able to fathom, but, as if grabbed by some unseen hand, the ball suddenly turned and hit—THE OFF STUMP.

Joe Hardstaff was shocked, and walked back to the pavilion as if dazed, and, when he saw me, exclaimed: "I must say I dislike it when this fellow loses his temper!"

So would any batsman after receiving such an amazing delivery. But then, O'Reilly got wickets all the time—and, as I said before, rarely, if ever, lost his temper.

Stan McCabe, the all-rounder, ranked among the most pleasant cricketers I have ever known. For young players, too, he was an object lesson in thoroughness. McCabe, whether batting, bowling or fielding, took great pains to make sure that everything was as it should be. He studied the field carefully before receiving every ball; he took trouble to make sure that his gear was always in the best possible condition; when he bowled it was to the field he had asked his skipper to set.

Yes, as cricketer and man, Stanley McCabe was an Australian to admire.

Lindsay Hassett, very much like Don Bradman in style during the 1938 tour, was another likeable fellow, full of fun, and always good company. As a batsman, and fielder, he was in the top-class.

What of Don Bradman? Although in later years I was to get to know him even better, the famous Australian has not altered. Is quiet, reserved, and does not talk a great deal, but once you get him on cricket it is to listen to one of the greatest living authorities.

You may have heard veteran cricket followers suggest that Bradman cannot be compared with the stylists of old—I have often been told this also applies to me—but there is no disputing, as a run-getter, he stands supreme. After you have listened to him discussing the various aspects of cricket you appreciate that the Australian, apart from being able to play the game, *knows* it, from A to Z.

These, then, were a few of the grand Australian cricketers against whom, in 1938, I furthered my cricket education. What is more, I think, because I had the opportunity of crossing bats with such distinguished opponents, that my game improved, for, I am sure, if a player, no matter how young he may be, wishes to make progress in the game, it is essential that he should play against the strongest possible opposition.

Many folk, I know, will disagree with this theory, but remember, I am writing from experience.

Apart from the satisfaction of playing in all five Tests, the 1938 season had many thrills for me when I played for my county, Middlesex, not the smallest being when I partnered my good friend, Bill Edrich, when he scored his thousandth run in May.

Don Bradman—yes, the match was against the Australians—declared with fifteen minutes to go, and this left
Edrich with a faint chance of getting the 21 runs he needed
for the coveted 1,000. I went out with Edrich to open the
innings, and the little man with the big heart faced the
bowling of McCabe and Waite. Do not get the idea that
the Australians were being kind and presenting Edrich with
his 1,000 "on a plate". Bill had to fight for his runs—and
how he fought! We managed to put on 22 runs before
stumps were drawn—and Edrich, to his delight, scored
21 of them, and so reached 1,000 in the month of May.

An interesting thing about Edrich's feat was that all his
runs were scored at Lord's.

It was when we entertained Gloucestershire at Lord's
that I played, for the first time in my life, in a match which
resulted in both sides scoring the same number of runs in
the first innings—478. During this match, too, "Big Jim"
Smith, our hard-hitting fast-bowler, used the long-handle
with wonderful success, and cracked up 50 runs in eleven
minutes!

Just you try doing this and I wager you will appreciate
how great was Jim Smith's feat!

Against Essex, when we played them at Chelmsford, I
had an experience that ranks among the most interesting
of my cricketing life. We had to take fourth knock on a
wicket that was crumbling fast, and with the Essex bowlers
taking full advantage of it, and making the ball turn a good
deal, our batsmen, as you would expect, walked into plenty
of trouble. Eventually, when A. D. Baxter joined me at
the crease, and nine wickets had fallen, we still needed 24
runs to win.

Remember, I was still only a youngster, and felt that a
great deal depended upon me being able to strike up a
quick understanding with the Middlesex amateur. Fortunately for me, A. D. Baxter knew what was expected of
him, and while I tried to nurse the bowling, and keep the
Essex spinners away from him, Baxter, when he did have
to face them, presented a very straight bat.

Playing for England

Slowly—very slowly it seemed to me—the runs began to come in. In singles and twos we crept forward, then, with the Essex fieldsmen nearly sitting on our bats, I managed to score the all-important run and we were winners by—one wicket!

As a matter of fact, of the 24 runs needed when Baxter linked up with me, I scored all but one of them.

"I don't think you'll play many better innings than that 87 not-out," said my skipper, R. W. V. Robins, as we made our way back to London, and I was inclined to agree with him, for, apart from helping to beat Essex, I had also managed to overcome one of my greatest failings at this time—impetuosity.

I'll put it this way. My great belief is that every cricketer, young or old, should invariably play his own game. In my own case that means, for the most part, attacking the bowling. Against Essex, though, with so much depending upon my ability to not only hold up an end, but help "nurse" my colleague, and still get runs, I had to forget my personal liking for attack, and mould my play to suit the conditions.

At Chelmsford, to my delight, I did succeed in this quest, and because I succeeded, Middlesex managed to gain a valuable win.

There's a moral somewhere in that . . .

7

*Opponent Forecast I'd Do Well Against Him—
Essex Give Us a Fright—The Wonderful "Canterbury Festival"—Jim Smith's Bitter Disappointment—The "Black Bradman" Shows His Greatness.*

I RARELY, if ever, take heed of any forecast as to how
I might play in a cricket or football match, but, when
returning from the second Test of the 1939 series at
Manchester, where we met the West Indies, I must confess
I took heed of my companion, who sat opposite me, as we
dined on the train that was speeding back to London.

"Why I should make such a forecast, beyond the fact
that you are playing so well, beats me," said my friend,
"but to-morrow, when we meet you at Lord's, I'm prepared
to see you—am willing to bet this will be the case!—make
your biggest score in top-class cricket."

As the train rattled over a crossing, and the soup rolled
back and forth in our bowls, I looked up at the man facing
me, for it was Bill Copson, with whom I had just played in
the Test, and who, on the morrow, would be bowling for
Derbyshire against me.

"Well, Bill," I said, "you're saying these things, not I,
so if anyone is disappointed it'll not be me."

Next day, when the time came for me to go to the wicket
it was to find Bill Copson, a big grin on his face, awaiting
me. "Here he comes," said the genial Bill to his colleagues.
Then, to me: "Don't forget what I said."

Well, thought I, Copson seems so confident there must
be something in what he says, so I faced the Derbyshire
bowling in quite a happy frame of mind.

I do not know if Bill Copson has powers to foretell the
future, but in this case he was 100 per cent correct, for I

73

did make my highest score in county cricket, knocking up 214 not-out, an innings that included one six and 26 boundaries, quite a few of them off my friend, Bill Copson.

"Well, and what did I tell you?" said Bill, when stumps were drawn for the day. "You *have* beaten your record."

This was the first occasion on which I had topped the double century. Scoring so many runs at a time demands more of a batsman than many folk in the crowd fully appreciate. Apart from the powers of concentration, your body muscles have great calls made upon them. I know football, you might say, should have hardened me to such exertion, but, believe it or not, a day playing cricket makes me much more tired than a game of football. Anyway, you are using entirely different muscles when batting at the wicket; muscles that are not used so often as those we call upon at soccer, and after my double-century at Lord's I felt stiffer than ever before in my life. Fortunately a masseur was able to help me; my father, too, gave me a rub, but next day, when I fielded, the stiffness was still with me and remained for some time.

"Maybe that'll teach you not to go scoring double-centuries," wisecracked one of my team-mates, but, having sampled such a success, I thought it worth while trying again!

By now, I had well and truly settled down to the career upon which I had set my heart from the very earliest days. Everyone was most helpful and understanding. My skipper, R. W. V. Robins, was always willing—anxious, I should say—to give me the benefit of his vast experience, while my colleagues were never slow in offering me hints that were to prove of value.

Apart from the joy of scoring runs, I also found that county cricket had much to offer. There were great friendships developed; you got around and met interesting people; and there were the various cricket festivals.

Without a doubt the Canterbury Festival must rank among the greatest in cricket. It was certainly an eye-opener for me with tents scattered around the famous St.

Lawrence Ground, women in long and colourful summer dresses, bands playing, and everywhere a happy atmosphere you will only find at festivals such as this.

Even the cricket was light-hearted, and "Big Jim" Smith, with his powerful hitting, gave everyone a thrill. "Big Jim", who had set his heart on winning the Lawrence Trophy for the quickest century of the season, was in terrific form, and when he did manage to connect the bat with the ball in the course of his mighty swipes, it invariably went either sizzling to the boundary or over the ropes for six. As it happened, though, quite a number of Smith's efforts did not quite connect properly—we must give the Kent bowlers, especially Wright and Davies, full marks for preventing Smith from dispatching everything past the field—so it naturally slowed down his rate of scoring. Altogether Smith, in cracking up 101—his only century of the season—took seven sixes and five fours off the Kent attack. To his chagrin, however, the century was nothing like so fast as he had hoped would be the case!

A remarkable fellow was Jim Smith. When he went to the wicket the giant looked as if he were holding some child's bat. Once he got going, though, there were few bowlers in the country able to stand up to his "Grand Slam" efforts.

Strangely enough, considering the manner in which he used to sally up to the wicket to clout slow bowlers, Jim Smith, during the course of his first-class career, was never stumped. The reason? I have heard many theories, but personally think that Smith had such a wonderful eye, and was so quick on his feet for a big man, that he was always capable of successfully "changing his mind".

There is also another thing to be considered: "Big Jim" rarely gave a slow bowler a chance to turn the ball. . . .

Yes, we liked the Canterbury Festival—incidentally, we defeated Kent by an innings and 64 runs and one of the most enjoyable features was the dance held at the close of playing. Never shall I forget seeing "Jim Smith the Giant", after his superb knock, dancing with a tiny girl of 5 ft. 4 in.!

Playing for England

On the whole, though, few cricketers I find are keen on dancing. That goes for me.

In Kent, you will gather, the match against Middlesex was played in a gay setting in a most light-hearted manner. How different it was when we played at Old Trafford, Manchester, against the men of Lancashire.

Now, do not get me wrong. The Lancastrians are grand sportsmen, while the Old Trafford spectators rank among the best-informed cricket followers in the world. Like their team, though, they like to see the home side winning, and, if you are to put it across Lancashire at Old Trafford, you have to do well.

It so happens that the Lancashire headquarters ranks among my favourite grounds. Apart from the hospitality extended to us all—they also have the best ice-cream I've ever tasted—I invariably seem to bat well on the Manchester ground, and when Middlesex went north, to play Lancashire, I was keenly looking forward to the visit.

The match, I might add, had been set apart as a benefit for Farrimond, the Lancashire and England stumper.

Well, once again, I "came off" at Old Trafford. I wondered, when dismissed in the first innings for seven, whether or not my run of luck had forsaken me, but at the second time of asking I collected 115.

What a wonderful and understanding crowd those Lancastrian folk are. I can well understand why, in the past, they have bred so many fine cricketers at Old Trafford, for those spectators, who understand and appreciate the finer points of the game, give a batsman, no matter whether he be a Lancastrian or a visitor, terrific encouragement. At least, that is my own personal feeling, and other cricketers hold a similar view.

Then, as if our batsmen had not done enough damage, Jim Smith completed a hat-trick—taking six wickets for 31 runs—and we managed to defeat Lancashire by 123 runs.

Just as Old Trafford is one of my "lucky" grounds, so there are grounds where I rarely do very well. Kennington

Oval comes under this classification. So, too, have I teams against whom I usually have a good game, and those who often get my wicket cheaply.

Essex are one of the teams against whom I have done well. In 1939 the good fairy who sits on the end of the bat was apparently not with me, for with only twelve and eight runs respectively in my two innings I was sent back to the pavilion wondering what it was all about.

The match, played on the Southend ground, had been awarded as a benefit to the late Laurie Eastman, and it so happened he was given a wonderful opportunity to finish the game in a blaze of glory.

Although suffering from water on the knee, and in some pain, Eastman, when nine Essex wickets had fallen, and 21 runs were needed for victory, gallantly decided to join Ray Smith at the wicket. As he could hardly walk, let alone run, the late Kenneth Farnes went out to act as runner for him.

With Middlesex in line for the championship, and every match tense as a Test for us, our bowlers, quite naturally, could not allow sentiment to interfere with the task of trying to force a win, but Laurie Eastman, a fine cricketer, was not going to give way without a fight, and, with Ray Smith supporting him in great style, started the uphill struggle for runs.

Slowly, but for all that surely, the Essex pair began to make the runs they needed. Then, with only four runs needed to tie, Jim Sims got one past Laurie Eastman's defence, let out an appeal, as the ball rattled the Essex man's pads and up went the umpire's hand—we had gained a narrow win in a truly first-class game.

But then, Essex are always a fine team to play against, for not only are they top-class cricketers but a grand set of fellows.

The same thing applies to Yorkshire, whom we journeyed north to meet late that season with an outside hope that we would defeat them and so strengthen our chances of winning the County Championship.

Playing for England

I have told you before of the sterling qualities of the Yorkshire cricketers; they are qualities to be found in few teams. In every branch of the game, as their past record shows, Yorkshire have always produced great players. I think they will continue to so do for years to come. Why? The answer is easy. They go out and seek promising cricketers, coach them, and then encourage the youngsters to reach the heights.

How frequently they do!

When, with the war clouds gathering, we met Yorkshire in 1939, those great players, Herbert Sutcliffe and Maurice Leyland, gave as perfect an exhibition of batsmanship as ever I've seen. What a contrasting pair they were, too, Sutcliffe with his elegance and polish, Leyland, dour when the situation demanded, but a rare hitter of a ball.

Against us this pair rattled up runs at a great pace, and when I eventually caught and bowled Sutcliffe "Our Herbert", as he was known to Yorkshire fans, had cracked 175.

The beauty of Herbert Sutcliffe's batsmanship was his great ability to make opposing bowlers, even if they were sending down first-class deliveries, feel that he was "the gov'nor". There was no showmanship, either, about the way in which Sutcliffe went about his work. He scored his runs the easy way. Did not use up too much energy, and, as a result, was able to bat for hours without taxing his strength too much. That, in my opinion, is one of the reasons why Herbert Sutcliffe kept at the top for so long.

He did his job without taking too much out of himself because, from the first, he took the scientific approach.

Maurice Leyland—who scored a not-out 186 in the match I am talking about—was another who kept going season after season without appearing to lose his form. Like Sutcliffe, he was a *cricketer*, not a *showman*.

What an object lesson for any young cricketer were Sutcliffe and Leyland.

The same thing applies to Bill Bowes, that towering, good-hearted, bespectacled bowler. What Bill Bowes doesn't know about "sending 'em down" isn't worth knowing, and when he helped skittle us out for 62, and 122, I appreciated why he has so often been called upon for England.

Bill Bowes is another example of a cricketer getting results without carrying exertion to the extreme. You may have seen, as have I, bowlers rushing up to the crease, taking a very long run, and then seemingly getting little pace. That is not the way Bill Bowes works. He does not overdo the run-up, but watch how he delivers the ball—there's a great art in it—and how it seems to nip off the pitch at great speed. It's all a question of practice, and taking the trouble to find out the best way to use your natural powers. Bowes took this trouble as a youngster. I've not the slightest doubt, if other young Englishmen took the trouble, they could have similar success to Bowes, and last as many seasons in the top-class in the manner of the Yorkshireman who has just retired from county cricket.

Yes, on reflection, I think batting against Bill Bowes, in that last pre-war match against Yorkshire, will rank among my most interesting memories, for Bowes, in the manner of the born bowler, made the ball turn both ways in a most disconcerting manner.

But then, in those days one was always prepared to learn, even if at a cost, from Yorkshire. . . .

In that last pre-war season we had visiting us in England the Test team from the West Indies, who included in their ranks George Headley who, as a result of wonderful batting at home, had been nicknamed by some alert cricket writers "The Black Bradman".

Now, although I had not seen Headley in action, it struck me that he had a big reputation to live up to if he was to be likened to the Australian wizard.

He well and truly justified all the nice things that were said about him, heading the English batting averages at the end of the season with an average of 72.70 and seven centuries under his belt.

George Alphonse Headley, to give him his full name, was born in Jamaica in 1909. He is not very tall—something like Bradman in build—but no sooner was he batting against us, when Middlesex met the West Indies at Lord's, than I was struck by his wrist-work. His wrists must be the most supple in the world. If Headley received a ball on the off he did not appear to hit it. He just wriggled his wrists, and, before you knew what had happened, the ball had rattled to the boundary.

Against Middlesex, Headley scored a wonderful 227. Once again, as a bowler, I had a close-up of this remarkable player and the impression I gained will never be forgotten. It was as if he were a tiger waiting to spring. On running up to the wicket to bowl you could "feel" his eyes watching your hand carefully. Maybe you would try and disguise the type of delivery you proposed making, but, in your heart—at least, that was my impression—something told you that the eyes of Mr. Headley had detected it.

Sure enough they had!

Headley, like Don Bradman, knew how to use his feet. By that I mean that he appreciated that a batsman, if he is to get runs, and at the same time not throw away his wicket, must take up the best possible position to deal with the delivery sent down to him. I remember, time and again, "wrapping up" a ball on which I had put a great deal of spin. Headley, quick to sense what I had in mind, was up the wicket and hitting that ball to the boundary long before it landed on the pitch and had an opportunity to turn.

When he played in the first Test of the 1939 series, at Lord's, George Headley once again proved that in addition to being a very great batsman—among the best four in the world—he possessed the ideal temperament for the big occasion. In the West Indies' first innings George scored 106 out of 277. In the second innings claimed 107 of the West Indies 225.

This scoring of a century in both innings of a Test at Lord's was a new record. Never before had such a feat been accomplished at Headquarters.

You may have noticed that I have often said how, after watching every great batsman, I invariably felt that I had learnt something new. Particularly was this so with George Headley. It was the West Indian batsman's ability to play spin bowling without taking undue risks that impressed itself most upon me, for in the past when playing against this type of attack I had a tendency to take chances that might have lost me my wicket. Through studying George Headley carefully I thought I understood how he succeeded in combating it so successfully.

When the time came for me to bat, and we had 147 runs on the board for the loss of Gimblett, Paynter and Hammond, I felt really good. Lord's, of course, is my "home-ground", and quite a number of my friends had come to see me bat in the hope that I would get some runs.

I was determined not to disappoint them.

The first ball I received was from E. A. Martindale, the West Indies fast bowler, and one of the speediest in the game—and I missed it. Martindale threw up his hands in disgust at this, and when, a few seconds later, off the second ball received, I was given a "life", I thought Martindale might break down and cry. Without a doubt he was bowling superbly and deserved to send me back to the pavilion. Having been given these "lives", though, I said to myself: "Your luck's in. Take advantage of it."

And I did.

How Len Hutton—who, by the way, never talks when he's at the wicket—and I enjoyed ourselves! Not since I'd left school had I had so many cracks at the ball, and boundaries seemed to roll out. First Len would crack one to the rails, then I would follow suit. We had a great race and put on 248 runs for the fourth wicket in the space of 140 minutes, which, you will appreciate, is fast scoring for any match let alone a Test. Altogether I knocked up 120, including 16 boundaries, before being caught off a big hit, by Stollmeyer, just in front of the ropes.

That century, before my home crowd, did me a great deal of good, for the West Indies fielding, as usual, was of very high standard, and to me, a young batsman, it was a wonderful experience to have to try and find a way through the tight ring that was so well-set by the various bowlers. Eventually, as you will have gathered, I did find a method of piercing this screen.

Yes, as I was to discover in the other two Tests, it was great fun opposing the men from the West Indies. Not only were they grand sportsmen, but really keen cricketers. Just the type you get a real kick out of playing against.

Learie Constantine, for example, will always be considered by me as one of the best examples of "perpetual motion" to be found this side of the great divide. On the cricket field Learie is here, there and everywhere. As a bowler he ranks high; his hurricane hitting when at the crease has delighted thousands of cricket fans; in the field he has rarely been equalled, and, I personally think, never bettered.

During the course of the Third Test at Kennington Oval, which was drawn, Learie Constantine was responsible for one of those terrific knocks about which people talk for years. I remember vividly how, when Learie went to the wicket, he appeared to be slowly gathering his strength for a terrific burst. He did not hurry, but took his time taking guard, looking around the field, and then, quite obviously, making a mental note of where we were positioned.

Then, when our bowlers commenced their attack, so did Learie Constantine leap into action and become the dynamic batsman against whom no bowler could hope to bowl "tight". Constantine fairly rocketed into action. He made us dizzy, and tired, by the manner he pulled and cracked the ball in all directions. One minute he would be straight driving with all his force. Next he would execute as classic a late-cut as you're likely to see in years.

In short, Constantine, at our bowlers' expense, presented the crowd with an exhibition of the type of batsmanship that had become his hall-mark of fame.

Altogether, in the course of that exhilarating innings he scored 79 runs, no fewer than 78 of them being in a stand of 103 he made with a colleague!

Playing for England

A mighty man was Learie Constantine in those days and with George Headley, and others of that fine West Indies team, gave us as fine an example of how cricket should be played as we ever want to see.

By now the war clouds had gathered ominously and talk of the impending clash of arms was on all sides. I do not think anyone of us felt like concentrating upon cricket with so much war-talk on hand, but like everyone else, we tried to grin and bear it.

Our last pre-war county match was against Warwickshire, and we introduced for the first time to the county side little Paul Brookes who, a few seasons before, when working as a ground-boy at Lord's, had hit the headlines because when bowling to Don Bradman in the nets, he had pierced the Australian's defence and knocked back his middle stump.

Often, when he and I were together in the nets, Paul Brookes used to confide in me and say how keen he was to make the grade in cricket. Paul, too, was always ready to listen to any advice that might be given him, and so rapid was his advance that it was felt, given reasonable fortune, he would blossom out into a truly great player.

Of medium-height, slim, and quietly-spoken, young Paul Brookes, who called everyone "Mr.", came into the Middlesex team as a left-handed batsman, and when he joined me at the wicket I knew, from the look on his face, that he was enjoying the happiest moment of his young life.

What is more, Paul absolutely "wallowed" in his batting, and with me as his partner, cracked up a wonderful unbeaten 45.

"You've a big find there," a Warwickshire player said to us, and we were in full agreement. But Paul Brookes—God bless him!—never lived to enjoy the success he had earned, for after lying three months in a hospital bed in England, after receiving a spine wound while fighting in Italy, he passed away.

After our match against Warwickshire, with war imminent, all our contracts were cancelled. Cricket, as we knew it, for so many years, was to take a back seat, and, before its return, many of those players who had delighted us so often were to lose their lives. I was to travel the world.

Cricket, though, is a great sport at binding men together, and before I finally returned "home" to Lord's, after my travels, I was to appreciate, more than ever before, just what a grand brotherhood exists between men who play the greatest of all games.

8

*I Join the Army—A "Mystery Ride" I Didn't
Enjoy—I Don't Think the Sergeant Liked Me!—
Cricket During an Air-Raid—The Army Made
Me Fit—Adventures in India—The Palace of
Gold—When a Mob Might Have Killed Me—
Indian Wickets Have Their Drawbacks.*

"JOIN the Army and See the World," was a poster I had
often seen on hoardings. I will confess that it had never
appealed to me. True, one of my ambitions was to see
new lands, and meet new people, but I anticipated doing so
with a cricket bat in my hand.

Hitler, though, when he caused the war that was to
bring disaster to so many, made it imperative that I, along
with many millions of other young fellows, should put on a
khaki uniform.

It was in November, 1939, that I registered for military
service, and when I presented myself at Finsbury Park
Labour Exchange, close to Arsenal Stadium, quite a number
of young fellows greeted me with "Up the Gunners", or
"Bit different to scoring centuries, eh, Denis?"

A week later I was summoned for a medical, and the
doctor, before giving me a thorough overhaul, said: "I
shouldn't really have to examine you. You're fit enough."
When, however, he discovered I had varicose veins, his face
looked a little grimmer. "It's the normal procedure to
grade men suffering with veins like yours," he said to me,
"but I suppose I'd be criticised if I did. They don't worry
you, do they?"

"Not on your life!" I replied, so he passed me fit for duty,
and I returned home to discuss with my mother and father

what the future might hold for me in the Royal Artillery, the regiment I asked to join.

December 12, 1939, will for ever be a red-letter day in my life. It was then that I was called for service in the British Army, and, I must admit, the prospect did not altogether fill me with glee. Still, there was a job on hand. . . .

I reported for duty at a large hall near London Bridge Station. About 150 other recruits were hanging around—that's the only expression one can use—when I arrived at eleven o'clock in the morning.

"Here he is!" someone exclaimed, and before I quite knew what had happened it was to find myself before an officer seated at a wooden table. He, while I looked on, had a long discussion with another officer as to what battery I was to join. Eventually, after a conversation that made me wonder, because of its length, whether or not they planned to use me to beat the German Army single-handed, I learnt that I was to go into "357 battery".

We were making progress!

Then began one of those long waits I was to learn were part and parcel of Army life before, just after eight o'clock in the evening, we were lined up in ranks of three, and, still wearing civilian suits, marched over London Bridge to the station.

If our feelings showed themselves I wager we looked a very sorry lot! But worse was to follow—from my point of view—for we were packed on to a train without even so much as a hint as to where we were destined, and after jolting through the black-out for what seemed hours, arrived at a station I recognised as being on the London-Brighton run.

It was East Grinstead.

Outside the station we were met by a number of Army trucks, ordered to climb aboard, and were immediately whisked once more into the night. Finally, after the trucks had halted, we were brought up before an Army major in a big hall.

"He's the C.O.," one of the "old sweats" who had driven

us to the hall whispered to me—and it didn't take us long to appreciate that he didn't appear to have a very high regard for the recruits that had been sent down to him. After eyeing us for a moment he said abruptly, and in the manner of "stage colonels": "You're here now—and in the Army." Not very intelligent, I thought. Then he went on: "We're going to make soldiers of you here. Good night!"

Most of us were, to use an old phrase, "out on our feet". So, after being told that there was straw upstairs, we climbed to the next floor as best our legs would let us, snuggled down, and with our attaché cases for pillows, were quickly far away from the new life in which we had suddenly found ourselves.

Next morning we received our uniforms, boots, and other kit, and in general began to feel a little more settled. One sergeant-major, though, at once showed that he had a "down" on me. On the first morning he sidled up to me and barked, without warning: "You're in the Army now, not playing football or cricket, so forget about it."

"I expect no favours," I replied, whereupon the sergeant-major barked back: "It's all right providing you understand that."

Four months later, when I was selected to play at outside-left for the British Army football team against the French Army, in Paris, I know that sergeant-major did not feel too pleased!

When I joined the Army one of the first things I was prepared to accept was that cricket would no longer be included among my fun, but that was not the case, for in the summer of 1940, when, like other servicemen, I was given a little free time, it was still possible to get an occasional game.

In that memorable summer of 1940 I shall never forget being chosen to appear in the Army *v.* R.A.F. match at Lord's. Things, you may remember, were very serious, but in the middle of the game, when the R.A.F. were bowling like men inspired, we suddenly noticed planes in the sky to the east. No-one paid much attention at the time, but when, without warning, a cloud of smoke suddenly billowed heavenwards, and the sirens began to wail, we all realised that danger was imminent.

We were not far wrong, either, for taking place before our eyes was the first great German aerial attack upon London.

As you will understand, the match came to a sudden conclusion!

Part of my Army training was a specialist course at the Army Physical Training Corps School, Aldershot, and if you think we had an easy time at this establishment you are wrong—very wrong! So hectic was the work that I discovered, at the end of two weeks, I had dropped over a stone in weight. In due course, after this, I was posted to the R.E. Depot at Aldershot prior to being sent overseas, and, when duties allowed, played for the Army at football and cricket.

By now the varicose veins that nearly prevented my entry into the Army had become extremely painful, so I decided to take expert advice and have them removed. I am right glad—especially to-day—that I took the doctor's suggestion to heart, for I felt like a new man when I returned to my unit, and in my first game after this operation, for the Army against the R.A.F., scored 87.

The young fellow who caught me, by the way, was named Alec Bedser. In the future, as England cricketers, we were to become great friends. . . .

At that moment, though, the needs of the Army came first, and when I received orders to proceed on embarkation leave—eleven days being allowed me—determined to have a good time. I did, and on my last day, playing for Arsenal against Luton in the afternoon, scored a hat-trick, and then proceeded north by the night train to Liverpool.

Although I held the rank of sergeant this did not appear to mean a very great deal when I climbed the gangplank of the s.s. *Stratheden*, for I found her as tightly-packed as a London tube during the rush-hour. Finally I did manage to burrow my way into some semblance of comfort, and for a month existed in this manner.

Playing for England

At last we reached our goal—INDIA!

Now, as I have said earlier, one of the places I had hoped to visit was India, but as a cricketer. This chance, though, of being able to see the great continent, without having to pay for the privilege, struck me as being too good to be missed, and from the first, although such posting had its obvious drawbacks, I determined to make the best of it.

What struck me as being amusing, however, was that I was a one-man draft. Carrying my rifle, full-pack, haversack, kitbag, and two cases, I looked as if the whole weight of the British Army rested upon my shoulders—and had a feeling that was the position! Eventually, after travelling a couple of days in a train that might well have been fashionable in the days of George Stephenson, I arrived at Ambala. I glanced at my watch. It was exactly six o'clock, and I looked in vain for someone to meet me. But then, I did not yet know my India, so after waiting about for three hours I hired a somewhat ancient-looking horse and cart, and aboard this was driven to the Army P.T. School of India.

The C.O., when I introduced myself, was kindness itself, and after a week at this delightful spot, with every opportunity given me to settle down, my next posting was to the Cadet Infantry School at Mhow. So far I had not met a soul with whom I had rubbed shoulders in the sporting world, but when alighting from the train at Mhow it was to find awaiting me, a big smile on his handsome face, none other than Ralph Birkett, the England, Middlesbrough and Arsenal right-winger. As soon as Ralph heard of my posting he made it his business to be on the platform to greet me, and, as we made our way towards the school—it was about 120° in the shade—I wondered how anyone stood up to it.

"Don't you worry about that," said Ralph Birkett. "Before you realise it the heat will mean nothing."

He was right.

One of the first things I asked, when I had struck up a friendship with various sportsmen at Mhow, was: "What's it like for cricket in these parts?"

Playing for England

The answer I received warmed my heart. "You'll enjoy every minute of it," I was told. "The wickets are full of runs."

It was not until six months later I was able to test the reliability of this story. I was chosen to play for the Europeans, against the Parsees, in the Bombay Pentangular Tournament. This is India's biggest cricket tournament, and when I saw the names of the players in our side I thought we stood an excellent chance of victory. They numbered among them Joe Hardstaff, R. T. Simpson and Fred Butler (Notts.), Dick Howorth (Worcester), Peter Cranmer (Warwickshire) and Peter Judge (Glamorgan), with Paddy Corrall (Leicester) to keep wicket. On paper this was a first-class team, and I think we were justified in thinking ourselves capable of holding our own when the match was played on the beautiful wicket at the Brabourne Stadium.

This stadium, which has a huge double-decker grand-stand behind one wicket, and a modern pavilion behind the other, is among the finest I have ever seen. Apart from its wonderful wicket, and other facilities, the stadium offers the cricketers wonder dressing-rooms containing lockers, shower-baths and massage tables. We have nothing to equal it in England.

As you will appreciate, being servicemen we had been unable to take with us to India flannels, white shirts and cricket gear in general, but the Bombay Europeans came to our assistance, loaning us the things we needed, and although they were not so loose fitting as many of us hoped—how tight my trousers were across the seat!—we made do.

Joe Hardstaff, who had come down from his regiment in Burma to take part in this match, was our captain, and when he won the toss, and the wicket looked so full of runs, wisely decided to bat.

I'm sorry to say that my baptism to Indian wickets was not a great success. Colah, a left-arm bowler, knocked back my middle stump when I had scored but seven, and we were all out for 300, Joe Hardstaff, who played a true captain's part, getting 159 of them.

When the Indians batted they did not begin too confidently, losing two wickets for 40 runs. Then Rusi Modi, about whom I had heard so much, came to the wicket, and we were treated to a wonderful exhibition of batsmanship. Modi, after being missed twice before he had scored ten, afterwards went forward without a mistake and made 215 of the 479 runs scored by the Parsees.

Tall, thin, but extremely elegant, Modi, in my opinion, is going to rank among the great batsmen of the age. He has a hawklike pair of eyes, and I noticed, when bowling against him, that like all ace batsmen, he does not stand still and wait for the ball. He uses his feet beautifully; is extremely light. Above everything else, too, he puts the whole weight of his body behind every stroke, and as a result gets boundaries by the dozen.

Any cricketer could learn much from studying the all-round-the-wicket strokes he makes with such obvious ease and confidence.

When we had a second innings I'd got used to the very bad glare that had at first unsettled me, and with Joe Hardstaff managed to find some semblance of my form. By the close of play, and the end of the match, we had forced a draw and were 185—2, Hardstaff being undefeated with 79 and myself 76 not-out.

This game of cricket—the first most of us had enjoyed for many long months—made everyone anxious to fix up another match. Eventually, early in December 1945, the Cricket Club of India arranged to play a selected Services XI, the game to be played upon the Brabourne Stadium.

We included in our team for this match the Indian Test stars, Mashtaq Ali and C. K. Nayudu, and on reflection I think we were fortunate to be able to call upon them. For instance in the first innings, when we were dismissed for 342—I scored 16—the two Indian Test players, between them, secured 181 of our total, and when we had to field, gave a perfect exhibition of a side of the game too many players are inclined to take anything but seriously.

Playing for England

It was when the Indian XI went to the crease that we saw something we had heard a great deal about, but had not, up to then, had the good fortune to see: Indian cricketers, on their own bone-hard wickets, going all out for runs.

Never, since Don Bradman was at the zenith of his power, had I watched such batsmanship as that produced against us by Vinoo Mankad, S. W. Sohoni, V. S. Hazare and V. M. Merchant, all of whom were to visit England in 1946. Merchant, who made 201 not-out, gave what can best be described as a charming display. Like most Indian batsmen, he is a rare artist with his wrists, while—notice how important this is—his footwork, to my way of thinking, has only been excelled by Don Bradman and Walter Hammond. It was grand stuff!

When the Indians had scored 615—4 they declared, and once more we started our fight against a first-class attack. Soon we were in trouble, and, maybe because good fortune was with me, I was the only one, apart from R. T. Simpson, who appeared capable of staying at the wicket for any length of time. Simpson scored a most valuable fifty, but, with the exception of the Nottingham batsman, I saw my colleagues frequently coming and going from the crease.

We were, I might add, all wearing borrowed kit, and as my shirt was very tight I cut it under the armpits to allow me more freedom!

Once more the Indian bowlers proved too good for us, finishing our innings for 238 of which I made 120, my first century in India, and, I think, one of the greatest fights I have ever had for runs.

Apart from the heat, which was terrific, one had to battle against fielding that needed to be seen to be believed. It was electric. No man was prepared to give away one run, and towards the end I wondered whether or not I had wandered into a Test match by accident!

It was around this time that the Australian Services XI that had proved so successful during their tour of England in 1945 arrived in India, on their way home, to take on the

best that the Indians could put into the field. As it happened, when the East Zone team to meet them at Calcutta
was chosen, I was rather surprised to discover that I—the
only Englishman as it so happened—had been invited to
take my place in it. As I was very anxious to try my luck
against the Australians, who had fared extremely well in
England, I was delighted to accept.

The Australians included such outstanding players as
Lindsay Hassett, against whom I had played in the Test
matches of 1938, and Keith Miller, one of the finest all-
rounders in the world, and it was with a great interest that
I watched them, when in the field, come and go to the
wicket.

The Australian batsmen—probably the unusual glare may
have upset them—could do little against the fine bowling
of Bannerjee, Sarwate, Nayudu and Choudbury, Hassett
and Workman being top-scorers with 25, and the visitors
were dismissed for 107.

No, I did not go to the wicket and crack the Australian
bowlers all over the field. As a matter of fact, my stay was
extremely short, and before I had scored, and as a result
of a misunderstanding, was run-out. Eventually the
Australians, due to some fine bowling by Cristofani, put
out the Indian side for 131.

In their second innings the Australians, thanks to a
brilliant 125 by Hassett, and a valuable 69 by Cristofani,
were able to take their score to 304, leaving us to get 284
for victory.

The Australians, sensing their chance of a win, began in
great style and two quick wickets brought together Mushtaq
Ali, the Indian Test batsman, and myself. Naturally, with
the Australian bowlers on their toes, we began carefully;
were beginning to settle down when something happened
for which none of us had bargained.

Rioters broke into the cricket ground!

Waving flags, and shouting, the mob, led by the biggest
Indian I have ever seen, paraded around the ground chanting
slogans, and in general making themselves anything but

Playing for England

blind ourselves to the fact that the opposition was first-class.

It was as well, for they scored 462 in their first innings, Modi collecting a classic 98, and Merchant 79. Holkar, in reply, also did well, scoring 360 of which Mushtaq Ali claimed 109, and myself 20.

If we thought our chances were good our opponents soon altered all that, Modi scoring 151, Merchant 279 and Cooper 104. Altogether Bombay amassed—and that's the only word to use—764 runs in their second innings, and when we again went in, we needed the mammoth total of 863 to win.

Once again Mushtaq Ali proved his greatness with a century, and to my delight, I was making runs confidently. It was, mind you, a terrific battle against bowlers who, because of the huge lead they had, were able to take great liberties against us, and at the same time experiment with different types of deliveries. Some of the overs I received were, to say the least, weird, and on every possible occasion I cracked the ball to the boundary.

In the heat I did not fancy running too much!

Before we went in for our second innings a wealthy merchant offered any member of the Holkar side 50 rupees for every run scored over 100. As you will understand, being on Army pay, I was naturally anxious to take advantage of this offer, and when I had passed my century, and runs began to come quite freely, began to think, as I sent the ball into the crowd: "There goes another 200 rupees."

In fact I visualised myself being quite a wealthy young man as a result of my good form.

Well, to cut a long story short, we did not get the runs needed for victory, scoring 492—and being beaten by 374 runs—but as I carried my bat for 249, and felt good for another hundred, it was with some pleasure I worked out what I had won as a result of the Indian merchant's offer.

Altogether, I reckoned, £550 was due to me.

The story, I understand, made newspaper headlines in many parts of the world. Dozens of friends wrote and congratulated me on my good fortune.

What they did not know was that the Indian merchant, round about the time I reached the 200 mark, rose from his seat and disappeared.

To this day I have not received a penny of the £550 the rest of the sporting world appears to have thought I collected after my innings for Holkar!

In that Ranji Trophy Final, by the way, a new world record was established, the aggregate of 2,078 for 40 wickets being the first time in history that two thousand runs had been scored in a first-class match.

It was in January 1946 that I had my last experience of playing upon Indian wickets before returning home to England after two-and-a-half years in the land of perpetual heat. It was for the Europeans against the Hindus in the Bombay Pentangular Tournament and our side, which included B. H. Lyon (Gloucester), R. T. Simpson (Notts), and C. H. Palmer (Worcester), to mention but a few well-known players, looked quite strong. But those Indian cricketers are good, especially on their own wickets. After first dismissing us for 212—I scored 91—they knocked up 505—7 declared, and then again dismissed us for 291, myself collecting 124.

Had I been able to score a century in both innings it would have set up a new record for the Pentangular Tournament, but even these innings did not save us from defeat, the Hindus winning by an innings—and ONE run!

In the course of my career I have played on many and varied wickets, but on looking back I feel sure, in my heart, that the experience gained in Indian cricket did nothing to improve my batsmanship. As you will have probably noticed from time to time, mammoth scores are made in this part of the world, and the wickets for the most part are responsible for this state of affairs.

To be quite blunt, Indian wickets are a batsman's paradise. Never once, during the course of batting in India, did I have to play a turning ball. When I returned to England, and found the ball turning, it took me some little time to settle down. But settle down I did, only after many hours

Playing for England

in the nets during which there were occasions when I wondered if ever again I would master English bowling.

They say "Practice makes perfect". From experience, after years in India, and returning to find a turning ball the bane of my cricket life, you can take it from me this is correct.

My summing up of Indian wickets, therefore, is this: "They are ideal for run-getting. Useless for developing batsmen capable of playing, as did Jack Hobbs, Wally Hammond, and Herbert Sutcliffe, superb cricket on whatever wicket they found themselves."

9

The Gay Cricketers from India—He Uses a Camera to Help Score Centuries—A Triumph for Bedser—Failure for Me—Beating the "Hoodoo"—I Score a Century With a Broken Bat—Century That Was Worth £100.

THE DISTINCTION of being the first Test team to visit these shores after World War II, fell to India, and right well did these fine cricketers rise to the occasion and give English cricket followers an opportunity to see the game played at its best.

Included in this gay party of cricket cavaliers were many players whose names were to become household words, but none stood out more, by reason of his elegant batting, than V. M. Merchant, the Indian vice-captain.

At home, Merchant is a most successful business man, but I say, without hesitation, that cricket must be his greatest love. You can see that by the manner in which he plays the game. As a stroke player I think V. M. Merchant ranks very high among world batsmen. He delighted everyone, I know, when during the third Test at Kennington Oval he scored 128, the highest score ever made by an Indian batsman in a Test match.

If you have seen Merchant in action, or are to have that pleasure, I do not think you will deny that he has a masterly way of going about things. But Merchant's skill has not just been born in him; it has developed to its present stage after years of patient study.

Whenever Merchant takes part in a cricket match in India he always takes with him a ciné-camera. When the time comes for the great Indian batsman to take his place at the wicket he asks a friend to take "shots" of him batting, and when he gets home Merchant, after the films have been developed, runs through them carefully on a screen, trying to locate his strong points and weakness; more important still, *how he came to be dismissed.*

That is a point about Indian cricketers I think many of us should never forget. They are so thorough in their study of the game, and use the knowledge they gain to such advantage, I do not think it will be many years before they come into the Australian category as Test opponents. That is praise, I know, my Indian friends will thoroughly appreciate.

Never shall I forget the ups and downs of that first postwar season of English cricket. I started off with a real bang. Runs flowed freely from my bat, and I felt in wonderful form. I might add, too, that my exertions were helping me in other directions, too, for I had returned from India plumper than I might otherwise have been, and in the course of just under three weeks of active cricket lost no less than a stone.

There was an interesting reason for this happy state of affairs. The outfields were all on the slow side, so when I hit a ball hard instead of it flying to the boundary as would normally have been the case, it stopped just short of it, a fieldsman picked it up, and we ran three.

In those opening weeks of the 1946 season I reckon to have covered miles. Remember, too, that I was wearing a sweater, pads, and carrying a heavy bat. It was more like being on army fatigue than playing cricket!

Then, as if a gremlin had perched itself on the handle of my bat, and did everything to prevent me getting runs, my luck departed. I tried every possible thing to overcome this lack of success, but nothing, it seemed, would bring me back to run-getting.

Often, following another failure, I'd go home to Kenton and after supper stand in front of a mirror going through the stroke that had cost me my wicket. Invariably did I satisfy myself that it would not happen again—but it was the same when I once more went to the wicket!

Photo : Sport and General

Don Bradman, the great Australian batsman.

Peter Smith, the Essex all-rounder, among the last
to know he had been picked for England.

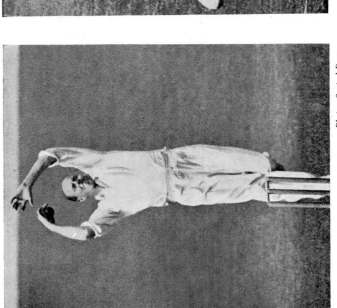

Bill O'Reilly, the great Australian bowler.

Photo : Central Press

Don Bradman is not being carried off in triumph. He has injured an ankle in the final Test of the 1938 series.

Photo : P.A. Reuter

The author puts a ball through the slips; one of his favourite shots.

Photo : Gopal Chitra Kuteer

The teams who met in the final of the Ranji trophy at Bombay in 1945. Denis Compton, the only Englishman to appear in the game, is seen second from right in the second row.

Photo : Sport and General

R. W. V. Robins, one of cricket's greatest captains, plays a late cut.

I will confess, too, it occurred to me that my place in the England Test team might be in jeopardy, for the five innings preceding the first Test against India were 0—0—8—0—1!

Hardly, you will agree, the kind of form expected from a player filling the number "three" position in the England team.

"Don't you worry, Denis," my father said to me, "things will work out all right in the end. The only thing you mustn't do is worry."

I agreed—but it was easier said than done!

From cricket followers, too, I received many letters giving me advice to follow. One sent a toy "duck", adding that he hoped it would be the last I'd ever receive. A noted dietician forwarded a diet he trusted I would follow, suggesting that my loss of form might have been due to certain foods disagreeing with me!

I did not, as you might think, cast away these letters into the waste-paper basket. The fact that I had lost my form had to be taken seriously and I was prepared to listen to any method of regaining it.

Practice, I finally told myself, was the only way. That is why I spent such a long time in the nets. And, when I was chosen to play against India at Lord's, I felt in my heart that I was going to break the "hoodoo" that had me in its grip.

When skipper Walter Hammond won the toss he naturally took the opportunity of batting first on a wicket that appeared to be full of runs. As usual Len Hutton and Cyril Washbrook opened our innings, but it did not take us long to appreciate that these Indians were going to be troublesome. With but fifteen runs on the score-board Hutton cocked up a catch to Nayudu, off a fine Amarnath delivery, and was given marching orders.

This meant that I had to take his place at the wicket.

Now, to be quite frank, in an effort to shake off my bad luck, I tried out two things for this match. Normally I prefer to bat with my sleeves down. Against the Indians I rolled them up. Rarely do I wear a cap. For this Test I

Playing for England

wore my "lucky" cap—the one I had won when first playing for England.

Having taken every possible "precaution" I also took my time in walking to the crease, giving my eyes an opportunity to get used to the "glare" after the shade of the pavilion, and by the time I had taken guard, and prepared to face the Indian bowling, felt "in the mood for runs".

My old friend, Amarnath, was the bowler I first had to face, and as he ran up to the wicket I watched his hand with utmost care. Over went his arm, and down came a fastish ball that broke in from the off.

"You've got this covered," I said to myself, as I moved my bat over. But I was wrong. In a natural anxiety to make the perfect stroke my bat slightly touched the top of my left pad, putting it a tiny bit out of line with the ball. That was enough to bring about my downfall, for the ball "stole" past me, and the click of it hitting my stumps told me the worst had happened.

I had been bowled first ball!

Naturally, in the course of my career, I've had several unhappy moments, but this "duck" against the Indians will easily rank among my most bitter. The walk back to the pavilion seemed endless, and although everyone was kindness itself to me I did not want sympathy so much as runs. . . .

To further my disappointment, I did not have another opportunity to justify myself, for I batted only once during that Test—we won by ten wickets. Then, when, immediately after this game, Middlesex were due to meet Warwickshire, I felt in my heart that my run of non-success simply had to turn against them.

"Don't you worry, Denis," my wife said to me. "We all have our runs of bad luck. I've an idea it has ended now."

When I went out to bat for Middlesex I wished the confidence my wife expressed had helped me, but, to be quite frank, I began to dread watching the bowler's arm come over.

On this particular occasion, I knew, the man I had to keep a very careful eye upon was Eric Hollies, the fair-haired Warwickshire "spinner" who played for England in Tests against the South Africans. Hollies, one of the most successful bowlers of his type in cricket, keeps a wonderful length and can "wrap up a wrong 'un" in a most disconcerting manner. Knowing him well from past experience, I was determined to play him carefully.

The first ball he sent down was of good length. I stepped forward to it. What quite happened I do not know, but after it hit the turf the ball seemed to "wriggle" past my bat, and a muffled "oh!" from the crowd made me wonder if the worst had happened. Fortunately for me a coat of varnish separated the ball from the stumps, and as Hollies, catching the ball thrown back to him by the wicket-keeper, prepared to send up another of his "specials", I wondered what new devilment awaited me.

Once more Hollies sent up a really first-class "spinner". Yet again I stepped forward, the ball evaded my bat, hit the top of my pad, and rolled slowly—very slowly—towards the wicket. I held my breath, hardly daring to look, as the ball tucked itself alongside the stumps. Quickly the umpire hurried forward to inspect the wicket. By some miracle the bails had not been moved—and I was still able to go on batting.

"Your luck has changed at last," I remember saying to myself. "Now, Denis, take advantage of that let-off."

And I did, cracking the next ball Eric Hollies sent down to the boundary, and starting on the road that was to once again lead me to success. Altogether, in that "come-back" innings, I cracked 13 boundaries, stayed 3 hours 20 min. at the wicket, and eventually scored 122.

Never did I go home feeling so happy as after this hundred. Apart from the satisfaction of reaching the coveted century, I had done much more than that. What was it? Regained my peace of mind. During this period of non-success I had done my utmost to try to prevent myself losing confidence. I think, to a great extent, I was successful. But to get runs

Playing for England

again was like finding water in a desert after you've been without it for a long time. . . .

When we played the Indians in the second Test, which was at Old Trafford, Manchester, I was returning to a ground at which I had invariably done well in the past. There is a warm-heartedness about the crowd who attend matches at the Lancashire C.C.C. headquarters that reaches the man out there in the middle. Apart from their kindness, and the encouragement one receives from them, a batsman, when doing well at Old Trafford, appreciates that the people applauding his efforts do know cricket.

In addition to their knowledge of cricket, the Old Trafford folk, as I said earlier, have something else that always makes a visit worth-while: their hospitality and the wonderful food served up at luncheon and tea.

When, therefore, I went out to bat for England at Old Trafford, my frame of mind, to put it nicely, was "very pleasant".

Hutton and Washbrook had put on 81, and although my old opponent, Amarnath, was making the ball turn a good deal, I was rather looking forward to crossing bats with him again. That failure at Lord's rather rankled with me, and only a good performance against him, I felt, would make me feel better.

This time fortune was with me, I got away to a good start, and before falling victim to Amarnath—lbw—collected 51 runs.

In the second innings, too, with my confidence rapidly returning, I collected an unbeaten 71, and in my heart felt, once more, that I was showing form expected from a Test cricketer.

"How does it feel to once more be playing in Test cricket after so many years in the Army?"

A former Army colleague, who called in to see me at Old Trafford, asked this question at the end of a match. It was not difficult to answer: "Not so strange as one would think."

While serving in the Army I had played against a large number of the Indian touring side, and, as you will appreciate, apart from the first Test, knew enough about them not to be unduly worried. In my heart I knew that I would be able to hold my own with them, but, apart from this, I was fortunate inasmuch that the majority of my colleagues in the England side were men with whom I had played before the war.

One of the newcomers was Alec Bedser; he and his identical twin, Eric, today rank among my best friends in cricket. Big, strong, and possessing a heart as big as a lion, Bedser made a most amazing Test début, taking 11 wickets to set up a new world record. His 7 wickets for 49 runs in India's first innings during the Lord's test was a grand performance.

Standing 6 ft. 2 in. and weighing just over 14 stone, the Bedser twins are terribly difficult to tell apart. I well remember, at the beginning of the 1946 season, going into the Surrey dressing-room, after Alec Bedser had bowled extremely well against the M.C.C., to congratulate him on his performance.

"That was really fine bowling, Alec," I said to him, and the big Surrey man smiled. So did his colleagues. For about five minutes I went on talking to him about his bowling, and still Bedser's colleagues went on grinning. Finally one of them said: "I don't like saying this, Denis, but you're wasting your time. That's not Alec you're talking with but brother Eric."

Was my face red!

Just now I mentioned how I enjoyed appearing at Old Trafford. It was here, after my Test match success, that I played two of the best innings of my career against Lancashire.

In Middlesex's first innings, when I was fortunate enough to get a century, I cracked my favourite bat—I had grown accustomed to its weight, just as a billiards player does his cue—and when next we had to bat, against this very fine Lancashire attack, I wondered whether or not I should take "my favourite" with me, risking the fact that I might destroy it.

Playing for England

I am pleased to say that I did the right thing, for having my trusty friend with me added to my confidence, and for the second innings in succession I got a century against Lancashire.

I was told that this was only the third time in history that a batsman had scored two hundreds in one match on the Old Trafford wicket.

The fact that I had scored my second century was the thing that mattered, but I doubt whether many of the crowd who were so kind to me appreciate just how fortunate I was in reaching three figures. Dick Pollard, the well-known Lancashire bowler, with my score at 96, sent down a good-length ball. By one of those strokes of fate the ball snicked the edge of my bat, and, before I knew what had happened, was over the ropes—and spectators and opponents were applauding my century!

After this I did feel a little embarrassed!

Although it may surprise you to hear me say this, the innings that delighted me most during the first full post-war season was not played by myself. I hand it to my Middlesex colleague, Andy Thompson, for giving me—and thousands of other folk—our biggest thrill when we met Surrey at Kennington Oval.

As you may guess, Surrey rank among our greatest rivals and we always try to do well against them. Anyway, when in our fourth innings we were left with 318 runs to get in two and a half hours to win, I do not think there were many folk who gave much for our chances.

R. W. V. Robins, our skipper, had most definite ideas upon the subject.

"We'll go all out for the runs," he said to us in the dressing-room. "Do not be afraid to take a risk if it means runs. We must get them."

Our Middlesex team is a grand team. With such a brilliant and inspired captain as R. W. V. Robins to lead us we have often risen to the occasion in a manner that astounded the critics. At Kennington Oval that afternoon the Middlesex side of which I am so proud to be a member gave a very great performance. From the beginning, against that very brilliant Alf Gover-Alec Bedser attack they went for the runs, and although wickets often tumbled in a disconcerting manner, quickly we proceeded towards the total that meant victory and kept us in the race for the County Championship.

When Andy Thompson, another product of the Lord's ground-staff, came out, the Surrey fieldsmen licked their hands and told themselves that the end could not be so very far off. Most of the recognised run-getters had been sent back to the pavilion in a big effort to force the pace, but it looked very much as if we were going to rely a great deal upon Andy Thompson staying with the skipper.

To many cricket followers Andy was more or less an "unknown". Like so many other cricketers who have made their names since the war, he learnt his game "the hard way". By that I mean he worked on the ground-staff, played in club and ground matches, bowled to members in the nets, and in general learnt every aspect of this great game we enjoy. So, when he gained a place in the Middlesex side Andy, although he did not possess a great deal of first-class experience, had a knowledge of cricket rarely equalled by one of his age. Quickly he settled down, made several useful scores, and went to the crease at Kennington Oval with the knowledge that he was at least in form.

What a wonderful exhibition of cricket did Andy Thompson give that afternoon! The Surrey bowlers, who had justly thought themselves "on top", suddenly found the thick-set young Middlesex batsman laying it on good and hard. One of his specialities was a cover-drive that ripped the ball to the boundary at an amazing pace, and although the Surrey skipper, Nigel Bennett, kept changing his field, the cool and collected Andy Thompson continued to pierce the lines of defending fieldsmen—and get runs in double-quick time.

With the skipper—how well he plays an attacking game! —also scoring runs quickly, the Surrey score was eventually passed, and Andy Thompson was unbeaten with 100— his first century in county cricket.

Playing for England

For a long time now I have played with the best cricketers in the world. Have visited India, Australia and New Zealand. Rarely, though, have I seen a finer display of *accurate hitting* than that served up by Andy Thompson at Kennington Oval.

This knock, by the way, won the £100 prize for the best century of the season. It was a well-deserved honour.

Quite a number of cricket enthusiasts, at the end of the 1946 season, remarked that it was noticeable, for the most part, that batting averages were not so high as before the war. Apart from seven batsmen, no other first-class players, they were quick to point out, had an average of 50 or more an innings. What so few appear to take into consideration, though, is the bad weather we had at the beginning of the summer.

Weather—apart from when he goes to the wicket in a match—plays a very much bigger part in the development of a batsman than many people appear to appreciate.

I have always said, for example, that a man learns how to bat really well by practising hard in the nets. Arguments, I know, will be put up against this theory, but you ask, as I have, any of the world's dozen leading batsmen whether or not this is true and they will agree that it is. Anyway, the early summer of 1946 brought with it showers by the dozen and we could rarely get into the nets for long spells of practice. In the nets a batsman has the opportunity to "get his eye in", and at the same time to develop various shots. He can do so without any fear of losing his wicket. Once— as many batsmen attempted—he starts testing out theories in a match he is asking for trouble.

That, in my opinion, is one of the reasons why many prominent players, from whom so much was expected, had such a poor opening to the season. I remember very well that I felt rather strange at first; badly missed my net practice. At the same time I had one advantage over my colleagues. Just a few weeks before I had been playing regularly in India!

Yes, net-practice, if you wish to make progress in cricket, is one of the essentials.

I am an elementary schoolboy and as such did not have so many opportunities as, say, a Public School cricketer, to have either coaching or frequent net-practice at school. The fact that I went on to the Lord's ground-staff at the age of fourteen, and there found an opportunity to bat and bowl in the nets, proved a wonderful blessing to me; made me appreciate why in the past the Public Schools and Universities have produced such a steady flow of cricketers. Do not misunderstand me. I am not suggesting that talent was not in these young men to be brought out. What I do say, though, is that net-practice, and coaching, brings out the talent to the best advantage.

In future I would like to see every school in Britain provided with a cricket net—and a matting wicket if they have no grass available—so that keen youngsters will be given an opportunity to play the game to the best of their advantage.

After all, not all of them can go to a Public School or work on the ground-staff of a county-club where such facilities are available. . . .

IO

*My Friends "The Bedsers"—I "Try Out" Gear for
My Rivals—Peter Smith Was Last to Know of His
Australian Selection—Laurie Fishlock Willingly
Loses Bet—Cricket and Football Have to Mix.*

FOOTBALL and cricket are my business—and my life.
In the course of my calling I have met some grand
folk in both spheres, but without wishing to hurt my
many friends in soccer, I would say that the spirit of
"brotherhood" in cricket is the stronger.

Take, for instance, the Surrey twins, Alec and Eric
Bedser. When I play for Middlesex against them these two
hefty young men try their hardest to get my wicket, and
knock the ball out of the ground when I am put on to bowl.
Yet, off the field, we are the greatest of friends and I know
they would do anything for me.

What an asset these Surrey players are to post-war cricket.
Alec, of course, is one of England's leading bowlers. Eric,
I predict, will one day be bang in the running for honours.
He is an excellent all-rounder. Apart from their cricket
ability—which is considerable—these Surrey cricketers have
something else which attracts cricket followers—"Colour
and personality". Other people, though, only want to see
what they term "Stars" or "Personalities" in action. Once
they watch cricket, though, they invariably follow it closely.
It is the "Stars", though, who develop their appetite for
the game.

The amazing resemblance of the Bedser twins quickly
caught the public imagination and folk who might never
have gone to watch a cricket match paid their money at the
gate for the pleasure of saying "I've seen the Bedsers". A
large proportion, too, enjoyed watching County Cricket, so

the Bedsers, in my opinion, apart from what they put into the game, have helped, in this post-war era, to further its popularity.

I have told how I was completely puzzled by the twins' resemblance during an M.C.C.-Surrey match at Lord's, but one of the most amazing stories about these brothers concerns an umpire in a club match.

It so happened that Eric, who usually bats earlier than Alec, had lost his wicket following a lengthy stay at the wicket, and after he had returned to the pavilion brother Alec followed him.

As the new arrival prepared to take guard the umpire at the other end looked hard at him, then waved his hand towards the pavilion. Alec Bedser took no notice of this but went on preparing to take the first ball. Eventually the umpire walked up the wicket to him and said : "There's no second chances in this game."

Alec looked at him, surprise on his face, and said : "What do you mean?"

"Why, you went out last ball," replied the umpire.

"You're wrong," countered Alec, "that was my brother."

The umpire, though, was not convinced, and it was not until Eric appeared on the scene that the man in the white coat realised that his leg was not being pulled!

Although the Bedser twins are great friends of mine, I wish they would not wear exactly the same kind of clothes —yes, even to shoes and socks!—for I would then be so much more certain whom I was addressing!

This "good fellowship" in cricket shows itself in many ways, one of the most helpful being in the willingness of one cricketer to play for another in the cause of charity or a benefit match. During the course of a season, I venture to say, very few cricketers have a Sunday free. After playing six days a week you will find them, more often than not, turning out in flannels on the "day of rest" so that someone will benefit by their appearance.

The "help each other" tradition of cricket frequently shows itself in unusual ways. For example, when I have a new bat that needs "breaking in" a colleague, going to the nets, will offer to try it out for me. Maybe I have purchased a new pair of pads. "Right," says a colleague, going in late, "I'll take the stiffening out of them for you." The good-spirit of cricketers shows itself.

During the course of the Oval centenary match played between Surrey and Kent *v.* Middlesex and Essex I had a rather novel experience. Before going out to bat I was talking to Essex's Peter Smith who mentioned that he had just bought a new bat. "I'd like your view of it, Denis," he said, "maybe you'd use it to-day." I agreed to do this, then got talking to Tommy Barling the Surrey batsman. In the course of conversation we began discussing gear, and it was then that Barling showed me a new pair of pads. "One of the best pairs I've ever bought," he said. "How'd you like to give them a trial, Denis?"

Readily I agreed, for it was not a Test match in which we were playing, so out I went to the crease wearing Barling's pads and carrying Smith's bat—a much heavier one, I might add, than that I use.

I thoroughly enjoyed the experience of playing with a new bat and pads—something I would never have dreamt of attempting in a vital match—and made a useful score. On reflection, though, I learnt enough to make me appreciate just why it is essential you play in big games with familiar gear.

So far as equipment is concerned, I have always had a great fad for keeping my bats, gloves and pads as long as possible. Why, the pads I wear to-day were given me as a present at the beginning of the 1939 season. Now they are so comfortable I would not change them for a pair inlaid with gold.

During this centenary match at Kennington Oval I had a long talk with Laurie Fishlock, the Surrey and England left-hander, who was showing wonderful form with the bat. Fishlock, one of the hardest hitters of a ball in the game, was scoring runs by the fifty and hundred. On all sides it was said that he must rank among the favourites for one of the final places in the Test team we were sending to Australia during the winter of 1946–47.

Although everyone appeared to take it for granted that Laurie Fishlock was a late certainty for the tour, the Surrey batsman was anything but confident, and when people were willing to wager with him that he would be chosen, Laurie was inclined to accept their bets. When, finally, Fishlock was selected he had to pay out small sums to many admirers —but I've no doubt he thought the outlay well worth such an honour.

Peter Smith, the Essex player, and one of our most talented all-rounders, was batting when news that he had been selected for the tour of Australia was received at the Oval, and everyone on the ground, in my opinion, must have known that Smith was going with the M.C.C. party before Peter did himself! Eventually cousin Ray Smith, who also plays for Essex, managed to get the news through to him.

Then the hard work began for Fishlock and Smith. They had little time to hurry round and get the necessary gear for such a long tour. They had to use every spare minute to purchase shirts, flannels, and be measured for blazers, etc. In fact, could have had little time for themselves.

I well remember, being anxious to buy a cabin trunk into which I could pack all my gear, travelling from store to store without any success. In the dressing-room one morning I chanced to mention this to Fred Price, the veteran Middlesex stumper, and at once he replied: "You can borrow the one I used when visiting the West Indies, Denis." And once again the friendship of one cricketer for the other showed itself!

I was thinking of this great comradeship when Alex Wilson, the former Arsenal goalkeeper, was giving me a massage after I had scored a century for Middlesex against Kent at Maidstone, which is one of my favourite grounds.

"Y'know, Alex," I said to Wilson, who was masseur to the Kent team, "you wouldn't find many trainers with time to give the opposition a hand, especially after they'd done well against them. But then, cricket is so different from any other game. Everyone is so sociable." "You're right," agreed Alex Wilson, "the sociability of everyone in cricket is something you quickly appreciate."

It was while I was at Maidstone that Mr. Tom Whittaker, then assistant-manager of Arsenal, and now secretary-manager, called to see me. By some oversight the club had not re-signed me and Tom Whittaker came down with the purpose of talking the matter over if I showed a reluctance to link up with Arsenal F.C. You can take it from me, though, that once an "Arsenal" man you are not anxious to make a change, so, after a discussion as to how we could make cricket and football mix, I once more signed on the dotted line for the Arsenal club.

As I had already been chosen for the Australian tour—a trip upon which I had set my heart from the day I joined the Lord's ground-staff at the age of fourteen—Arsenal appreciated that football was out of the question, for the most part, so far as the 1946-47 season was concerned, although I promised, if possible, to return to play in some games when the Test matches ended. What is more, to the surprise of many folk I was able to keep my promise—but that is jumping ahead quite a bit. . . .

It was at Maidstone that I once again had the pleasure of meeting Godfrey Evans, the Kent wicket-keeper, who had shot to the top of the stumpers' ladder and "made" his place in the England Test team.

In 1943, when first I played with Godfrey Evans—for the Army against the R.A.F.—before leaving for India—I was greatly impressed by the way Evans could gather the ball so cleanly, and quickly, on the leg-side. He has one of the smallest pairs of hands I think to be found among top-class wicket-keepers, but they are safety itself, and the manner in which he is always "wide awake" behind the stumps gives bowlers—and I am talking from personal experience—a great deal of confidence.

He, too, had been chosen for the Australian tour, and naturally, as you will understand, we had plenty to discuss. But, for all his friendship off the field, Godfrey Evans, as usual, was out for my wicket on it.

Playing for England

Doubtless you will be surprised to know that Evans was born in Middlesex—at Finchley—but Kent fans need not worry. He was brought up in Kent.

Just as a good goalkeeper, like Frank Swift, is of paramount importance in football, so is a first-class stumper essential in cricket. Fortunate are England to have Godfrey Evans to call upon. Like goalkeeper Frank Swift, too, he is full of confidence and "colour". In fact, just the type of man to have with a touring side.

A fieldsman who is extremely reliable, can also play a big part in a team's success. At Lord's we had a truly grand fielding side and no player was more successful than Sydney Brown, who was a ground-staff junior with me.

For hours, I know, Sydney had practised fielding, and this, coupled with his powerful batting, brought him right to the front during the season, and at the same time brought to light something that caused a big surprise.

It was taken for granted that Brown, who had proved such a valuable member of the team, had been awarded his county cap. Everyone, I am sure, imagined Sydney possessed the coveted headgear way back in 1939. One day, though, during conversation, it transpired that our opening batsman did *not* possess a Middlesex cap, so, there and then, arrangements were made for one to be presented to him.

Never was a county cap more deserved—and appreciated!

Mention of cricket caps reminds me that many youngsters have asked me if I receive—as does a footballer—a cap every time I play for England in a Test match. The answer is "No." When a man makes his début in international cricket he does, as a matter of course, receive a cap. After that he will probably receive another cap at the commencement of a new series of Tests.

For Tests in this country the cap—a blue one—depicts three lions surmounted by a crown; the same badge as worn on the blazer. When playing abroad, though, the badge is of St. George and the Dragon, while the blazer, which also has this badge upon the breast pocket, has the red and yellow braid of the M.C.C. round the edges. You see, when we go abroad the party is organised by the M.C.C., a fact that is often overlooked by cricket enthusiasts.

My own initial England cricket cap is the most prized possession of my cricket career. Now I hope to add a soccer one to it and so join the small body of men who have been "capped" at both sports.

No, although I have played on twelve occasions for England in wartime internationals and once in a "Victory International", I did not automatically get a cap because they were not awarded during the war years. Instead I received, from the kindly English Football Association, an illuminated address giving details of my appearances on the football field for England.

It is a handsome trophy—but I still want that soccer cap and am determined to try and win it in the future. . . .

*Cricket as a Career—The £ s. d. Has to be Consi-
dered—Fees for Test Matches Have Gone Up—Kit
Costs Money—So Does Laundry—Fan Mail has
to be Answered—My Footballer-Cricketers can Make
Progress.*

"AM I likely to be able to make money if I select
cricket as my career?"

I have been asked this question dozens of times
by young players of promise who have considered making
cricket their calling. Well, there is an old adage: "Life is
what you make it." Especially is this applicable so far as
cricket is concerned.

There is no uniformity about wages; different counties
follow different systems, and because of this I can only quote
my personal experience in top-class cricket. It will, though,
give you an idea how the financial position works, and
the reward at the end of a six-day week.

On returning from India in 1945 I commenced a three-
year contract with Middlesex C.C.C. Under this agreement I receive £6 a week all the year round, and during
the season £8 per match and all expenses paid. As, like
other professional cricketers and footballers, I come under
the Pay-As-You-Earn system, tax is stopped at source
and, as a result, I received, after the Inland Revenue
had deducted their dues, something like £15 a week during
the season.

It is the custom in first-class cricket to reward a good
servant by putting aside a match for his benefit. This frequently happens after ten years' service, and a player so
rewarded, stands an excellent chance, providing the weather
is kind, of pocketing a large sum. Unlike the benefits

E

Playing for England

granted to professional footballers, those awarded cricketers are not subject to income tax, and in the past many a player has made sums exceeding £2,000. But it should also be pointed out that when a cricketer is awarded a benefit he has to cover all expenses. He also shows his appreciation of the occasion by celebrating with his colleagues, who, in turn, take collecting boxes around the ground for him and help in the organising of dances and charity matches to help swell the sum raised on behalf of the benefit.

Apart from county cricket a man, if fortunate enough to gain recognition in Test and other important matches, gets a good financial reward.

Let us, to commence with, examine Test cricket. For appearing against India, New Zealand and the West Indies, a cricketer receives £36 a match. This figure is raised to £60 when he's chosen to play against either Australia or South Africa, and, as in the case of the other three countries, all expenses are paid.

We receive our match-fee on the second day of every Test, the secretary of the club on whose ground the Test is being played bringing it into the players' room. He has, of course, deducted tax, our code numbers having been sent him by the secretary of our own county.

What of special matches such as the Gentlemen v. Players fixture? For this famous match the fee paid to the professionals is £25. As Middlesex were playing in a county match at the time I naturally did not receive an £8 match fee from them, but at the end of the week, as a result of being honoured for selection by the Players, was approximately £8 10s. "in pocket".

As you will have noticed by my earlier remarks, Middlesex no longer favour the old bonus system, but some counties still award, I am told, an extra fee for a win. I believe this sometimes works out at £2–£4, depending upon the club you are assisting.

A successful cricketer also often receives invitations from manufacturers of sports goods to advertise their wares. If he considers the offer worth-while, and the goods of quality, the player might accede to their request. I mention this just to show another gate that sometimes opens.

Other opportunities sometimes occur during the close-season. In the Commonwealth there are many clubs—at least, this was the position just before the war—who appreciate nothing more than having a well-known English cricketer visit them as coach during the close-season. Insisted they were the best in the world at helping develop youthful players.

A good reward, in addition to a pleasant holiday, was always the lot of a cricketer who used to go "a-coaching" in the close-season. As a point of interest, before I returned home from serving with the Army in India I was offered one of these coaching engagements—but the call of Lord's was too strong!

So far we have dealt with the income—and possible "extras"—of a cricketer. Now, we must remember, he also has his "overheads" just as the baker, butcher and tailor.

In the course of a season I need eight pairs of white flannels. This works out at about £40. Four shirts cost me £2, and a dozen thin singlets another forty shillings. A sweater demands £2, two pairs of boots work out at £2 10s. a pair, and I reckon to use over a dozen pairs of socks during the course of a season. I happen to be heavy on socks, and to prevent my feet getting sore, always wear two pairs. My wife knits me special-type socks, and apart from her labours, this means adding another £2 to my bill.

Then, of course, there are bats, pads, batting gloves, and other items which come under the heading "etc." to be bought. . . .

My laundry bill, too, works out, approximately, at about £50 during the course of the season. I know this may, to the average sportsman, sound a very great deal, but it should never be forgotten that we county cricketers put in a six-day week, and there are occasions, especially if you are having a successful time, when every single shirt and pair of flannels you possess are called upon.

Playing for England

During the 1947 season, for example, when I was doing well with bat and ball, I reckoned to use about five pairs of flannels, and the same number of shirts and singlets, during every game.

Why is this so?

The answer, if you study it, will explain a great deal. On a particularly hot day, if you bowl for long spells—as I frequently did—and then spent hours at the wicket, you find that your clothes really do "stick" to you. The only thing to do is to have a shower, and a complete change of clothing, once you find the heat is likely to interfere with your play. There is no half-measure about it. You must be "fresh" to play really well in cricket.

A short time ago, during a particularly hot spell of weather, I started to bowl really well—and at the same time was still expected to get runs. Well, I followed the old policy of changing my kit—and then had the shock of my life on returning from a tour. All my flannels and shirts were at the laundry. As I was due the same morning to appear for the Players against the Gentlemen I naturally began to get worried.

Once again, though, the spirit of cricket fellowship saw me through, and my Middlesex colleague, Jack Robertson, loaned me some of his kit.

So, in one of "the" matches of the season I turned out in borrowed gear—and no one, I hope, was the wiser!

Another item—a small one that costs me £1 1s. a year—is my subscription to the Cricketers' Friendly Society. Few people outside of the game appear to have heard of its existence, but this body is the counterpart of soccer's "Players' Union". If a player is put out of county cricket through injury the Cricketers' Friendly Society pay him £1 10s. a week until he is able to return to the game. For permanent disablement, as a result of cricket, they pay £1 10s. a week.

The organisation, which goes about its valuable work so quietly, is of great value to cricketers, that is why the majority of players belong to it.

Entertaining celebrities, I can assure you, also makes something of a hole in one's pocket—and, believe me, one has to return hospitality—while cricket enthusiasts who write me can also assist in not reducing the size of my bank balance by enclosing a stamped addressed envelope.

Before the war, when I used to answer every letter—even those without a stamped addressed envelope!—I reckoned the outlay, including the buying of photographs, worked out at nearly forty shillings a week. At my rate of progress in those days I could not have saved very much for the future.

I should like to make it clear that I like to hear from cricket followers. If they did not write me I should worry and feel that I must be slipping. What I do dislike, though, is the letter that requests dozens of things—and fails to even enclose a stamp. . . . Since the war, however, I have noticed a great difference in the types of letters I receive. In nearly every case they are from folk who love cricket and only request an autograph or a piece of information.

Schoolboys, especially, appear to write more intelligently, and some of the questions asked prove without doubt they do know cricket.

My wife—what a wonderful help she is!—looks after all my mail for me these days and sorts out the various requests. On one occasion, after I had arrived back at Lord's after a week's absence, I returned home with no fewer than 200 letters for her to sort out!

The autograph position at Lord's has been to a large extent solved by "pooling" them. When a letter arrives addressed to a specific player, requesting that all the Middlesex men should sign a book, the envelope is attached to the book, it is then placed upon a table in the dressing-room, and the 12th man makes sure that everyone pens their signature.

In this way we try our hardest not to disappoint anyone, but, as I said earlier, answering the requests of cricket fans can be a most expensive hobby!

To most young men the picture I have drawn of county cricket may appear most attractive, but do not forget that

Playing for England

cricket is only a seasonal job, and that you do not hear of the young players of promise who have failed.

Remember—and never forget it!—cricket, like football, asks much of a man before it gives anything worthwhile in return.

Quite a feature of cricket to-day is the large number of players who, before they hit the highlights on the field of play, made sure they had a trade or profession behind them. If they failed at cricket they knew there was another career to which they could turn. In nearly every case, too, it gave them confidence in their ability as cricketers.

Last season, for instance, I noted a number of players who made their mark had other callings behind them. Miles Coope, the Somerset batsman, is an organ-tuner; Allen Watkins, who made such an impression with Glamorgan, a professional footballer. In fact, I can quote dozens of examples, and personally think it a good thing for cricket and cricketers.

The stage has been reached when more and still more professional footballers are entering top-class cricket. I am, as you know, an Arsenal player. At Lord's, apart from myself, there is my brother Leslie (Arsenal), and Jack Chisholm (Brentford), Yorkshire have Willie Watson (Sunderland), Worcester, George Dews (Plymouth Argyle) and Henry Horton (Blackburn Rovers), Leicester, Maurice Tompkin (Huddersfield), Nottinghamshire, Arthur Jepson (Stoke City), Northamptonshire, Billy Barron (Northampton Town). And so I could go on producing examples of footballer-cricketers. The day when such a sportsman was a novelty has entirely disappeared.

I stand to be corrected, but I think the financial position has something to do with this, for a man, keen to make his living at sport, must, I think, if he is to remain solvent, have all-the-year employment.

Professional football, providing you make some headway and join a good club, can be a most happy medium by which one earns a living. Especially, from a financial point of view, is it worth dove-tailing with cricket, for a man at the top of the ladder receives £12 a week during the soccer season, plus £2 for a win, and £1 for a draw, and during the summer—again if he is on top pay—£10 a week.

It should not be forgotten, either, that a professional footballer may, at the end of five years, receive a maximum benefit of £750. Note I say "may", for there is no law forcing a club to pay out a benefit, although the majority follow this principle.

Unlike a cricket benefit, those awarded to professional footballers are subject to income tax.

What of the man transferred from one club to another for, say, £20,000? No, he does not receive a percentage of the fee, although some folk think he should, but £10 as a signing-on fee, plus a percentage of benefit money due to him from the club he is leaving.

In view of the fact that I have known no other life, since leaving school at the age of fourteen, but professional sport, I feel that it is with experience that I can write on the subject. That is why, without hesitation, I would allow my son Brian, if he wanted it that way, to follow in my footsteps as a professional sportsman.

I know it is rare to hear a professional talk in this manner, but there is no finer life for a young man than an outdoor one. In addition, you meet, as I have, many fine and interesting people; learn far more from experience than from books. What is more, the financial reward, although small compared with the enormous sums won by boxers such as Joe Louis, and baseball stars of the calibre of America's Babe Ruth, is steady and a man with his feet planted firmly on the ground can save enough so that he might prepare for the day when he can no longer follow sport as a living.

I will be perfectly candid and admit that from the first week I worked on the ground-staff at Lord's I have saved money. To a great extent I owe my outlook in this direction to my mother. From the moment I left school she impressed upon me that being thrifty, without being mean, was a virtue, and, as I appreciated it, every week a sum, growing larger as I made progress, went into the bank.

Playing for England

Every penny I made selling match-cards at Lord's—and during Tests this could be pretty considerable for a lad of fifteen—went into the bank. Right lucky was I to be guided so wisely.

To-day I am fortunate in having a wife who also gives me the benefit of her business experience and clear outlook on things. Apart from looking after me, she knits the type of socks I have to wear for cricket—very thick ones—attends to my mail, and in every possible way proves a friend to me.

I often stop to wonder if the folk who go along to cricket matches to cheer on their favourites ever stop to think about the women behind the various players. I must confess the wife of a cricketer does not have a very pleasant time during the summer months. Take my own wife for an example. I rise at about 7.30, have breakfast, and leave home for Lord's at about nine o'clock. Often, until gone nine in the evening, she does not again set eyes upon me. Then, after a meal, it is time to retire for the night. If Middlesex are playing away she will not see me for four days.

Sometimes, on a Sunday too, I leave her to play in a charity match, so, until cricket finishes for the season, Mrs. Compton does not see her husband so very much.

That is one of the reasons I did not go to the West Indies with the M.C.C. team last winter, for, after being away in India for two-and-a-half years, I returned home for six months, and then went away with the M.C.C. to Australia for a further six months. To keep up this kind of thing just is not fair.

Yet professional cricket, despite its drawbacks, has plenty to be said in its favour, and speaking for myself, I have never regretted making it my career. From a personal point of view, though, it can interfere with your home life, especially with so many matches to be played away from home.

I am fortunate, though. My wife appreciates just what cricket demands of a player, and understands why it has a hold upon me. It is to her kindness, and sympathetic understanding, that I owe more than words can tell during the past few years.

When I have been "down" she has tried to encourage me; when things are going extremely well she was the first to remind me that they would not always be that way. In short, she has been my off-field captain.

No cricketer ever played under a more thoughtful skipper.

12

*Wise Words from Pat Hendren—Australia is an
Education—Why They Produce Great Players—
New-Type Wickets Can Be Puzzling—Bowlers Who
Can really Bowl—Don Bradman the Master—
The Australians Treated us Very Well.*

"NO CRICKETER can really say he has much experience until he has played in Australia," Patsy Hendren, the former England and Middlesex batsman
said to me, a few days before I boarded the *Stirling Castle*
with the M.C.C. touring side. "You'll find the conditions a
bit strange at first," went on Pat, and then proceeded to
give me some hints that proved extremely useful when I
commenced playing "Down Under".

Those great England captains of former years, R. W. V.
Robins and G. O. Allen, were others who gave me the value
of their vast experience, and when I set sail for Australia it
was with the knowledge that everyone had given me the
opportunity of planning my own campaign.

It did not take me long to appreciate that what the Test
stars of yesteryear had told me was correct. There is a
great difference between playing cricket in England and
Australia. I would not have thought anything could have
been so marked. It is only, though, when a man has switched
from one country to the other, after only a short break,
that the difference is fully appreciated.

I had been told, because of the lack of moisture in the
grass, fast bowlers get little assistance from the wicket,
neither does the ball turn a great deal but tends to come
straight through. At first, I must confess, I wondered if all
this was accurate, but after visiting the crease a few times
I appreciated the truth of the story. One had only to watch

the crack Australian batsmen at work to understand that
the wickets were not of great assistance to bowlers, for they
took chances few batsmen in England would have attempted,
knowing that there was little chance of the ball turning at
the last moment.

In England, if you watch carefully, most batsmen follow
a policy of playing the bowling carefully, for you never know
what to expect on wickets that have their share of rain.
In Australia, though, the bone-hard pitches rarely aid the
fast-medium men, and we batsmen opposing the Australians
soon understood why in the past our opponents have so
frequently produced top-class spin bowlers.

In Australia we met quite a number of them, outstandingly
Colin McCool, Ian Johnson and George Tribe.

A noticeable thing about these Australian bowlers was
their willingness to give the ball plenty of air. In England
there are few men willing to toss the ball up, but there is no
doubt, as we found to our disadvantage, that it does help.
These Australian spinners have to impart much more spin
to the ball than bowlers of their type in England. If they
did not the ball would not "bite" the pitch, so you can be
sure, when an Australian "spinner" starts bowling very
well he can make the ball do some very remarkable
things.

I was reminded of this fact when the Australian team to
visit England for the first post-war Test series was announced,
for among the seventeen players were a number of bowlers
who struck me as having the necessary spinning ability to
really make their mark on our wickets.

Running carefully through the team one thing stood
out a mile : the all-round balance of the side. To my way of
thinking the Australians are past-masters in the art of blend-
ing youth with experience and it is this ability, I feel sure,
that has played no small part in them having a constant
flow of young men to take the place of the old favourites
at the top of the tree when they begin to approach the
veteran stage or for other reasons have to quit top-class
cricket.

Playing for England

But, for a moment, let us examine carefully the list of players who made history by being included in the first Australian Test team to visit England since 1938.

Skipper, of course, was Donald Bradman, the idol of every young cricketer "Down Under", as I found, and, to my way of thinking, he stands out as the perfect example of a grand sportsman.

Don, a broker back home in Australia, has broken so many records it would not be serving a purpose to list them all in the limited space I have available. I should like to point out, however, that Bradman is not one of those fellows who sits back and rests on his laurels. From the moment I first opposed him "The Don" has stood out because of one important thing: he is always looking for runs.

It is his wonderful captaincy that has played no small part in Australia's great run of cricket successes, and the attitude he adopts towards the game is the correct one when a Test win or defeat is involved. Bradman, under these conditions, once he has topped 100 does not think of throwing his wicket away but looks upon it as a step towards a second hundred, and so on. This is an outlook that helps Australia win matches, as past events have proved.

Arthur Lindsay Hassett, vice-captain to Bradman, and a commercial traveller in Australia, is one of the prettiest batsmen I've ever played against—when he is in form. Hassett, whom it will be recalled captained the Australian Services team that played in England during the summer of 1945, figured in all the Tests in Australia during the winter of 1946–7, and although in this series Lindsay did not show anything approaching the form that made him such a formidable pre-war figure, he made a great come back during the 1948 tour of England.

What strikes one about Hassett, when the "vest-pocket Bradman"—as he was called by an English journalist—is at the wicket is the power he can, for such a small man, get behind his shots. Reason for this? Next time you have the opportunity of watching Hassett either at the wicket, on the films, or, maybe, in an action photograph, note his perfect balance. This, as much as anything else, is why he gets so much "beef" into his strokes.

Billy Brown, whom I remember first coming to this country as the "Baby" of the Australian side in 1934, caught my eye when I was but a groundstaff lad at Lord's. I suppose it was because Billy was only a youngster—he is now in his middle-thirties—that I paid so much attention to him, but soon those of us who studied his stroke play appreciated that Billy Brown had plenty to commend him.

In 1938, when he visited this country with the Australians, he played one of the most magnificent innings it has ever been my pleasure to watch, an undefeated 206 at Lord's when he carried his bat in a manner that justified him taking a place among the immortals.

When the M.C.C. visited Australia in 1946–7 Bill, who was ill, could not appear against us.

But, if only for a moment, let us turn away from run-getters and switch our spotlight upon the men who made the long voyage for the purpose of getting the wickets of Len Hutton, Cyril Washbrook, Bill Edrich, Norman Yardley, and other English batting stars.

I always think it interesting—and invaluable—to make a careful study of your opponents. More often than not you can learn a good deal you did not earlier know, especially, if by means of discussion, you can encourage friends or colleagues to join in your "summing-up".

Colin McCool, who is a commercial traveller when he is not bowling or batting, has since the war proved himself one of the best bowlers produced by the Australians for a long time. Blond, sturdy, and possessing fingers that really can make a ball spin, some people claim that Colin is a first-rate "googlie" bowler, but I must confess that he has not so far produced such a delivery against me. Right-handed, possessing a beautifully-easy action, he looks as if he can go on bowling for hours and, even if an opposing batsman does succeed in taking runs off him, McCool, in my opinion, never loses that wonderful length he possesses.

I feel that Colin McCool must, like most other Australian

Playing for England

bowlers, make a keen study of local conditions. These men from "Down Under", you probably appreciate by now, leave nothing at all to chance. They are successful cricketers because they are thorough in their approach to the game.

Colin McCool, I might add, is one of that always-dangerous band of bowlers who bowl with their brains, not only their arms. Personally I enjoy playing against such men, for when you're at the wicket the spirit of a duel is felt.

So long as the sporting spirit remains I think this adds to the interest in the game.

Ian Johnson, like McCool, is another bowler who developed a perfect length before attempting to do things in the cricket world. His success in one direction inevitably saw Test distinction follow, and this clever attacker, who works as a warehouseman, must give the ball much more air than a normal bowler. His confidence in this direction is justified, however, for Ian has perfect control of the ball all the time, and on softer English wickets there were many experts, bearing in mind Ian's ability to make the ball turn a good deal, who, from the moment he landed, expected him to quickly get among the wickets. He did!

I personally think Ian ranks among the best bowlers of his particular type in world cricket and suggest any young cricketer who has ambitions so far as becoming a slow bowler to make a very careful study of Johnson.

"What kind of bowlers rank among the most valuable in the game?" is a stock question asked me by youngsters when I attend youth clubs, or invariably crops up when, with my wife, I run through my mail. Local conditions, of course, make this a difficult question to answer, but I think a really top-class left-arm slow bowler, if he possesses the ability to make the ball turn both ways, wants some beating.

Australia have such a bowler to call upon: his name is Ernest Toshak.

Back home they used to consider Toshak something of a defensive bowler, but this well-built cricketer, who is in the building trade when he is not taking wickets, soon began to dismiss many top-class batsmen, and when he made his Test début against us collected nine wickets for ninety runs, which, if nothing else, proves Ernest knows how to bowl.

Against the Indians, when they visited Australia, Toshak did even better, collecting, in the first innings, five wickets for two runs.

Why, as a London schoolboy, such a feat in one of our matches would have put the bowler among the probable winners of a Jack Hobbs bat presented by *The Star*!

Reverting to Ernest Toshak, however, he is one of the very few Australian cricketers I know who appears to have concentrated all his energies upon one side of the game. As a bowler he has few equals; as a batsman, however, Ernest, I'm sure, would be the first to admit that he is fortunate to even get in at number eleven!

The Australian selectors, no doubt noticing the success of Ray Lindwall and Keith Miller, their opening fast bowlers when they played against us during the last tour, did not hesitate to automatically select them for the visit to the Mother Country, and English cricket lovers studied them with very great interest.

No, we have no fast bowlers in England to touch these Australians at the moment, and, although Lindwall had no previous experience of English wickets, the dynamic Keith Miller was successful here, with ball and bat, with the Australian Services side in 1945. He topped the Test averages for the Services' side with an average of 63.28, including two centuries, both at Lord's, and took ten wickets for an average cost of 27.70. Judging by what I saw in Australia, and in England in 1948, however, Miller must have improved his bowling a good deal, although, to be quite honest, he is still a little erratic.

Lindwall, on the other hand, is icy cool, thorough, and quite out on his own as a fast bowler. Although, as you may have noticed, there was a good deal of discussion about his run-up to the wicket, from a technical point of view, and if one is a student of poise, I have no hesitation in saying that Ray Lindwall is the best all-round fast bowler we have had visit us for a number of years.

Playing for England

Now, to conclude with our quick "spotlight" upon many of the Australian stars, we'll turn towards their great opening pair, Arthur Morris, a left-hander of elegance, and Sydney Barnes, a run-getter who has developed so much he is little if anything behind the one and only Don.

Morris, who is a motor-car salesman, will for ever be linked in my memory with the Fourth Test at Adelaide during the 1946–7 tour. Arthur, you see, scored two separate hundreds in that match. So did I. Maybe that is one of the reasons we have become such good friends. Anyway, so quickly has Arthur developed as a cricket personality that the Australians thought enough of his judgment to make him, along with Don Bradman and vice-captain Hassett, a member of the Selection Committee.

This, to me, suggests we shall hear a good deal of Arthur Morris in the future. . . .

Partner of Arthur Morris in many an opening stand, Sydney Barnes is one of cricket's comedians, although, on occasions, I have seen crowds fail to appreciate one of his little jokes. Barnes, who made his second visit with an Australian team to England when he landed at Tilbury, is, like Bradman, something of a machine once the runs begin to flow. His defensive skill is tremendous, and in this direction he ranks as Australia's number one batsman—Bradman apart—in my view.

As a fieldsman Barnes, I should add, has few equals at short-leg, while his slow leg-breaks do get wickets.

In short, Sydney is just the type of player a skipper likes to be able to call upon!

When a team makes a tour one thing quickly makes itself evident: every side you oppose is out to lower your colours. We had this experience in Australia. While visiting this country our cousins, I'm sure, found a similar spirit entering into their games. In fact, when a team makes a tour it can look forward to one thing above all others—a hard game every time they take the field.

This, of course, helps develop a wonderful team-spirit, and the side, as I know from past experience, invariably

V. M. Merchant (India), one of the world's classiest batsmen.
Patience and a keen eye are the reasons for his success.

Bowled for a duck by Amarnath in the first Test of 1946 against
India. The peak of the bad period.

Denis Compton meets King George.

Photo : *Sport and General*

The " Middlesex Marvels." Bill Edrich and the author go out to
bat at Lord's.

Compton here demonstrates how he delivers his
"Fleetwood Smith".

rises to great heights, but, for all that, playing all-out without respite can be most tiring. The constant travelling, too, does nothing to ease the situation. . . .

Fortunate are the Australians to be able to have good food at home, for, I must confess, from experience "Down Under", I appreciate the big part it plays in providing extra stamina so necessary in Test cricket. Because of this our visitors may find tours a little less tiring than might otherwise be the case.

Just now I mentioned how the majority of teams, big or small, we met during our M.C.C. visit were all out to defeat us. That, I should stress, was one of the reasons we played, for the most part, serious cricket, for, as members of the M.C.C., we had a high prestige to maintain.

It should be explained, I think, that many of the players assisting minor teams we met during the last tour were well up to English County standard. On no occasion can they be treated lightly, as these Aussies know the wickets upon which they play as well as the back of their own hands . . .

This, of course, brings to mind an incident when last the M.C.C. visited Australia.

I remember going to a small country town called Newcastle a couple of days before Christmas 1946. Naturally, as the town was composed of either English folk, or those descended from natives of these shores, we were made royal welcome—the hospitality all over Australia was terrific—but they made no secret of the fact that the local team would be more than delighted if they gave us a close game.

The little ground on which the match was played could not have been laid out better by one of the town-planning experts about whom we hear so much to-day. It was oval in shape, had benches laid out around the ring, tents were placed behind them, and in these various foods were served, foods which make my mouth water when I recall them. In short, there was an air about the match such as one finds at cricket festivals in England.

The wicket at Newcastle was similar to those on which we

are accustomed to play at home, and our batsmen, for the most part, took full advantage of it, Laurie Fishlock getting 110, and Walter Hammond 142 out of a total of 395. I was dismissed for six, caught and bowled.

If we had expected the Newcastle batsmen to be over-awed because they were facing an England side, we soon found our mistake, for these "Saturday afternoon cricketers" batted well against such fine bowlers as Bill Voce, Dick Pollard and Bill Edrich before we got them out for 202. We thought that we might well win then, but the Newcastle bowlers soon knocked this notion on the head, sending back six of our batsmen for 40 runs!

When Walter Hammond joined me at the wicket we both understood the danger that faced us. That is why the skipper, who had spent such a time at the wicket during the first innings, decided to again go to the wicket and endeavour to save the situation.

The Newcastle attack, relying a great deal upon two medium-paced bowlers named Pickles and Sullivan, was without a doubt really good, and at first Hammond and I had to treat it carefully. Then, when the skipper began to open those broad shoulders of his I followed suit, and in the course of an hour we put on 106 runs, bringing to an end the prospect of a Newcastle win, the match fizzling out into a draw.

But a match we had looked upon as valuable practice might well have developed into a defeat!

Our English bowlers, during the Australian tour, did not find the wickets very helpful, only Douglas Wright, despite atrocious luck, getting anything near the form we know him capable of producing. Yet Wright, who missed the stumps by inches more than any other bowler I have seen, only once found a wicket to his liking, and then ran through the opposition.

For the most part, though, he was fighting what eventually proved a losing battle against wickets that are so very different to those found at home.

What of the batsmen? As time progressed, and we settled

down, so run-getting appeared easier. Speaking for myself, towards the end of the tour I found runs coming as if I were having a really good season in England. In my last ten innings, for example, I scored 882 runs—including four centuries—and finished up with an average of 110.25 for the last ten innings played in Australia including two centuries in the fourth test at Adelaide.

Altogether, during the Australian tour I scored 1,660 runs in first-class matches—a new record for an England batsman—and altogether collected 2,066 runs during the course of the tour.

I mention this fact because, early in the visit, I experienced several setbacks that might have upset me had not I early taken to heart the advice given me by former Test cricketers. "Don't worry if runs do not come at first," they said. "Take your time, settle down, and it won't be so very different from playing in England." They were, to some extent, right!

I think the heat upsets the Englishman, new to such conditions, if he is an all-rounder and expected to do well with bat and ball.

My friend, Bill Edrich, is a typical example of what I mean. Bill, a wonderful little fellow and as compact a bunch of energy you will find anywhere, scored 1,040 runs—averaging 49.52—bowled 261 overs, secured 29 wickets, and made 18 catches.

A good job of work.

How Edrich, despite his enthusiasm and terrific physical fitness managed to produce such grand cricket is beyond me. I know, after the end of the tour—in which I bowled 102 overs—my body felt very, very tired.

Apart from Bill Edrich's great skill as a cricketer, he possesses something else that plays a big part in his success in sport—a big heart and a will-to-win spirit that is worth many runs to the side he assists.

I well remember, early on the first day of the Third Test at Melbourne, Sydney Barnes cut hard at a fastish ball and it struck Edrich on the knee. The little all-rounder did not utter a word, although most men would have shouted out with pain, but although he would have preferred to remain on the field, had to limp off for treatment from Tom Langridge, our Australian masseur.

"That's the last we're going to see of Bill in this match," I said to myself, remembering how the ball had cracked his knee, but Bill, with the masseur working upon him all that day, and half the night, was determined to take his place in the side next morning.

What is more he did, resumed his fast bowling as if nothing had happened, and with one of his first deliveries got an Australian wicket—encouraging Don Tallon to flick at a ball that was going away—and Godfrey Evans, behind the stumps, did the rest! Even then Bill Edrich was not finished, for when we batted the Middlesex all-rounder, against some really first-class bowling, and despite his injured knee, knocked up a fine 89. You will appreciate, now, what I mean about a cricketer being invaluable when he possesses, in addition to skill, a big heart. No wonder the Australian crowd admired Bill Edrich!

Godfrey Evans, our wicket-keeper, was another who gave everyone great confidence. Considering he was little known until the season of 1946 the Kent wicket-keeper's rise is among the great stories of post-war sport. As a matter of fact, the only man who did not seem surprised at Evans' advance was Godfrey himself!

Behind the stumps he simply "oozed" with confidence, and his perky air, even when things were not going too well for us, gave everyone encouragement. The fact, too, that Evans possesses the safest pair of hands most of us have ever seen, meant more than folk in the crowd might understand. The Kent stumper became one of the outstanding successes of the Australian tour, and as the trip progressed improved enormously as a batsman. Maybe, after standing for hours behind run-getters such as Bradman and Barnes, he picked up some valuable hints!

One of Evans' finest innings was in partnership with me during the second innings of the Fourth Test at Adelaide. Between us we put on 85, without being parted, during a stay of 135 minutes at the crease, after coming together a very difficult situation. At the time eight wickets had fallen; the Australians were on their toes and definitely all out for the "kill".

When Godfrey Evans appeared at the wicket Don Bradman at once called upon his battery of star bowlers to try to send Evans back to the dressing-room before he had settled down. The Kent man, though, showed the bowlers as straight a bat as ever you've seen, and for 95 minutes, while I tried to batter the bowling, did not score a single run!

Although, for the spectators, this may not have been very entertaining, Godfrey Evans, by such tactics, proved himself a very valuable batsman to have in the side, and although when the time arrived for the skipper to declare he had only knocked up 10, that innings was worth more than a hundred considering the circumstances under which it was made.

As you know, the Australians defeated us in the 1946-7 Test series, kept a tight hold on the "Ashes", and proved themselves a truly fine cricket team. What, though, did we think of the Australians, apart from their cricket prowess? They were grand fellows, every one of them, while the hospitality of Australia towards us had to be seen to be fully appreciated. All over the Dominion we were taken into hearts and homes, treated as brothers, and given everything we wanted.

As for that Australian food. . . .

After eating the steaks and fresh fruits we all felt champion, and understood why Australian cricketers appear to have so much stamina. There is no doubt, I will repeat, that beefsteaks do help you in sport.

In future—beefsteaks apart—I hope to visit Australia again, for, as cricketers and gentlemen, the fellows I met in the Dominion are of the type we all like to call "friend". No praise—and I want it that way—could be greater.

*…ary Travellers" Return—They Call Us
…iddlesex Marvels"—Norman Yardley's
Smart …love Foils South Africans—I Try to Emulate
Fleetwood-Smith—Diet, Smoking and Test Cricket.*

13

RETURNING to first-class cricket in England, following a winter of intense endeavour "Down Under", was, you may be surprised to hear, like being asked to work overtime after you have put in a very hard day at the factory or office.

Of course, after I'd "loosened up" a little the thrill of playing against some of the world's greatest cricketers made me forget the tired feeling, but I often wonder how such great-hearted bowlers as Duggie Wright, Alec Bedser and Dick Pollard, to mention but a few, got down to bowling out batsmen after spending a winter hard at work on the sun-drenched Australian wickets.

One of the first things I did, after a fortnight's holiday at Bournemouth, was to go down to Arsenal Stadium and put in a spell of training, and play a couple of games for the club. I felt that I must, if only for a few days, try and forget cricket so that when the season opened in England I would, to some extent, start a little fresher than might otherwise have been the case. My friends agreed that this was a good idea, and after putting it into practice I felt pleased.

It did give me, if only for a short time, an opportunity to relax from thinking about wickets and runs.

Just before the opening of the 1947 season I made it my business to spend a number of hours each day in the nets at Lord's. Maybe you will think it surprising that a cricketer, after six months' playing, should return to start practice. Never forget, though, that in Australia we had been playing under conditions vastly different to those found in England. The light, in addition to the wickets, was entirely different to Australia's, and the only way, in my opinion, a cricketer could prepare himself and so avoid letting down his side in early matches while "acclimatising" himself, was to prepare in the nets. My friend, Bill Edrich, agreed with me, and before the season commenced in earnest we put in a great deal of practice.

When the Australians were in England for the 1938 tour I became friendly with that genial left-arm spin bowler, Fleetwood-Smith. In addition to his wonderful ability as a cricketer, the Australian attracted me because of his cheerful outlook, and the fact that cricket, first and foremost, was a game so far as he was concerned.

Fleetwood-Smith's unusual over-the-wicket type of bowling interested me a great deal. Apart from the number of wickets he secured—in two visits to England, 1934 and 1938 he secured an aggregate of 194 wickets—it was the Australian's method that caught my fancy. For hours I would watch him in action; when at the wicket batting against him, I made a greater study of his methods than those of any other man. In fact, the genius of Fleetwood-Smith became something of an obsession for me, and I made up my mind one day to try to emulate him.

I find that it is not generally understood how hard the men who reach the top of the bowling ladder practice so that success may come their way. Fleetwood-Smith told me that he spent years perfecting his style of bowling, and when I first began attempting to emulate him it did not take me long to understand that the road ahead was likely to be long.

Anyway, soon after returning from India I started to practise this over-the-wicket type of bowling in the nets. At first the fellows batting really did give me the "stick", and hit the ball about in a manner that was at first disconcerting. I remembered, though, that Fleetwood-Smith had once told me that he was clouted about the field unmercifully when he began bowling his new-type deliveries, so I consoled myself with the fact that I was at least being spared that indignity while keeping to the nets.

After the Australian tour, realising the value of a good all-rounder, I "swotted up" this type of bowling once more. For hours, even when I could have been elsewhere, I used to practise my "Fleetwood-Smith stuff" at Lord's. Slowly— very, very slowly at first—I started to improve. Fellows against whom I bowled began to notice the ball performing tricks that were not noticeable a short time before. Often I pierced their guard and hit the stumps.

"Why don't you try bowling your new-style overs in a county match?" one batsman asked me, after I had twice bowled him during a knock in the nets, and I replied: "I will—when I think they're good enough."

I have never lacked confidence in cricket, but it was my opinion that it would be unfair to take an unnecessary chance with my county running hard for the Championship, and so give away valuable runs.

It was when we visited Leicestershire, however, that Bill Edrich, who was acting as captain, put me on to bowl, and, as I had decided that the Fleetwood-Smith technique might prove useful on such a wicket, tried out my new-type bowling.

To my surprise the Leicestershire batsman appeared a little puzzled when I went on, and five wickets fell to me as a result of this "secret bowling" I had so long practised.

Later, against Northamptonshire, I again tried out this technique and took nine wickets in the course of the game after scoring a century!

Returning to the Leicestershire-Middlesex game, I rank this one of the finest matches in which I have ever played. It had everything: good cricket, thrills, and a grand sense of sportsmanship on both sides.

On the last day, I well remember, we needed 66 runs for victory and 20 minutes were left for play. As we returned to the pavilion Bill Edrich walked up alongside me and said: "We'll go in first, Denis, and get those runs."

As every second counted Bill and I went out on the resumption with the Leicestershire fieldsmen, and although it meant taking a chance—and well worth it under the circumstances—we went for the bowling, and with but a minute or so to spare got the necessary 66 runs for victory.

During the 1947 season Bill Edrich and I were associated in many an exciting partnership on the cricket field. Maybe it would be as batsmen; sometimes he and I would have a duel success with the ball. Anyway, some of the newspapers began to christen us "The Middlesex Marvels", and questions were asked us as to how we managed to succeed so often.

There was no mystery about it. We had not worked out any deep-laid schemes for success. It so happened that Bill and I had run into form at precisely the same time. If we had both been failing together I doubt if it would have attracted so much attention. That we both kept getting runs and wickets, naturally caught the public imagination.

Although Bill Edrich and I are so often associated on the cricket field, it is one of those chances of Fate that we linked at Lord's. As I have told, since my schooldays I have been a regular visitor to cricket headquarters, but Edrich was born at Lingwood, in Norfolk, hundreds of miles away, and grew up in a vastly different atmosphere to me. I started out on the ground-staff at Lord's. Bill spent his off-cricket hours on the farm. And what a great cricketing family these Edrich folk have proved to be. Apart from the great William, there is Brian (Kent), and E. H. and G. A. Edrich, other brothers playing for Lancashire. In fact, you can always be sure to find at least one Edrich doing something worth while, in at least one county match, at any time during the course of a cricket season.

"Our Bill," as he is affectionately known to enthusiasts at Lord's, joined the staff after making a big reputation for himself with Norfolk. His talent, and great enthusiasm, quickly marked him down as a player with a future, and from the moment we first found ourselves partners at the wicket I knew Edrich was a cricketer with whom I had a natural understanding. My first reaction has, time and again, proved correct.

Playing for England

As he and I have both played at outside-left for League clubs—Bill for Spurs and me for Arsenal—we naturally started on common ground. At the same time, we both enjoyed taking those snappy short runs that get the opposing fieldsmen "on edge". In fact, our partnership became "a natural" from the first.

Although Bill, like me, takes his cricket as a matter of course, accepting failure just as he does success, he has one or two little fads—some might call them superstitions—as have so many of us. For instance, he always puts his left pad on first when going out to bat; claims that he has a favourite shirt which, once donned, frequently brings him luck.

During the war years, when Bill Edrich, a bomber pilot, took part in the first-ever 1,000 bomber raid—he was a squadron-leader and won the D.F.C.—the great all-rounder, even then, had a little "fad". Beneath his tunic he wore his M.C.C. sweater. . . .

Although Bill Edrich is now such a great success—so much that he has become a national institution—fame did not come easily to the little man from Norfolk. Only his stout heart pulled him through and has put him among the game's immortals.

In the Middlesex county side Edrich, almost as soon as he had qualified, began to hit the headlines. Runs flowed from his bat in an unceasing stream. Then, when he began to be chosen for England, nothing would go right for him. In 1938, for instance, Edrich played in all five Tests against the Australians, yet the man who thought nothing of scoring a century in a county match could seemingly do little right in representative cricket. In fact, all he could rattle up, in the course of five Tests, was 67 runs as a result of six visits to the wicket.

Many enthusiasts were surprised when Bill Edrich continued to get chances after that, but the selectors had faith in him. In South Africa, though, things continued to go badly for Bill Edrich until the second innings of the last Test. Then, just as everyone in cricket knew would be the case, he blossomed out with a brilliant 219, and from that day has never looked back.

I think there is a great lesson to be learnt from Bill Edrich; a lesson that applies to cricketers and cricket clubs all over the country. It is that if a man has cricket ability in him he should be given every possible encouragement. What does it matter if he fails a few times? Given the proper opportunity he invariably "makes good", and more than repays for previous failures. That is what has happened in the case of Bill Edrich, now ranked among the greatest all-rounders in world cricket. Now, supposing he had not been encouraged so much by the M.C.C. when things were going badly. . . .

Len Hutton, the pride of Yorkshire, and prince of opening batsmen, is another who went through a spell of ill-fortune last season. Did the selectors panic and drop Hutton? Of course not. Again the wisdom of the men who choose England's Test teams proved correct, for Hutton came back with a real bang and showed the brilliance we all knew he possessed.

Often, too, there is mental worry that upsets some players. For instance, one season Willie Watson, Yorkshire's brilliant left-handed batsman, whom I rank among my cricketing-footballing friends, kept reaching a high score, but then, when he seemed set for a century, failed in a most surprising manner.

"Why does he fail when everything looks set for him making a big score?" folk asked.

The answer was not difficult to give. At the time Watson's small son was very ill, and, although he might not have known it, such worry cannot but help interfere with one's powers of concentration. Eventually Willie Watson, with a grand 150 against Surrey, started off on the "century path", but I feel that his personal worry may well have prevented him taking it earlier.

To be a cricket success a man must go to the wicket with his mind free from everything else but the job on hand. He has to concentrate all he possesses upon outwitting the bowler. If he cannot do this a batsman invariably fails.

Playing for England

When we played the first Test match against the South Africans at Trent Bridge, Nottingham, in 1947, our skipper, Norman Yardley, a keen student of the game, understood how important it was that our remaining batsmen had an opportunity of "seeing the ball" and concentrating upon the task on hand.

It so happened that the South Africans, a fine cricketing side, and grand sportsmen, had surprised us by getting some cheap wickets in the early stages of our innings. Fortune was with me, and I was able to hold my ground until the close of play. The following morning, though, I received a personal letter from Sir Pelham Warner, my mentor in cricket, and that kind gentleman and grand captain of yesteryear, gave me some advice I knew to be good.

"May I suggest," he wrote, "that you go out into the nets before resuming your innings so that you might get a sight of the ball? I am sure you will find it valuable."

They say that great cricket minds think alike. In this case it was true, for Norman Yardley, the England captain, had already told all the remaining batsmen—most of them the "tail-enders"—to spend some time in the nets before play was resumed. Yardley, himself due to bat, went with the players, and I am sure this pre-match practice played a big part in the success of so many of our bowlers when the time came for them to go to the wicket as run-getters.

Speaking from my own point of view, I found the net-practice most useful, for when I resumed in the Test the ball seemed much "bigger" than might otherwise have been the case. Other men, who followed, agreed with me that this was so.

Net-practice, you see, a subject I have advocated so often in these pages, played a big part in the probable saving of the day for an England Test team.

Quite a number of other teams I find have followed this system when men relied upon to get runs have failed. In most cases, too, the move has proved worth while and runs that might not normally have been secured have helped to make the score look much more "respectable".

The Australians looked upon such practice as a matter of course. But then, the always-thorough Aussies would!

When a cricketer is playing in a Test match—and I write from personal experience—you cannot be too careful. Apart from making sure that gear is in order, flannels and boots comfortable, there is another item that always comes high on the list of "Take Cares".

It is food and drink!

As I have said before, when a man is playing first-class cricket he cannot afford to have any worry if he is to succeed, and food, believe me, can be most upsetting if taken at the wrong time and too large a portion.

Soon after I had gained the Middlesex side—remember I was a growing lad!—I ignored the warnings of several veterans to "Lay Off The Food" during the luncheon interval. In the past, I reasoned, food had not interfered with my game—although first-class cricket is much more exacting than any other sport I know—but, out in the middle again, with a blazing sun overhead, and a large meal tucked away beneath my belt, I soon felt anything but fit, and lost my wicket when I might, under normal circumstances, have been set for a good score.

That experience taught me a lesson I shall never forget, and since then going careful so far as eating is concerned has been an item of major importance to me. Never, for instance, do I eat many potatoes or puddings. If I happen to be batting when the luncheon interval comes around I eat very little; at the most a little salad. At the tea interval, if "on duty" at the crease, I eat nothing, enjoying nothing more than a cup of luke-warm tea.

The same thing applies to smoking. I have never been what you might term a heavy smoker, although I enjoy about four a day, and do not think this harmful. "Chain-smoking", of course, can upset a cricketer, or footballer, but no sportsman I know would think of asking for trouble in this direction.

When Test matches come around, though, I take a special little precaution and reduce my smoking by half.

Playing for England

What of rest?

Ever since I first signed on the dotted line at cricket and football I have made a point of getting eight hours' sleep every night. No sportsman can hope to give of his best if he does not rest limbs and mind.

All the star sportsmen with whom I have come into contact have agreed that it is necessary for a fellow to get eight hours' sleep if he is to keep in the finest condition. Often, during Tests, I retire to bed at nine o'clock in the evening, for I believe the story that the rest you get before midnight is all-important. Anyway, I always feel better for it.

This reminds me of a story—and a true one a that—concerning a player who developed into one of the best all-rounders in the game. When he gained his county side a distinguished batsman was the "star" of the team, and the youngster, who looked upon the great cricketer as something of a god, would have done anything to please him. Why, the thought of playing in the same team made the lad bristle with pride!

On the first night of the team's arrival at a well-known provincial hotel the county "joker"—a stumper, I might add—went up to the youngster and said to him: "As old —— goes to bed early, when you pass his room take off your shoes, like us. On no account must he be disturbed. . . ."

It so happened that the youngster's bedroom was in a position that meant he had to pass the "star's" apartment whenever he went to and from the room. What is more, not realising he was having his leg pulled, the newcomer religiously took off his shoes and tip-toed past the bedroom belonging to his idol.

Fortunately he was a good-natured young man, and laughed a good deal when told that he was having his leg pulled.

Seriously, though, this world-famous batsman did make a point of going to bed early and saving up all his energy for cricket.

He was a wise man and a great player.

14

*English   Umpires   Know   their   Job—Meet   Frank
Chester—Poet of the Crease—£. s. d. of Umpiring—
Wisecracks in the Middle.*

THERE is no doubting that an umpire has one of the
most difficult jobs in sport. If he pleases everyone an
official has performed a miracle; if both sides say
that he is "all right" the umpire has made a first-class job
of it.   But, as everyone agrees, the standard of umpiring
in England is not to be bettered elsewhere.   In the course
of my travels I have played under the jurisdiction of umpires
hailing from many parts of the globe, but for quick-thinking,
and the knowledge of the game, the men who officiate in
county cricket take some equalling.

Look carefully through the list of first-class umpires for
any season and it is not difficult to appreciate why they are
so successful: a very large percentage of them were formerly
cricketers of great distinction.   They "live" the game they
grace so well.

Perhaps the best-known of all umpires is Frank Chester,
who has been in charge at so many Test matches.   Cool,
calm and collected, Frank, in the opinion of many experts,
is the leading umpire in world cricket.   He certainly has as
many admirers outside this country as in it, which proves
just how efficient Chester has proved himself.

On the field, although affable, with a ready smile, Frank
Chester never gets friendly with the players—a fact that is
important if at some time there is any little dispute—and in
short sets a perfect example to anyone who has ambitions to
become "A Man in a white coat".

Frank Chester is not one of the umpires who formerly
had a big following as a cricketer.   But for a terrible injury

in the Great War, though, there is no doubting that he would have put himself in the running for national honours. In 1914 he was one of Worcestershire's most promising players, but when he returned from France, without one arm, first-class cricket was out of the question for him, so he determined to become one of the leading umpires. How well he has succeeded!

It was in 1921 that Frank Chester was appointed to the list of first-class umpires, and when the youthful-looking official arrived at a certain county ground to "take" his first big match, the official at the gate thought he was having his leg pulled when Frank announced that he was one of the umpires. In due course the gateman appreciated that Chester was serious, scratched his head, and then allowed him to pass!

In that match Frank used, to count the various deliveries, half-a-dozen small pebbles he picked up outside the ground. Now, over twenty years later, these same pebbles are still in use. . . .

What makes Frank Chester such a great official and called by some "Prince of Umpires"? I think it is the attitude in which he stands, coupled with his quick eyes and full appreciation of the game. Unlike the Australian umpires, who stand on one side when the bowler is approaching the crease, Frank Chester is looking up-wicket all the time, and when he keeps an eye upon the bowler's feet is once more looking at the batsman receiving the ball as soon as it had left the bowler's hand.

Years at the game, too, has made Chester familiar with the likes, dislikes, and weaknesses of various batsmen and bowlers. He knows what to expect from many of them—and it is not often that you can catch out Frank Chester!

These wearers of the white coat, as those who rub shoulders with them understand, are cricket enthusiasts of the old school, but, for all their love of the game, they cannot be expected to spend eight hours a day, six days a week, out in the middle without receiving a return for their services.

Playing for England

These days first-class umpires receive a match fee of £12, plus £1 a night for hotel expenses, and third-class fare. If honoured by being entrusted with a Test match, like Frank Chester, Harry Baldwin or Jack Smart, to mention only three, last season, their reward is £40 plus hotel accommodation.

To those not familiar with the duties of an umpire these fees may sound a good return for their services, but do not shut your eyes to the fact that an umpire has to deeply concentrate all the time. He cannot have a rest but must watch every ball so keenly that I can understand umpires, at the end of a long day, with the sun shining down on them, going home with a headache.

Apart from deciding whether or not a batsman is out, or a bowler sends down a no-ball, an umpire has numerous other duties that take time. For example, they have to report to the management of the ground on which the match they are umpiring is being played half an hour before play is due to commence, and, if necessary, in the management's opinion, have to remain on the ground for half an hour after stumps have been drawn for the day.

It does not seem to be appreciated by some cricket enthusiasts for instance, that the umpires are the *sole* judges as to whether or not play is possible. If, too, an umpire thinks that a bowler is sending down unfair deliveries with the intention of injuring the batsman facing him, he can caution him. If this does not prove effective, the next step he takes is to tell the other umpire and the fielding side's skipper.

Such a thing would hardly happen, but if a bowler did continue to bowl unfairly, the umpire, at the first repetition of the dangerous delivery would call "Dead Ball", the over would be ranked as completed, and a request would be made to the bowler's captain for him to be taken off. Apart from meaning that he could not again bowl in that innings, the umpire would have to report the matter to the captain of the batting side.

F

Playing for England

I mention these few instances just to show you that the men who umpire in first-class cricket have a great responsibility. They cannot afford to be "caught out". Always must they be ready to deal with any strange incident that might arise. Never, in my experience, have I met a first-class umpire who has not had a ready answer to any appeal.

Incidentally, do you know there is only one reason—apart from illness—why an umpire, in the course of a match, can be displaced without the consent of both teams? The one reason is—betting!

Another point, so far as the umpire is concerned which few of those who follow county cricket appear to appreciate, is that every time he makes a signal to the scorers he has to await their answer before continuing with the game. Perhaps, if they were aware of this, those bright lads who shout "Get on with it!" when an umpire is waiting for the scorers to answer his signal, would cease their misplaced "guidance" to the man in charge.

Yes, the umpires, who have so much depending upon their skill, possess a knowledge of the game that cannot be equalled. That is why they are, as a body, so greatly respected, and their decisions accepted without any suggestion that they are biased in any way.

Considering the importance of their job, I always wonder how it is that so many of these officials can go about the task of umpiring in such a light-hearted manner. Out in the middle, though, you find among the umpires some grand comedians; men who, in a flash, can bring out a wisecrack to equal anything produced by an American funster.

In this respect, Alex Skelding, the former Leicestershire fast bowler, who went on to the list of first-class umpires in 1929, is one of the "stars". To look at him you would never credit the fact that Skelding, although his hair is greying, was nearly sixty years of age. Not only is he fast-moving and light of foot, but has the enthusiasm for cricket one normally associates with schoolboys, and when we hear that Alex Skelding is down to take charge of one end, everyone looks forward to hearing some amusing remarks.

Playing for England

When the fielding side and batsmen, for instance, have walked out to the middle of the arena and everyone is ready, Alex Skelding always says with a smile: "Gentlemen, the entertainment will now commence." At the end of the day's play, after picking the bails off the stumps, Alex invariably remarks: "And that, gentlemen, concludes the entertainment for to-day."

Often, when the weather is bad, and play is held up, Alex Skelding, who is no mean poet and a great teller of cricket stories, will provide us with first-class entertainment as we await the sun. As a player of experience I have learnt much through talking to him, but it is when Skelding commences to recite some of his poems that the lads crowd round to listen.

Here is the final verse of one effort which he calls "Skell's Elegy":

" So now you willow wielders
And you volley-catching fielders,
You who stand there at the wicket
Injured innocence—didn't snick it,
Bowlers who are apt to squeal
At a negative appeal,
Think of umpires Jack or Jim,
Think kindly, please, and pity him! "

Naturally, of course, you will hear dozens of amusing stories concerning umpires, but one of the funniest to reach my ears concerned Jack Hearne, one of my great predecessors in the Middlesex and England team.

Jack, according to the story, was a youngster about to make his batting debut in county cricket. As he sat in the pavilion, pads on, bat by his side, one of the older professionals came up to Jack and commenced giving him some valuable advice. The final piece of "guidance" left some impression upon young Jack Hearne: "Now," said the veteran, "when you go to the wicket try and be pleasant to the umpire. Don't hesitate to say 'Good-morning'."

Playing for England

Jack Hearne, when the time arrived for him to take his place at the crease, gave the umpire who was to face him when he "took guard" a big grin, nodded and said: "Good morning. How are you getting on?"

"Fine," replied the umpire, adding, as an afterthought: "Three more decisions and I'll have given a hundred batsmen out this season!"

Jack couldn't add anything to that!

Denis Hendren, brother of the colourful Pat, and an umpire of distinction, is an official with a big reputation for joking. Why, last summer, during the course of one county match, a loud-voiced spectator, when the visiting batsmen were faring too well to his liking, commenced a one-man blitz upon the bowlers who were battling hard beneath a broiling sun. "What about showing us the middle stump!" he kept shouting. As this call was repeated so often, Denis Hendren couldn't resist, after one particularly noisy effort, walking up to the wicket, hauling up the middle stump, and holding it aloft.

The crowd roared with laughter, and no more was heard from the noisy spectator!

On one occasion, when Denis Hendren, together with the famous Bill Reeves—a rare wit—was umpiring at Swansea, he was concerned in an incident that made nearly every player within earshot double up with laughter.

At the time, Denis Hendren was at square-leg, and when a batsman suddenly turned on his heel and hit a ball hard in his direction the umpire, realising that his only chance of escaping injury was to fall flat, did so in double-quick time.

It so happened, at this precise moment, the sound of shots came from the direction of the rifle-range at The Mumbles, and Bill Reeves, a serious expression on his face, remarked: "I've frequently heard spectators say they'd shoot Denis for some of his decisions, but I didn't think they meant it!"

It isn't always the umpires, though, who have the last laugh, for I know of one cricketer, noted for his comic tendencies, who "took the wind completely out of the sails" of one official who prided himself he knew all the answers. On going to the crease the batsman at once prepared for action, and the umpire called up to him: "I say, don't you want centre?"

The batsman looked surprised, then hurt, as he replied: "No, thank you. I played in this match last year and took it then!"

15

These Men Have Made Their Mark in Cricket.

WHEN I worked on the ground-staff at Lord's the duties I had to perform enabled me on many occasions to get a "close-up" of most of the great players of the day. On looking back I realise how fortunate I was in this respect, for as a student of the game, and one who realised that I could learn much from others, the opportunities I had of seeing star batsmen and bowlers in the nets, as well as on the field of play, proved a real blessing.

Although I am not a veteran in years, I have followed cricket for twenty-one years. Thanks to my father, who never hesitated, on Saturday afternoons, when he had finished work, to take me to see the fine cricketers who performed at Lord's or Kennington Oval, I have memories of scores of "names" that have gone down in cricket history: the classic and super batsmanship of Jack Hobbs; Frank Woolley, prince of left-arm all-rounders; Pat Hendren, the little man with the big smile and even bigger reputation; Herbert Sutcliffe, the Yorkshireman whose name will for ever be associated with that of Hobbs; Harold Larwood, speediest bowler of my generation. These players, and dozens more of their calibre, come to me as I sit down and bring to mind the reasons—and they are many—why these cricketers climbed out of the general run of things and made for themselves a cricket reputation that will live through the ages.

Jack Hobbs, I suppose, because he has scored more centuries in first-class cricket than any other man—197—is the batsman who caught my eye in a manner that has never been equalled by any other player. From my earliest days Jack Hobbs was my idol, and when, one August Bank

Playing for England

Holiday Monday at Kennington Oval, I secured his autograph, there was not a prouder lad in the whole of England. Years later, when I got to know Jack Hobbs well, I appreciated him still more, for England's greatest-ever opening batsman, in addition to being such a renowned cricketer, proved to be one of the kindest and most likeable men it has ever been my pleasure to meet. Do not run away with the idea, though, that Jack Hobbs is ultra-reserved. He is not. Hobbs is a quiet man with a subtle sense of humour that befits him; has never been known to "put on side". In fact, to meet Jack, and enjoy the pleasure of his friendship ranks among the great experiences of my cricketing life.

What made him such a wonderful batsman? As a youth I used to spend hours watching Jack Hobbs perform and ask myself the same question. After gaining experience in county cricket I think the answer is that he refused to allow the opposing bowlers to get the impression they were on top and could dictate to him. Apart from this very important trait in his make-up, Jack Hobbs, as he proved on so many occasions, could produce his best form on many varied kinds of wickets. You may have heard some batsmen say they are at their best on a particular type of wicket. Hobbs went out in the middle—to the joy of England and Surrey—to score runs on whatever kind of wicket faced him. All over the world Jack produced the form that made him the idol of English cricket and one of our finest sporting ambassadors. Consistency, too, should have been his Christian name, for a glance through the records will prove the value of Hobbs as a run-getter.

I have heard him described as "The daddy of the short run". It is justified. Time and again have I seen Hobbs, with perfect judgment, "steal" a run that did not really exist, and his ability to continually do this was prone to upset even the best fielding side. A batsman with all the strokes, and an ease and artistry I would willingly travel thousands of miles to see, Jack Hobbs is the master batsman of his generation.

Batsmanship apart, however, Jack Hobbs was among the three or four best cover-points the game has ever known.

Playing for England

I remember well how he used to stand when fielding in this position: loose, but for all that ready to pounce on the ball and flash back to the wicket-keeper a perfect return. By hard practice Hobbs became such an accepted expert at throwing down the wicket when the ball went in his direction, no batsman would dare to take a liberty.

Many cover-points to-day invariably move in towards the batsman when the ball is being bowled. I never saw Hobbs do that. But then, Jack never was one to waste valuable energy. That was why he was able to keep at the top for nearly thirty years!

As a cricketer, and as a gentleman, I can well understand why Jack Hobbs became the favourite not only of me, but millions of folk all over England.

"How does Bradman compare with Hobbs?"

If this question has been put to me once it has been a thousand times. At first glance it may seem a good one. Think, though, for a moment, and it becomes a little pointless, for you cannot really compare one batsman with another.

Jack Hobbs was the supreme artist. Bradman, in his way, is also an artist, but without the copy-book play of Hobbs. As a run-getter, pure and simple, Bradman, however, is in a class of his own.

Hobbs, it is on record, received no coaching, as he fought his way up the ladder. As a matter of interest neither did Don Bradman until he made for himself a mighty reputation in the team that represented his village, Bowral. Bradman was only twelve when he made his first century. At the age of seventeen "The Don", as he was to become known to cricketdom, played successive innings of 320, 300 and 230 for Bowral; went for two years without losing his wicket.

Such brilliance did not escape the eye of Australia's cricket authorities, and Bradman, after accepting employment in a Sydney estate office, was coached at the noted Sydney "nursery", in due course gained the New South Wales team, and in this first match, against South Australia, scored a century.

"The Don" has since been scoring them consistently!

Playing for England

I have batted and bowled against Don Bradman on many occasions and the things that always impresses itself upon you is the fact that the great Australian, from the moment he takes up his place at the wicket, means to dominate the scene, just as did Jack Hobbs. The difference in style of Hobbs and "The Don" is much more pronounced than may seem the case when sitting in the pavilion or around the ground, although each, in his way, has a certain similarity one with the other. Both, for instance, take infinite care to make sure that they "know the pitch". In other words, they constantly keep running their eye over it to try and detect anything that might assist the bowlers.

As fieldsmen, too—both were truly great cover-points—they were alike inasmuch that their deadly throwing-in was worth many runs to their side. Hobbs, as I have said, was an expert at hitting the stumps. Bradman could learn little from him in this direction. As a boy, I am told, he used to spend hours at a time throwing a golf ball at a five-barred gate. If he missed the result was a long walk to retrieve the ball, so to avoid this, Bradman became very careful with his "heaves" and, in due course, really deadly.

I know, when opposing Don Bradman in Tests, that you cannot afford to "steal" any runs.

"The Don's" batting, as many qualified writers have pointed out, is not of the copy-book variety, but there is no disputing, as I said earlier, the fact that he is the greatest run-getting machine the game has ever known. In 1938, for instance, Bradman was in terrific form. He scored 1,000 runs by May 27, secured 13 centuries during the course of the Australian tour, and finished up with an aggregate of 2,429 runs, and an average of 115.60.

A truly wonderful performance.

Unlike Jack Hobbs, who had so often opened those broad shoulders of his and gone for the bowling—to the crowd's delight—when once past the century, Bradman always looks upon making a hundred as the first step towards getting a double-century. When two-hundred are on the board Bradman then thinks in terms of another century.

Playing for England

Yes, this very remarkable little man who has eyes like a hawk, and watches the opposing bowler's hands and fingers as if mesmerised by them, has wonderful powers of concentration and a stamina that amazes when you consider how frail he is.

It is when you bowl against Bradman that a full appreciation of his wonderful footwork—and "cheek"—is yours. Note I use the word "cheek". I mean it, too, for the little Australian is the most audacious batsman it has ever been my lot to try and dismiss. Once he has his "eye in" little short of a miracle—and miracle is the correct word—can rid the bowlers of Bradman.

Unlike such classic batsmen as Hobbs, Woolley, Nourse, Merchant, Hutton, to mention a few, Bradman is never afraid to step away from the "copy-book"—and play a shot that will upset those who love artistic batting—if it means getting runs. Sometimes, when I have bowled against him, Bradman has amazed me by producing shots that even a schoolboy would consider venturesome, such as stepping to a ball pitched outside the off-stump and pulling it round to leg.

Only a batsman possessing an ultra-keen eye and wonderful footwork could afford to make such an effort, and bowlers must be thankful that Bradmans are not born every minute.

An English batsman with whom I have been honoured to partner in Test cricket and had a style somewhat similar to that of Don Bradman was the little Lancashire man, Eddie Paynter. Now Eddie, as it happened, was born at Oswaldthistle, and, as if that were not enough for those who delight in cracking a joke at the Lancashire town's expense, Paynter first saw the light of day on November 5th!

But that is where the amusing part—except for his own light-hearted approach to cricket—ended, for so good a cricketer was Paynter that he quickly forced his way into Test cricket. He is one of the greatest partners it has been my pleasure to have in a Test. Like Don Bradman—and the illustrious Hobbs—Paynter was a born cricketer and had but little coaching. I have even heard it said that he played little as a boy because there was no ground near his home. Eddie, though, quickly became a cricket enthusiast and must have spent all his pocket money in purchasing books dealing with the game and the personalities who popularise it.

It happened, in 1920, that Lancashire spotted this tiny fellow with the "happy bat" and cheerful disposition and decided that he was a "prospect". It fell to the lot of J. T. Tyldesley, the coach, to polish the "rough edges" off Eddie Paynter. Fortunately he did not interfere with the gay cavalier-like style that was to endear Paynter to the followers of cricket, but, because of the county strength at the time Eddie had to wait ten long years before he could consider himself a regular member of the Lancashire team.

But Eddie Paynter never wasted a minute during his period in the Lancashire second eleven. He studied the art of batting; improved his fielding until he became the recognised star among outfielders, and took such a delight in bowling that many thought he could have become a leading bowler. Paynter though, decided to concentrate more upon his batting.

The wisdom of Paynter's patience and thoroughness in preparing himself for the future was shown by the way in which, in 1931, he scored his first 1,000 runs, and opened the England innings—with Herbert Sutcliffe as his partner—against New Zealand. Many folk sat up and took notice when this "unknown" was chosen, but Paynter more than proved his worth.

Like Bradman, who has all the strokes, Eddie Paynter can use the "long handle", and produce the audacious stroke, when the occasion demands. It was his ability, too, to rise above the occasion that left a lasting impression upon me, and I was fortunate to play with him in my first Test against the Australians. In his quietly confident Lancashire accent, Eddie, from the moment we met, did his utmost to put me at ease. When we were at the wicket together he did all he could to encourage the "new boy", and in general proved to be a good friend.

What is more, by watching Eddie Paynter I learnt a great deal, not the least important being that a big heart in cricket is just as vital as good stroke play.

Playing for England

In mixing with north countrymen I have noticed, for the most part, that they approach the game with a different attitude to the cricketers of the south. Eddie Paynter, mind you, was an exception, but Len Hutton and Cyril Washbrook, who have opened the England innings so successfully of recent years, are a case in point. Both are quiet and thoughtful men. I cannot imagine either of them losing their temper, but once you get them talking about cricket the best thing to do is sit back and listen. You will learn plenty. England's "opening pair", you see, are the type who know a great deal but have to be "drawn out". Especially so is this with Len Hutton, one of the greatest stroke players I have ever seen.

Hutton, who has been reared in the traditional Yorkshire school, will never be hurried. He takes his time, chooses the right ball to hit, and in general, as all good batsmen should, sets out to dominate the scene. So does Washbrook, and when this opening pair get settled they really do take some shifting.

Both are classic stroke players, although Washbrook, in the past, has shown a tendency to "flick" at a ball going away from the offstump, but he appears now to have overcome this weakness. Patience, they say, is one of the great factors in determining success or failure with an opening batsman. Len Hutton and Cyril Washbrook have this in abundance.

My friend, Joe Hardstaff, with whom I have played in some thrilling Test matches, is another batsman who might be termed "classic". Rather I think the Nottinghamshire man, once he gets cracking, might be termed "majestic". I have seen him play some glorious innings, and it is my opinion that he is the hardest hitter of a ball among recognised batsmen. His bat—as I earlier revealed—weighs 2 lbs. 7 ozs.—and Hardstaff gets terrific power behind his shots. His flashes through the covers, the result of perfect timing and balance, give the fieldsmen little chance of cutting down a possible boundary, while his defensive play, when the situation demands, gives confidence to the fellow at the other end. It is as an attacking batsman, though, that the blond and handsome Joe is at his best. Once he gets the better of the bowling it is a joy to sit back and watch him open his shoulders and hit. But if you happen to be partnering him at the time, it can become very tiring!

Mention of the word "partnering" at once brings to mind those two grand Kent and England players Leslie Ames and "Tich" Freeman. What a grand team they proved to be in the years preceding World War II! I wonder if we shall ever again see such a wonderful understanding between wicket-keeper and bowler as that which existed between Leslie and "Tich". As a youngster I watched this pair "diddle" out many a star batsman, and when the time came for me to cross bat with them I was determined to try and outwit them. Oh yes, when you played this Kentish pair it was a battle of wits, for they planned, long beforehand, how a certain batsman was to meet his end, and by means of a secret code of some kind, which they developed over the years, were in constant touch with each other. If, for instance, Freeman was to send down a slightly-faster ball, he would give Ames the signal they both knew. In fact, by means of signs this bowler and stumper were all the time working out a way of sending you to the pavilion. That it worked so successfully can be judged by the hundreds of victims that fell to Leslie and "Tich".

I can even now see "Tich" Freeman, with his bald pate and short run up to the wicket, sending down those deliveries behind which there was so much guile. At times, it was said, Freeman "bought" his wickets, but judging by the stars he "bagged", he did his "shopping" successfully. In one match, I well remember, a well-known batsman turned "Tich" round to the square-leg boundary with as perfect a stroke as you could wish to see. Exactly the same ball was sent down next time, and once more the ball hit the fence. For the third time Freeman sent down an identical delivery —at least—it looked like that—and the batsman, feeling pleased with himself, made another perfect stroke. What happened I do not know but the ball seemed to jump a little, and a man Freeman had quietly moved round to square-leg gathered the easiest of catches.

That was "Tich" Freeman, the bowler who looked upon cricket as a game to be enjoyed—and to be won by the man who was smart enough to outwit the other fellow.

Bill "Tiger" O'Reilly, one of the many great spin bowlers produced by the Australians, ranks among the most deadly I have ever met. Off the field you could not wish to meet a more pleasant or hospitable fellow than O'Reilly. Once you got on the field of play, though, he became a different person and was out to dismiss you as quickly as possible.

As he pounded up to the wicket, a fearsome expression on his face, the ball grasped in his huge hand, O'Reilly looked deadly. His deliveries, too, were packed with guile, but if you managed to get on top of him, and dispatched balls he thought would get your wicket to the boundary, O'Reilly was liable to get a little annoyed.

Strangely enough, it was when in this mood that he could be at his best. Why? Because O'Reilly, when hit, did not become hostile to the opposing batsman as an individual; he felt that his skill should have deserved a better reward, and, more often than not, pulled something extra-special from out of his bag of tricks.

A great "kidder" was Bill O'Reilly, but there was nothing vicious in what he did on the cricket field. In fact, I'm sure he played the game with his tongue in his cheek when the myth was built up around the nick-name "Tiger".

The secret of his success on Australian and England wickets? First he had a wonderful length and could keep plugging away, without losing it, for hours on end. Secondly, like most Australian spinners, he had to put extra spin to make the ball "grip" wickets down under. Appreciating that to be really good he had to spin the ball more than usual O'Reilly set his long fingers to work and succeeded in his aim. When he came to England, therefore, where the wickets were more susceptible to spin, he was an immediate success, and during the 1938 tour became a real "Jonah" to me.

But then, it was an honour to be "outed" by Bill O'Reilly, one of the finest bowlers Australia ever sent to these shores.

Among English bowlers Hedley Verity, Bill Bowes, Harold Larwood, Tom Goddard, Bill Copson and Alf. Gover, have left an everlasting impression upon me. Verity, who lost his life serving with the Army in Italy, was a master of length. The silver-haired Yorkshireman, who, like Eddie Paynter, waited a long time for his big chance in county cricket, often used to talk with me about bowling.

"Denis," he said on one occasion, as we awaited our turn to bat in a Test match, "once a bowler is able to develop a good length, and keep it for long periods, he is half-way towards becoming successful. Once the length is there you can concentrate upon building up your store of tricks. Without a length, though, no trick is worth while."

Hedley told me that as a younger man he must have spent many weary hours trying to drop a ball accurately on a piece of paper at one end of a net. At first it was a full sheet of newspaper. Slowly, as he made progress, Verity reduced the paper in size. Eventually he became so accomplished that more often than not he could pitch the ball on a piece of paper no bigger than the ball itself.

"The importance of being able to do this," said Verity, "can quickly be appreciated. Once you discover a piece of turf that is of assistance to you, and you can drop the ball on it, you're well on your way to getting wickets."

This quiet-spoken Yorkshireman was more than a good bowler; he was a cricket scientist. Most folk, especially those in Yorkshire, say that he was a natural left-arm genius. After talks with him, though, I am convinced that Hedley Verity was a steady bowler who, by hard work in the nets, and listening to what the great Wilfred Rhodes had to say, developed himself into a genius, which is as nice a thing as one can say about a man whose loss English cricket feels to this day.

His Yorkshire colleague, Bill Bowes, is another who has "got there" by hard work. A most deceiving bowler is Bowes. Many a time, when sitting in the crowd, I have heard

Playing for England

people ask, as he trots up to the wicket, why he is termed a "fast-medium" bowler. What they appear to overlook is that a man does not have to run-up to the wicket, arms flailing, to be a quick bowler. Bowes, as it so happens, makes the ball do the work. There is timing and precision in Bill Bowes' delivery, and the ball, after it lands on the wicket, come up at you with terrific speed. Maurice Tate, I well remember, was another able to accomplish this, much to the discomfort of opposing batsmen. So, too, can Alec Bedser.

Harold Larwood, though, as a fast bowler, was a law unto himself. He is the speediest and most accurate bowler of this type I have ever faced. In fact, you will only find a Larwood once in a generation, and no matter how hard you might coach a man for this tiring work, I am sure really great fast bowlers are born, not made.

Larwood was born to the job.

By reason of his stature—Harold was on the small side for a fast bowler—he did not bump the ball much. Instead, as it hit the turf the ball would come through at terrific speed and a batsman needed good eyes, and a smart pair of feet, to stop a "fast 'un" from the Nottinghamshire man if it happened to be on the target.

What impressed me most of all about Larwood was his approach to the wicket. Although this fleet-footed ex-miner ran up towards the batsman at great speed, there was an air of "comfort" about him that made Harold look dangerous long before the ball left his hand. He was, in fact, the perfect fast bowler. A man of pace who, coupling his brain with the phenomenal speed he was able to work up, Harold gave opposing batsmen the kind of experience they found it hard to forget.

Like Verity, and other great bowlers, Harold Larwood, although pace was his prime weapon, kept a wonderful length. That is why so many of his victims were bowled.

As a lesson for would-be fast bowlers a day watching Harold Larwood in action was *the* thing. I consider myself fortunate in being able to say that I had the opportunity of facing the "Notts Express".

Playing for England

In the same way was I lucky in being able to bat with Patsy Hendren of Middlesex and England fame. You see, apart from Jack Hobbs, Patsy was my big schoolboy favourite. When I joined the ground-staff at Lord's, too, I was fired with an enthusiasm to follow in Hendren's footsteps—he was once a ground-boy—and climb to the top of the cricket ladder. That he helped me in my quest is one of those romantic little touches that are to be found on all sides in cricket.

Apart from giving me some words of advice—Pat would do this in the course of conversation, not by putting on the "old campaigner" act—it was at the wicket that I learnt so much from this merry little man who had also played, with success, as a professional footballer for Brentford and England. As he prepared to take the bowling at the other end of the wicket I have often studied hard this short and sturdy batsman, and it did not take me long to understand why he made so many runs.

Hendren, you see, looked upon a cricket bat as an offensive weapon, not as something with which to defend his wicket. Like Don Bradman—and long before the Australian star was even thought about—Hendren went to the crease with the set purpose of looking for runs. Often, when sitting around the ropes, I heard people who have "copybook play" on the mind comment that Hendren's hooks and pulls looked more like the effort of a village cricketer. That they brought him valuable runs—and quickly at that—was too often forgotten. What the critics did not know, however, was that Patsy, a great believer in net-practice, had spent many hours perfecting those strokes. That there was nothing "chancy" about them. Hendren, with his wonderful stroke play, and attacking tendencies, was a grand partner for a youngster. I remember how he used to inspire me with confidence by his actions, while, when in the field, the little man, always on his toes, gave everyone a perfect example. The crowd loved Hendren in England, Australia, West Indies and wherever the great game is played.

Apart from his ability with the bat, Hendren had something else that endeared him to the crowd: a sense of humour.

Playing for England

On one occasion, for instance, when we were fielding at Lord's, one of the opposing batsmen made a late cut, but Hendren, in the slips, snapped it up. At the same time he turned on his heel and pointed in the direction of the boundary. Like a hare one of our outfielders tore round the ropes—and pulled up with a jerk. What he thought was the ball was in reality a sparrow, and Hendren was tossing the ball back to the bowler!

Another time Pat brought down "the house" at Lord's, when soon after all the body-line controversy, he went to the wicket wearing a contraption half-way between a speedway rider's crash helmet and a flying cap!

As a teller of cricket stories Patsy Hendren is in a class of his own, and although I did not have very long with him as a colleague in the Middlesex side, the stories I heard him tell will never be forgotten.

On one occasion, according to Patsy, he and Walter Hammond were travelling to Manchester for a Test match. As it had been a rush to catch the train, and there was no time to have lunch, they had taken with them a few sandwiches.

After settling down comfortably in a compartment, and the train was about to move off, a clergyman, flushed and obviously a little tired following his rush, sank down in a seat opposite Walter Hammond. Nothing was said, however, and as the journey passed so did the two cricketers open their parcel of sandwiches and settle down to enjoy their lunch.

When the last sandwich had disappeared Hammond rolled up his paper and tossed it out of the window. At least, he intended it to go through the window, but the paper, catching the frame, was blown back into the compartment and landed in the clergyman's lap. Without so much as a smile he picked up the paper and remarked: "Obviously not a cricketer, sir!"

This, mind you, to the man who was for years recognised as the world's greatest holder of slip catches, and one of the best fieldsmen of this or any other generation!

Playing for England

I used to get a great kick out of hearing Pat Hendren talk about his experiences when with touring sides, and two, which have remained with me, rank among the most amusing I've ever heard.

When with an M.C.C. side in Australia he was included in a yachting party that made a trip from Sydney to Killarney Island, a local beauty spot where folk used to go and enjoy a meal in the open and in general laze in the sun. As the cricketers made their way ashore a youngster detached himself from a game of cricket which had attracted the Englishmen's attention, went up to Phil Mead, the Hampshire batsman, and asked how many there were in his party. "About twelve," replied Mead. At once the reply was flashed: "Right, we'll challenge you to a game of cricket."

Apparently the captain of the "Australian" side imagined the men they had challenged were novices at the game, and when it came to Pat Hendren's turn to bat the cheery little Middlesex batsman was determined to keep up the impression. First he held the bat incorrectly, placing the right hand above the left, whereupon the wicket-keeper, a most friendly chap, stepped forward and showed him the correct method to hold it. "You'll be much more comfortable," he added, and when Hendren cracked the first ball he received into the sea his "coach" was a very proud young man. "See what I mean about holding your bat correctly?" he said. "It makes all the difference."

In the meantime one of the lads had stripped off his clothes, swam out to sea, and recovered the ball.

The game was about to be re-commenced when the wicket-keeper, noting Hendren again holding his bat incorrectly, halted the bowler and once more showed Hendren the correct way to place his hands upon the handle of the bat. The rest of the team objected to this, but the stumper, who had a pride in his work, ignored their protests, and when Pat clouted the next ball so far out to sea there was no chance of recovering it, the match was brought to an abrupt conclusion.

Playing for England

At this stage the rest of the "Australian" team began an argument among themselves as to whether or not this stranger had ever before played cricket. The general feeling was that none of the other side were really novices, but the stumper was quick to reply: "Why, the last batsman didn't even know how to hold a bat."

This proved too much for the suffering bowler who snapped: "Well, he didn't do so badly smacking the ball twice into the sea, which is something none of you've done!"

As the Englishmen were returning to the yacht one of the Australians went up to Patsy and said: "You know, I believe you're Hendren." His friends, though, laughed their heads off. "Why," one said, "if he's Hendren I'm Charlie McCartney!" (referring to the great Australian Test star.)

"To this day," Pat Hendren said to us, "I doubt whether they appreciated how we were pulling their legs."

The Australian spectators—very critical at times, as I know from recent experience—loved Pat Hendren because of his ready wit. He was more often than not ready with a snappy reply to their banter.

On one occasion, during the course of a Test, Pat Hendren was fielding on the boundary when the crowd, in their usual chatty mood, began asking Hendren questions.

"Why haven't you brought out —— with you?" he was asked. In his usual cheery manner Pat replied: "Oh, they only decided to bring out the good-looking fellows."

A low whistle followed this, and then an Australian voice roared back: "How the heck, then, did they manage to pick you!"

No one laughed louder than Hendren.

But then, you would expect nothing else from Hendren, a great cricketer who, apart from his skill, had something more than that: personality and colour, and a kindly character that made everyone who shook his hand feel all the better for their meeting.

16

*All-Rounders Prove Their Worth—Australians
Have Set Us an Example—Why Edrich and I Became
Batsmen-Bowlers—Team Comes Before Records—
The Value of a "Bowling Stumper".*

IN MODERN cricket the man who can bat, bowl, and field, is worth his weight in gold. Although there will always be need for a "specialist"—batsman or bowler—the game has changed so much in the last few years that more and more all-rounders are finding their way into county teams.

I personally think it a good sign, and in some ways an insurance for the future when we meet Australia in Tests. The Australians, you see, are great believers in all-rounders, and in the side that defeated us in 1946–7 and 1948 there was more than the normal number of "bat and ball" men to be relied upon by skipper Don Bradman.

An all-round cricketer gives every team balance, at the same time there is a strength which is not always apparent, in a side that includes men who are either batsmen or bowlers.

When in Australia Bill Edrich and I noticed how the various young cricketers in the Dominion take a delight in being able to bat and bowl well, and when I returned home one of the things I determined to do was improve my own bowling, for once again, to make your way in cricket, as I have said so often before, practice is the only path to the top.

It should be stressed that you cannot "make" an all-rounder any more than you can a batsman or bowler. A young chap has to have it in him to be a good cricketer. The rest is up to him, patience, and a good deal of perseverance.

A point that should not be overlooked is that few all-rounders have succeeded as fast bowler–batsmen. There are one or two very great exceptions, most noticeable being Bill Edrich, but this is not the rule. Most all-rounders are either medium-paced or slow bowlers; wisely conserve their energy for the job of getting runs and wickets.

"How do men become all-rounders?" is a question that has been fired at me dozens of times during the past few months. The answer is not so difficult; can be summed up in one word: "Success."

When Bill Edrich, always a good bowler, began to get regularly among the wickets, he said to himself: "I rather enjoy bowling. Now I must try hard to improve." And the man who was already recognised as one of the world's greatest batsmen began to practise hard his bowling in the nets. He improved his length; controlled the ball better. To-day, his bowling and batting, coupled with alert fielding, have made Bill Edrich, along with Keith Miller of Australia, the finest all-rounder in the game.

I have explained earlier that I made my debut in first-class cricket as a left-arm bowler. When my batting began to take first place, however, I did not send down so many overs, then, while in Australia with the M.C.C. team, began to experiment with my left-arm googlies in the nets. "Why don't you take a chance and try out those deliveries in a match?" both Edrich and Laurie Fishlock said to me, after I had spent some time bowling to them.

"What!" I exclaimed, "and have every ball I send down knocked out of the ground? No thank you!"

But the suggestion of Bill and Laurie set me thinking. When I returned home to England, and commenced practice in the nets, it was, as I remarked earlier, to find other batsmen sharing a similar view; that the "googly" balls I sent down were really worth developing. Eventually I had the "courage" to try out this type of bowling in public, the move proved successful, and at the end of the season I had collected 73 wickets.

"Will bowling interfere with my batting?" That question was asked me by a young fellow when I took a coaching class not so long ago. Again, the answer was not difficult.

If you are physically fit, make sure that you have eight
hours' sleep every night and do not over-work yourself,
there is no reason at all why a cricketer should find one
part of his game interfering with another. By "over-work"
I mean you should not, after putting in a long spell of
bowling, at once hurry out to the wicket and attempt to
knock the opposing bowlers all over the field. In fact, if
you wish to become a successful all-rounder I think the
best examples are Keith Miller, Colin McCool and Ian
Johnson, the Australians. They do everything in modera-
tion—and as a result have proved of very great value to
their team.

To be a successful all-rounder demands a great deal of
hard net practice, more so as the majority of all-rounders,
for reasons I have explained, are either medium-paced or
spin bowlers. The latter type, apart from "spinning
powers", also has to have a complete control of length.
This only comes with experience, and Duggie Wright, one
of the greatest of our exponents in this type of delivery,
spent many weary months perfecting it at an indoor cricket
school. Speaking for myself, when at net-practice I prefer
to have a batsman facing me, for I can ask his opinion as
to how I'm bowling, but some fellows prefer to experiment
on their own.

Greatest of all the men who have shone with bat and ball
was Yorkshire's George Hirst. Way back in 1906 George,
who later became coach to the county he served so wonder-
fully on the field, took 208 wickets and scored 2,385 runs.
An amazing performance during an era when cricket was at a
terrifically high standard, and one that will take some beating.

It is heartening to find, though, that young cricketers
are now appreciating the value of an all-rounder, and at the
same time understanding that they can enjoy their game
even more by taking an over or two with the ball if they are
batsmen, or knocking up a few runs if their main calling
had previously been to get wickets.

Middlesex County Cricket Club do everything possible
to encourage cricketers who show signs of being able to do

well with bat and ball. Why my big brother, Leslie, even when keeping wicket, was sometimes asked to take off his pads and gauntlets, hand them over to one of our colleagues, and try his hand at trying to break a partnership that looked dangerous. Surrey, whose brilliant little stumper, Arthur McIntyre, was called upon to do a similar thing, found it worked, too. "Mac," who used to be a slow bowler, apparently had kept up his practice in the nets, and it was he, like my brother, who made folk sit up and understand how valuable it is for a skipper to have such a "reserve" to call upon.

Since the war all-rounders have commenced to make their presence felt in the first-class average. In successive years Dick Howorth, of Worcestershire and England, has completed the cricketer's "double"—100 wickets and 1,000 runs in a season—and many other players are shining with the bat and ball.

Alec Bedser, the England and Surrey bowler, is typical of what I mean. When we were in Australia, and England found themselves in difficulties, Bedser quite often pulled "out of the bag" batting skill few folk would have credited him with possessing. Alec produced classy shots all round the wicket, and Australians said: "What a batsman he could become!"

"Down Under" Alec Bedser, I guess, must have learnt to enjoy his batting, and at the same time appreciate that to be a good run-getter would not upset his bowling. During the 1947 season, too, apart from getting 130 wickets, he scored 727 runs, a good performance considering that he often went in low down in the batting order. What is more, he scored his first century in county cricket.

This all-round ability of Bedser was noted with interest, for Ray Lindwall, Australia's brilliant fast bowler, even found time in a Test to crack a fine 100 against us. Such efforts, you will appreciate, do help win matches!

You will have noted, too, that most of the leading county sides can call upon many men who come under the classification of "all-rounders". In the Middlesex side we have utilised as batsmen-bowlers Jack Robertson, Bill Edrich, Jim Sims, Leslie Compton, R. W. V. Robins, Andy Thompson, and myself, which gives any captain a wide choice, and means that he can switch the changes so much there is no chance of a few men getting over-worked and tired.

Yes, I am all out for young cricketers trying their arm— if they are talented enough—as all-rounders. It gives increased power to the team they assist, and, at the same time, adds to their own personal enjoyment of the game. *And enjoyment of cricket, more than anything else, is the thing that matters.*

A final word to young cricketers so far as this side of the game is concerned. Have you noticed how successful Kenneth Cranston, Bill Edrich, and skipper Norman Yardley, have been in several Test matches? If one of them failed with the bat, more often than not he proved successful with the ball. In the case of Norman Yardley, when we went to Australia in the winter of 1946–7, he was recognised as a steady batsman. No one, however, took much interest in his bowling—until we were short of a change-bowler "Down Under". Then our captain, Walter Hammond, tossed the ball to Yardley, and the vice-captain proceeded to "try his arm". They do say you never know your capabilities until you try. This proved to be the case with Norman. At least, he played in a Yorkshire team that had so many star bowlers he never had to be called upon. In Australia, though, our vice-skipper surprised everyone, especially the Australians, by his ability to send down a consistently good-length ball. What is more, Norman got Don Bradman's wicket on three occasions, and returned home established as an "all-rounder"!

There must be many more cricketers with all-round ability such as Norman Yardley proved he possessed. I hope, for the good of the game, and themselves, that they try their hand at doing well with bat and ball, for there is always room in the game for the good all-rounder.

17

Fitness and the Cricketer—Fielding Success Comes with Practice—Bowling Hints—Wicket-Keepers are Born—Batsmen Should Note these Things.

THERE are no hard and fast rules for cricket success. To put it bluntly, a young man either "has what it takes" to be a player, or must be prepared to accept the fact that he will never be anything above the ordinary. Even if he has natural ability, however, our cricket "hope" must be prepared to accept that success will not go his way by just wishing for it. Every great cricketer has had to work hard before he reached the top of the ladder, and an aspect that must never be overlooked is physical fitness and the keeping of oneself in the most alert mental state. First and foremost, as I have said before, eight hours' sleep every night is essential. If you have ambitions to succeed in county cricket never forget that it is a hard game to play day after day. The concentration, whether you are batting, bowling, or fielding, is terrific, and it is only when you have spent a season or so playing in county cricket that you appreciate the immensity of the strain.

I am not suggesting that every young cricketer should go into a match with the same outlook as a county player— although there is nothing wrong with it—but he should always remember that if he is to enjoy his game, and get the best out of himself, physical fitness is most essential.

It is most heartening to discover, as I have, during the course of my travels around the country, that the standard of fielding in every class of cricket has risen a great deal of recent years. In the past, especially in club cricket and schoolboy matches, not enough interest was attached to the importance of fielding, and in many instances it was looked upon more as a hardship than a branch of the game to be enjoyed.

When we won the County Championship in 1947 many tributes were paid to the quality of our fielding which had considerably reduced the run-getting powers of teams we opposed. This fielding ability did not just "come" to our side. We worked hard for this before the season opened, and never lost sight of the fact that a run saved in the field was as good as one scored with the bat.

This is a view I strongly suggest every cricketer should bear in mind when he is fielding.

One of our little stunts, when we put in evening practice, was for a number of men to spread themselves out over the field, and a batsman would hit the ball hard in any and every direction. For half an hour we would put in this kind of training. There was no "pulling of punches", either. The batsman would hit the ball good and hard, and the fieldsmen would find it coming at them from all angles, and at various heights. In fact, the practice was as good as playing in a match.

Accurate fielding really can be encouraged by this type of whole-hearted practice.

When I was a youngster at Lord's many were the occasions I heard distinguished cricketing figures discussing the fielding side of the game, and the remarks made, for some reason, stuck in my mind and I have never forgotten them. Putting them into practice helped me to improve my own standard.

I shall never forget on one occasion having a long talk with Patsy Hendren on the subject of fielding. "Always be on the move and ready to dart into action," I remember Patsy saying, and from that moment onwards I made sure that I would not be caught unprepared when in the field. Cyril Washbrook, whose fielding is a perfect example for any young cricketer, is a firm believer in this view. If you have the good fortune to see Cyril at cover-point watch how he is always ready for action. Invariably on his toes. Rarely does Washbrook miss anything.

Playing for England

For fieldsmen who prefer to be close to the wicket, I would recommend a careful study of Cyril Washbrook's methods. To commence with, you will never see him, when returning the ball to either the stumper or bowler, throw it "from the shoulder". Washbrook, rightly, more or less "flicks" the ball back with his wrist. Apart from saving energy—and the possibility, judging by the way some youths throw a ball, of putting out his elbow—it saves valuable time. Remember that a split second may mean all the difference between a batsman being run-out and staying to make a hundred.

On many occasions remarks have been passed about the accurate throwing powers of many of our leading fieldsmen. Washbrook, from cover-point, has been responsible for the throwing-down of many wickets, yet it does not appear to be fully appreciated that such ability is not always "born in" a cricketer. Like everything else, even if a cricketer has natural skill only hard practice will help him "polish it" and develop into a top-class player.

So far as throwing down the wicket is concerned, like many other players, I myself have spent long hours, often alone, to develop accuracy. One of the best methods I found was to erect a stump in a field, then, from various angles, and distances from it, try hard to knock it down. At first, I must admit, so many times did I miss the stump—and had to run after the ball!—that I felt like calling it a day. Something inside of me, however, said "get on with it", and I am right glad that such "advice" was forthcoming!

Accurate fielding, especially if you are a chap who prefers to go close to the wicket, is essential for the success not only of yourself, but the side you assist. Hard practice is the only way you can reach a really high standard, and the stars, I know, will be the first to admit how they found this the only way to the top of the ladder.

Sidney Brown, the Middlesex player, is a typical example of what I mean. When he joined the Lord's staff—like me he was a ground-boy—Sidney, as he will admit, was anything but a first-class field. It was to his advantage to admit that his fielding was his drawback, and accordingly Brown went about the job of learning the art. He succeeded, too, and when we won the County Championship was outstanding not only as a batsman, but as a saver of runs.

Reverting to fieldsmen who take up a position near the batsmen, I have always felt, in club and juvenile cricket, that too many players do not appreciate the importance of slip-fielding. I may be wrong, but from personal experience in the past I know that the position was not looked upon with the seriousness it demands. In modern cricket—and again I am open to criticism—the slip-fieldsman has become as vital to his side as a first-rate wicket-keeper.

"If I want to become a good slip, how do you suggest I go about it?" I can hear a number of you asking. Well, providing you have a good eye, possess an ultra-safe pair of hands, and can concentrate for hours, you are well on the way to developing into a fellow whom fast bowlers pat on the back and are proud to call "friend!"

There is, however, more in slip-fielding than possessing these three essentials for success. Another very important item is anticipation. Like a goal-keeper, every slip-fieldsman has to anticipate where a batsman will try to place a shot, and next time the opportunity goes your way of watching a star slip-fielder such as Bill Edrich, note how he concentrates all the time, is ever on his toes, and, quite often, moves slightly just as the ball leaves the bowler's hand. Edrich, after long and careful study, can more or less tell, with some certainty, the re-action of certain batsmen to a particular ball—oh, yes, first-class cricketers do build up a first-rate picture of the strong and weak points of opponents—and accordingly he is always ready to pounce on any chance that may materialise.

Another important word of advice for budding slip-fieldsmen: never snatch at the ball: always take it calmly.

Walter Hammond, greatest slip-fieldsman of my generation, was noted for this high-quality, plus, of course, his uncanny anticipation. Wally, I recollect, made a study of **every first-class batsman and how he re-acted to certain** balls that were destined for the slip-fieldsman. His great speed—and he was fast as a younger man—was what caught the eye, but the real reason Hammond was so successful at slip could be traced to the fact he could anticipate a shot before the batsman had even received the ball!

I do not think anyone would have a better example of success than Hammond in this particular branch of the game.

One of my greatest delights is fielding on the boundary. Apart from the good-natured banter and "advice" that comes from the spectators, the thrill of tearing round the ground trying to save valuable runs has, even with the years I have spent in top-class cricket, never left me.

There is, though, more in fielding on the boundary than just chasing a ball. I learnt that on joining the ground-staff and seeing a cricketer, noted for the quality of his fielding, doing nothing else but short, sharp bursts, of about 20 yards.

"It's keeping on the move, and being ready for a swift 20 yard run, and a clean pick-up, that makes the successful out-fielder," Archie Fowler, the Lord's coach said to me, and the cricketer I had noted practising his sprinting, although at the top, he realised that the only way to keep in this proud position was by training.

For a long time now this has been one of my favourite little training stunts—it also helps me as a footballer—but starting, although very important is not the beginning and ending of outfielding.

Throwing-in to the wicket is just as vital, and the aim of a "boundary man" should be to pick up the ball and return it to the wicket all in one movement. I appreciate that it is easy to suggest such a move—but with patience you will find it comes naturally.

So far as returns are concerned, do not try to hit the sun with the ball. Throw it hard and low so that it reaches the wicket-keeper just above stump high. Apart from helping the man wearing the gauntlets, long-throwing saves vital seconds.

The saving of seconds, remember, means the cutting down of runs.

Just now I mentioned the wicket-keeper. My recollection as a schoolboy and junior is that nearly every fellow had the idea he was a potential George Duckworth or Leslie Ames. Too often, though, to his chagrin he discovered that to have ambition and to possess skill are different things, and it possibly dawned on him that great wicket-keepers are born, not made.

You will gather, from this remark, that my view is that you cannot make anyone a good wicket-keeper unless he has ability. All the coaching in the world will not pay dividends if the cricketer concerned does not possess a keen eye, safe hands, patience, and, once again—how it has cropped up since we began "talking fielding!"—that priceless gift, anticipation.

Like a slip-fielder, too, a stumper must not snatch at the ball.

Godfrey Evans, the Kent and present English wicket-keeper, is the perfect example of a successful stumper. At the end of a long day he is on his toes, and "alive for chances", with the same vim that characterised his play during the morning. I would suggest to any would-be wicket-keeper spending a day or two watching Godfrey. A study of him, and his methods is a first-class lesson not only for schoolboy 'keepers, but men who play in good-class club cricket.

In the course of my travels, I have been a little disappointed to find that youngsters are not taking to bowling with the same seriousness they do batting. This is a thousand pities, for there is no doubt, in the years ahead, we shall need young men in the Tests, for in Australia, as I noted when in that country, they have an abundance of youthful bowlers making headway in the various grades of cricket.

At the moment, in England, there is a dearth of fast bowlers. On a number of occasions, when talking to young cricketers about this type of bowling, I have met with the answer: "If I take up fast bowling I won't last long.

Playing for England

By bowling slow I'll be able to go on for very much longer."

This argument, when you are over 30 years old, may stand up, but if a youth starts talking this way to me I feel like laughing. Providing a young chap is in the best possible physical condition, possesses a good pair of shoulders, and, just as important, can smile when things are not going too well for him, he ought, if his heart is in the job, to develop with coaching into a useful man of pace.

Before any young bowler attempts to become really fast there are a number of points he should sit down and think over. They are: 1. How to develop an easy and comfortable action. 2. Find one set distance he will use as his run-up to the wicket. 3. Learn how to "get his body" into every delivery as did the great Harold Larwood.

Among modern fast bowlers Ray Lindwall, the Australian, is the nearest approach I have seen to Larwood for this particular essential.

When a fast bowler is making a delivery his left shoulder should be in direct line with the batsman, and if you are accurate in this respect, it will be to find that the "follow through", which is most important, will also come.

For years fast bowlers hailing from many countries have found their approach to the wicket a great concern. I have known even great stars to worry. To ease their fears they invariably put in plenty of practice over various distances, measuring out their strides, and in general doing everything possible to not only regain their easy action—if you have "no-ball" barked in your ear by the umpire it can be most upsetting—but the confidence that goes with an easy mind.

One of the most successful fast bowlers in the game, after a season in which he had been "no-balled" more than the normal number of times, went to his home, laid down a cricket pitch in his garden, and during the winter months, when conditions allowed, did nothing else but practise running up to the wicket.

"I bet I'll not be stepping over the line so much this season," he confided to the umpire, as he handed him his

Photo . Sport and General

The one and only Jack Hobbs, Denis Compton's greatest idol.
Scorer of the record number of centuries (197) in first-class cricket.

Photo : Central Press

Denis plays one towards mid-off. Note his perfect balance.

sweater in the opening game of the season, and then, after measuring up the distance he had found best for his approach to the crease, commenced to pound up to the wicket. Over went his arm, and at the same time the umpire shouted: "No ball!"

That poor bowler, who had spent the whole of the winter trying to overcome his great weakness, nearly cried—but for the rest of the game never again stepped over the line.

"Anxiousness, I am sure, was responsible for me making that early mistake," he said to me.

He was right, but might also have added: "And because I wanted to bowl too fast to begin with." That is a thing every young fast bowler should remember. Work up speed gradually. Do not sacrifice accuracy. The two combined get you wickets, not pace alone.

These days not enough fast or medium-paced bowlers, in my opinion, make the ball go away from the batsman. This—and I am speaking from personal experience—is one of the most difficult of all balls to play, and the man who sends it down can only achieve it by finding out his best method of delivery. Get hold of a cricket ball, experiment with various ways of holding it, and try to make the ball go away from the bat. If you can do this—and I say this with all seriousness—you're a bowler who is going to prove mighty useful to some team.

In England, especially since the war, the number of cricketers who have become spin-bowlers must be out of all proportion to those who tried their arm at it before 1940.

There are many schools of thought on what helps make the ideal spin bowler. Many say a consistently good length; my view is the amount of spin you are able to put upon the ball. The general impression, especially among juvenile cricketers, is that the best way of achieving most success as a "spinner" is to use your fingers. The Australians—with whom I agree on this point—have found that the ball would not "bite" on their wickets with finger-spin, so they devised a method of spinning the ball with the wrist. It is much more effective, and Douglas Wright, the great Kent and England bowler, is one of the men who call upon this style with success.

What, therefore, do I consider an ambitious leg-spin-bowler should do in his efforts to succeed in this particular branch of the game? First I would advise him to learn how to spin a ball. No doubt he will commence by "spinning" with his fingers and then, if he wants to make headway, learn to spin with the wrist. This side of the business settled, he should next develop a length. One of the favoured methods is to place a small piece of cloth on a certain spot, and then learn how to pitch the ball on to it. At first it is anything but easy. With practice—how that expression has constantly crept in—you will find yourself in the position of being able to place the ball more or less where you want it. Then—and at first it will be extremely difficult—try combining spin and length. When you have accomplished this—and determination should assure you of some success—it will be to find that leg-spinning, apart from its wicket-getting qualities, can be most enjoyable, for you really feel yourself pitting your skill against that of the batsman.

By comparison with the leg-spinner, bowlers who con-centrate upon off-breaks use their fingers more to get the necessary spin. Quite a number of the stars, I find through talking with them, built up their spinning qualities by starting with underhand deliveries. Try it yourself with underhand deliveries and then attempt the same thing by bowling over-arm. With practice you will find the ball beginning to turn to your liking.

One last word to the "spinners". Make a special point of varying your pace and attempt to make every ball different from the one before.

Do not hesitate, every now and again, to send down a much faster ball. Douglas Wright does this, but not until, by means of a code, he has pointed out to his wicket-keeper and fieldsmen that he is about to bowl a "fast 'un". Were he not to do this colleagues, in addition to opponents, might be caught unawares and a valuable chance missed—and that is the last thing anyone would wish!

18

Batsmanship and You.

"I AM very keen on cricket, play a good deal, but do not seem to have much success. Can you tell me how I can become a successful batsman?"

This is part of a letter I received a short time ago—one of many in a similar vein, I might add—and to each and every one my reply is: "It is up to you. If you possess no natural cricket ability nothing will make you a batsman. On the other hand, if you have a natural aptitude for the game, the best thing is to study every possible side of the batting art, and use your ability to the best advantage and *practice.*"

The first thing any young cricketer should learn is how to hold the bat correctly. It is surprising to find so many pay little attention to this important essential, but, before you can even think of scoring runs, you must be able to swing the bat freely and hit the ball in the middle of the blade. You must, too, learn how to judge whether to play forward or back.

"But how can I learn to judge whether to play forward or back?" I can hear many a youngster ask. Again the answer is easy: "By constant practice." The only way— and I must stress this—to become a really proficient batsman, is by constantly facing up to bowlers, and learning by your mistakes.

I well remember, at the age of twelve, standing in front of a mirror for the first time and practising various strokes. I had read in books the importance of footwork. Not until I began to play cricket regularly did I appreciate in full how true this was. By studying myself in the mirror I found that many faults I had could very quickly be spotted, and— I hoped—rectified.

Playing for England

Balance, of course, is another great essential for batting success. All the great run-getters of to-day such as Len Hutton, Cyril Washbrook, Bill Edrich, and Jack Robertson, to mention but a few, have perfect control over their body, in addition to the bat they hold. Again—and I do not want you to get tired of me repeating this—balance, like perfect footwork, and timing of the ball, only comes with practice and experience.

Although a great believer in the value of a first-class coach, I would like to point out to young cricketers that they should never be afraid to continue making strokes, even if they are not of the "copy-book" type, providing they bring runs. So far as I am concerned my driving is the despair of the "purists", for my foot is not near the ball, but it works because I find I have more room in which to let my arm swing, and so get more force behind it.

Good coaches, I am sure, take the view that a youngster should never have his natural style upset. In the past the zeal of some coaches, I am afraid, has spoilt many an up-and-coming lad because they tried to end strokes that did not look good, but paid dividends.

From my earliest cricketing days I have looked upon my bat as an offensive weapon, at the same time remembering that a purely defensive batsman rarely develops run-scoring shots. It should not be overlooked that a batsman with a wide range of strokes is always a difficult proposition for a bowler to keep quiet, and, if a batsman goes on getting runs, the fellow whose job it is to dismiss him cannot help getting disappointed. On the other hand, if a man does nothing else but defend his wicket the bowlers opposing him get the idea they are on top and half the battle, so far as they're concerned, has been won.

Don Bradman is typical of the batsman who never lets the bowlers get on top of him. "The Don" has every shot in the book and others that would not qualify for honours among the stylists.

Every batsman has his favourite shot, and none gives me greater pleasure than an off-drive. The elegance with which such great batsmen as Don Bradman, Wally Hammond, and Len Hutton, send the ball flashing through the covers to the boundary, has never ceased to give me a thrill, but I am all for a batsman developing his shots not only on the off, but on the other side of the wicket. If a player is equally strong on either side a captain will find it most difficult to set a field to him. There are some batsmen a captain will know, from past experience, who favour one set of strokes. He can, accordingly, plan ways and means of keeping them quiet. As a bowler, and a batsman, I can understand how a skipper feels when opposed to run-getters who can make scoring shots all round the wicket.

As a youngster I was always very keen on watching the stroke play of great batsmen, taking the view that you can learn a very great deal by a careful study of their methods. I recollected in a cuttings book hundreds of photographs including some of Jack Hobbs, Patsy Hendren, Don Bradman, and Wally Hammond, to mention a few. For hours I would examine them, and in due course formed my own opinion as to how various shots should be made.

From photographs illustrating my point, you will see on other pages how certain shots should be made, but I think for all that you would like a word from me.

Let us commence with the cut (square and late) which these days appears to have caught the fancy of many budding batsmen. There is one great rule when you are making this stroke. With the bat square from your body, make sure that it comes down *on* to the ball; always be certain that you are over the top of the ball. If you follow this rule the chances are that success will go your way. Don Bradman and Cyril Washbrook are fellows I'd advise you to study —possibly by looking at photos—when planning to develop this stroke. Again, do not be disappointed if at first you are not very successful. Only practice in the nets, and actual matches, will help you improve your technique.

The same thing applies so far as the hook is concerned. This shot which has proved quite a run-getter for me, demands first-class footwork. You hook off your back foot, taking up an upright position, and, just as when cutting, hook the ball *down*.

Bowlers, you know, are intelligent fellows who watch carefully for any weakness on the part of a batsman. Quite a number of run-getters—even some in first-class cricket—have developed a tendency to hook the ball up instead of on to the ground, with the result some bowlers purposely send down a short ball, have a fieldsman placed in a set position, and make a catch out of a delivery that should have been sent to the boundary.

Among schoolboy and youthful club cricketers I should say that the leg-shot is easily the most popular. It seems a pity, though, that so many young batsmen prefer to use this without a thought for any other, for the shot on the leg-side is for certain types of delivery. Your job is to pick out the right ball.

Take for example the fine-leg glance. This shot should only be made when the ball is pitched outside the leg stump, otherwise you are courting trouble. Always, this shot apart, show the ball the full face of your bat, without exception, when it is on the wicket. Always make it a cardinal rule to cover your wicket. That is the thing you have to defend above everything else. Your whole batting structure, apart from getting runs, should be built around ways and means of upholding it.

When selecting your bat, too, take a good deal of trouble to make sure that you not only find it easy to handle, but that it also brings with it a confidence one must have if runs are to come with ease. Personally I favour a light bat, but some of the best players in the game prefer a heavier one. Whatever your fancy, stick to it, for remember a bat is going to be your best friend. Take care of it in the same way a billiards player does his cue.

The same thing applies to pads. I have never enjoyed wearing a new pair—have had my present pads nine years—and more often than not receive a helping hand from colleagues who break them in while batting in the nets. Just as a cricket bat, so with a pair of pads—when you find a pair you like, stick to them.

Another hint so far as pads are concerned: do not wear them too tightly. If you do the blood circulation will possibly be affected and serious trouble may develop.

Just as a footballer takes care of his shooting boots, so should every cricketer make sure that his footwear is comfortable, in the best possible condition, and suitable for the conditions under which the match will be played. Comfortable boots, as we all know, mean a good deal to anyone; especially does this apply to a batsman or bowler who must not have anything to cause him to take his mind off the task at hand.

You may be surprised to hear that among the cricket fraternity there are many players who just will not break in new boots; they prefer a colleague, while playing in the nets, to do so. Maybe this is a sound idea, but it can be dangerous if you allow the other fellow to wear them too often, for the boots begin to take the shape of *his* foot, and you will, as a result, find yourself in difficulties trying to make your *own* feet take to them.

Make sure, without fail, that your boots are carefully studded—four studs on the sole, and two on the heel are quite enough—and if the summer is particularly hot, and there has been little rain, do not hesitate to use rubber-soled boots or shoes. They are most comfortable but, again, are only to be worn when conditions justify it.

One last suggestion. When you go to the wicket as a batsman try your very hardest to put every other thought, but the one on hand, in the background. The great art of being a successful batsman is concentration, knowing how to use your feet, and picking out the right kind of ball to hit.

Only the fellow who thinks of nothing else but doing this job well can hope to succeed.

19

Captains Can Win Matches.

IF I WERE asked the most important man in cricket
there would be only one answer: The Captain.

Skippers, more than anyone else, win matches, and
it is a fact that really first-class captains are rarer things
than great batsmen, bowlers, or wicket-keepers.

What goes in the making of a first-rate captain? Four
things, in my opinion, dominate. They are:

1. He must have made a careful study of the game.
2. Personality is essential.
3. He should possess the ability to draw the best out of
   everyone under his command.
4. He must study the opposition in such a manner that
   he can denote their strength and weakness in double-
   quick time, and, more important still, work out a
   plan of campaign to take advantage of anything and
   everything.

In the course of my career I have played under the
captaincy of several great skippers, including R. W. V.
Robins, Walter Hammond, G. O. Allen, and Norman Yardley, all of whom have led England in Test Matches. All, in
their way, possessed the qualifications needed for success.

The captain beneath whom I have served the longest is
R. W. V. Robins, and in the 1947 season, he led Middlesex
to the County Championship. Mr. Robins is typical of the
"terrific captains" we hear so much about, but which too
often do not exist. In my opinion he is the ideal captain
for any would-be skipper to mould himself upon. Apart
from his skill as a batsman and bowler, "R.W.V." is always
planning the downfall of the opposition.

"We're here to win matches, not draw," is Mr. Robins' attitude, and I think it should be the outlook of everyone who skippers a cricket team. Such a viewpoint brings about entertaining cricket which makes things enjoyable for not only the players but the spectators.

When he is in the field you can always sense that "R.W.V." is planning something, and when we played Kent at Canterbury during our Championship run I had a first-hand example of what shrewd captaincy could do.

After a somewhat see-saw game Kent, in their second innings, were left with just over 200 runs needed to win, and an hour and a half to get them. Bearing in mind the strength of the Kent batting it seemed an impossible task for our bowlers to dismiss them in the time, but our opponents, among the most sporting sides in the country, decided to go for the runs. In doing so Kent lost four quick wickets, so, when Brian Valentine, their captain, joined forces with Pawson, the young amateur batsman, he naturally decided not to take too many chances and so lose the game. He and Pawson, therefore, "put up the shutters" and showed the full face of the blade to our bowlers.

With the clock ticking on the Kent men, who had hoped for a victory, began to find themselves behind time if the necessary runs were to be secured. It was then that Skipper R. W. V. Robins put his tactical skill to work. He called upon me to bowl at one end, and then took a turn at the other, shifted fieldsmen away from vulnerable points, and then, with me aiding him, encouraged Valentine and Pawson to go for the runs. They did, found the "chinks" in our defensive armour, before long were once more ahead of the clock, and began to take chances in an effort to force a win.

It was then that R. W. V. Robins, with a rapier-like thrust, brought back our stock bowlers, and before the Kent side quite knew what had happened, three more quick wickets had fallen!

By studying the opposition keenly, *and* putting himself in their position, Mr. Robins had appreciated the right time to attack. But for some steady batting, too, on the part of Leslie Todd and Ray Dovey, who defended resolutely, we might well have won. As it was, Kent forced a draw.

Another instance of R. W. V. Robins' tactical outlook can be judged by the following little story that went the rounds last year. Apparently, according to the tale, after one particular Middlesex match our skipper, sitting by himself in one corner of a room, suddenly rose to his feet and said: "I should have bowled Jack Young (he's our slow bowler) with the wind behind him. Then we might have got some catches."

During this particular game Young had been bowling into the wind and one particular batsman, opening his shoulders, had cracked Jack good and hard, the following breeze taking the ball over the boundary line for six. Our skipper reasoned—and quite understandably—that had that batsman hit the balls delivered by Young *into* the breeze it might have acted as a "stopper", and, instead of going for six, the ball would have fallen short, and into the hands of one of our fieldsmen in the deep!

That is R. W. V. Robins all over. To his mind nothing is ever perfect. Always is he working on plans to improve his team, the players in the side, and, just as important, himself. I well remember, when I was sitting alone in the Press Box at Lord's one mid-summer afternoon, writing this book— no match was in progress—watching "R.W.V." in flannels, come out of the dressing-room, a cricket ball in his hand, and commence running around, all by himself, throwing the ball into the air and catching it. For over thirty minutes he did nothing else but practise throwing, and catching—he did not even suspect I was watching.

Then, at the end of it all, he trotted round the ground, and back to the dressing-room.

A man who, even after he has captained England, becomes a Selector, and puts himself among cricket's immortals, realises that practice is still needed, stands out in my mind as a very great cricketer.

Apart from a captain's skill as a tactician, he has something just as important to consider: the handling of the men in his side. A brainy captain can either make or break a young cricketer, and again, holding up Mr. Robins as a first-rate example, I will give you the case of eighteen-year-old Ian Bedford.

In 1947 Ian, although still attending school, proved such a capable spin bowler that the Middlesex Committee decided that he was worthy of inclusion in the County side. To play in top-class cricket for the first time is a strain for anyone; it could not have been anything else for young Ian. At once, however, our captain put the young man at his ease; showed confidence in his bowling ability by giving him an early turn with the ball. To the delight of us all, Bedford quickly got among the wickets.

That was all very well, but there came a time when the opposing batsman began to take runs off Bedford as he tired and the accuracy of his deliveries departed, even if only slightly. At once our keen-eyed skipper noted that Bedford needed a rest, and took him off.

The ability of "R.W.V." to sense that the time had come for Ian Bedford to have a "breather" probably saved the young bowler not only a disappointing time, but possibly from having unnecessary runs taken off him.

A bold and imaginative captain is the man who is prepared to take chances if he has a "hunch" that might swing the game round in his side's favour. Again quoting R. W. V. Robins as an example, I will tell you what happened to my big brother, Leslie, during our Championship run.

Leslie, as you may know, has developed into quite a good wicket-keeper and "keeps" regularly for the County. Apart from his skill as a stumper, Leslie is also a useful seam bowler, and it was when a couple of opposing batsmen had withstood our main attack, and one of our fast bowlers was injured, that the skipper decided to take a chance.

"Take the new ball and see what luck you have," he said to my brother, so while Sydney Brown took from him the pads and gauntlets, Leslie commenced loosening himself up. Then he began to bowl against the batsmen who had made a stand. What is more, before R. W. V. Robins decided to take him off, my brother had broken the partnership that seemed so difficult, proving, once again, that a good captain, if he has a "hunch", is doing the right thing by working upon it.

Don Bradman is another captain who in my opinion is entitled to rank among the greatest of our time. The Australian skipper, whom I once christened "The man with the photographic memory", has an uncanny habit of being able to place his field to the best batsmen in the world. Don, who is a great student of cricket, may not say a great deal, but when an opposing team is batting takes a mental note of every strong and weak point in their make-up.

I do not think there is one England batsman "The Don" has not at some time or another had beneath the "Bradman Microscope", and his ability to place specific fields for particular batsmen must have saved his team many hundreds of runs.

Bradman's judgment so far as bowlers are concerned, too, is first-class. I remember, when I have opposed teams under his captaincy, that Bradman has tried out a variety of bowlers, and, sure enough, picked out the one or two for whom I had shown the greatest respect. Even if I had been fortunate enough to take runs off them, the astute Bradman's eagle-eye had detected that they were the most likely to get my wicket.

Every star captain builds up a fairly good idea of the strong and weak points of the opposition. Bradman, though, has brought it to a fine art, and although you are less conscious of his planning by comparison with R. W. V. Robins, you have only to play against "The Don" to appreciate in full the brilliance of his handling of a cricket team.

Norman Yardley, the Yorkshire amateur under whose captaincy I have been honoured to serve in the England team, has not had the experience or opportunities of gaining it as have Robins and Bradman, but already has shown a judgment that suggests he knows the business of a skipper.

First and foremost, apart from his knowledge of cricket, which is considerable, Norman Yardley possesses the ability to make everyone who serves under him conscious of his responsibilities and by reason of his encouragement, brings the best out of everyone. Speaking for myself, I would do anything for Norman Yardley and know that I am not alone in speaking in this manner.

As an all-round cricketer, too, Norman Yardley—how well the Australians have found this out!—proved worth his place in the Test team for his ability alone.

That, you can believe me, means a great deal.

Brian Valentine, for years the Kent skipper, is another player of the same type. He is a fine cricketer, is prepared to take a chance if there is an opportunity to win by so doing, and in general stands out as the type of skipper I would advise any youngster to try and emulate.

In 1947, when Middlesex had neither our skipper or vice-captain available, Bill Edrich, who had turned amateur, was invited to lead the side, and, as you would expect from one who has devoted a greater part of his life to studying the game, did extremely well. Bill, in fact, showed that he is something of an inspired leader, and, on this occasion, displayed much of the R. W. V. Robins' touch, and we won a thrilling victory when few folk thought we stood a chance.

I have found it interesting to note that many of the great batsmen have it in them to become outstanding captains. Jack Hobbs, of course, was one; among modern players that grand Yorkshireman, Len Hutton, is another; so is Joe Hardstaff, who has captained the Players against the Gentlemen. Their ability to "size up" the opposition, after years of experience, is naturally their outstanding quality, but each and every one, you will find, have theories and advice any cricketer would be wise to heed.

Summing up, the truly great captains are those who go into a cricket match with a plan of campaign, just as a general does, and are able, if things do not work out as they expect, to switch to an alternate method of overcoming the opposition.

Such captains, I understand, are not easy to come by, but every young man with ambitions towards captaincy should set himself this goal, for his team, just as much as he himself, will get a good deal of satisfaction from his success.

20

*Breaking Records Cost—Weight! Keeping Dapper
is Expensive—One Bat is the Order—I Lost My Heel
but Kept My Boots—The Hardest-Earned Century
of Them All.*

RECORD-BREAKING can be a most hectic affair.
At least, that is my experience, gained when I set
up a new record for most centuries in a season,
passing Jack Hobbs' sixteen by two, and scoring 3,816
runs, to beat Tom Hayward's aggregate of 3,518, set up in
1906.

At the beginning of May, 1947, I weighed 13st. 8lbs. By
the time I had made my last run, in September, it had
dropped to 12st. 8lbs! Yes, run-getting can be most tiring
work, and, at the same time, quite a costly affair so far as
clean gear is concerned. In the course of the season I wore
the following:

150 Clean Shirts.
100 pairs of Laundered Flannels.
200 Clean Singlets.
200 pairs of Clean Socks.

At the start of the season no thought of record-breaking
ever entered my head. True I "kicked off" with a knock
of seventy, but following this several medium scores went
my way and some folk thought I had played too much cricket
in Australia. Then, for some unknown reason, I suddenly
found myself playing better than ever before in my life.
Maybe the experience of batting on Australian wickets had
something to do with this, but I cannot but help feeling
that good fortune was with me, for everything I attempted

came off. At the same time, because of the attitude I have adopted towards cricket my play did not suffer. It does not matter much to me whether I make a century, or a good average score, providing I play in the way I enjoy, and, at the same time, in a manner that will assist my side. When runs began to flow, therefore, I did not worry whenever I went to the crease that I might fail!

In the third week of the season, after a period of up-and-down form, I decided to try out in a County match the bat I had been "breaking in" while at net-practice. At once this new bat seemed to bring me luck, and for the rest of the season I used no other. It weighed 2 lbs. 3 oz., was short-handled, and in general proved one of the best friends I've ever had in cricket.

At the same time, with the hard grounds so prevalent, I decided to try out the rubber-soled boots I'd bought for use in Australia. "Down Under" I had only worn them once. In England, however, I found them exceedingly comfortable, and even when one of the heels came off, continued to use them. In all my record-breaking innings those rubber-soled boots were my "foundation", and I can thoroughly recommend them to anyone suffering, as I was, from "foot weariness".

It was after I had scored about twelve centuries that cricket lovers began to write me and give encouragement, and advice, as to how I could beat Jack Hobbs' record of sixteen centuries in one season. I must confess that these letters, to some extent, amused me, for I did not anticipate being able to keep up with the spate of centuries that had "flowed", but when first the thirteenth, and then the fourteenth century were secured, decided that the critics and fans might, after all, have proved right in thinking I might break the record.

I should like to stress—especially to youngsters—that record-breaking has never been one of my life ambitions. Enjoying cricket, to my way of thinking, is more important, and even when I neared Jack Hobbs' 16 centuries in a season tried my utmost to play my normal game.

Playing for England

On glancing back at reports of these matches I think I succeeded.

My best innings during the course of that—for me—memorable season? The 168 scored against Kent at Lord's. By far the hardest century, though, was my sixteenth, obtained against Lancashire at Lord's, after Middlesex had made certain of the County Championship, and when the north countrymen were right on their toes and determined to defeat the Southerners.

I have always had a respect for Lancashire, even though many of my best scores have been made against them. At Lord's on the afternoon of September 2nd, the Lancastrians proved, just as in the past, among the best fielding sides in the game. With Dick Pollard, one of my colleagues in Australia, bowling very "tight", and the fieldsmen, with Jack Ikin outstanding, playing like men inspired, I found runs harder to get than at any other period during the summer. Ikin, with Price, backed up Pollard exceedingly well, and when Middlesex wickets began to totter, my hopes—which had been roused by now—of scoring another century to equal Hobbs, began to fall. Fortunately, for the side and myself, our skipper, R. W. V. Robins, was able to stay with me, and together we put on 92.

As my score neared the century the Lancashire fielding, always on a high note, seemed to become even more impressive and I had to take very great care when choosing my runs, for Cyril Washbrook is a "terror" at throwing down the wicket of daredevil batsmen. Then, with my score at 98, and the field closing in on me, I managed to put Dick Pollard behind square leg for a boundary. The sixteenth century of the season had become a fact. I had equalled the record set up by Jack Hobbs twenty-two years ago!

I must confess that I heaved a huge sigh of relief, and had not fully recovered my composure when Kenneth Cranston, the Lancashire captain, and other members of his side, came forward to congratulate me. It was, as you will understand, a very great moment for Denis Compton, but even in the excitement of the moment I remembered Jack

Hobbs, my schoolboy idol, and knew how he must have felt; thought, even when flushed with victory, that one day in the future I might be in the same position as Jack, for records are only made to be beaten. *This is a fact that should never be forgotten.*

It always amuses me to think of such things, but as a result of me equalling the record a deluge of letters and telegrams descended upon me, most of them from folk I had never even met, but among those I shall cherish most of all was one from Jack Hobbs himself. You see, to me it seems but yesterday that I waited patiently for "The Master's" autograph. . . .

Having succeeded in equalling the Hobbs record, and with a couple more matches to be played, for the first time I really thought I stood an excellent chance of setting up figures. No, I did not go into "special training", as a boxer would do, but tried hard to live and play the game, as if nothing had happened.

It was against the South Africans, at Hastings, that my big opportunity to break the record came. As you may remember, during the 1947 season I experienced a great deal of success against the Tourists, and on this occasion once again found runs easy to get. Slowly at first, but gradually speeding up as I settled down, the score mounted. Then, when I was at 97, play was held up for tea. All I wanted was a glass of milk, which I drank at the wicket. Then, from the second delivery after the interval I turned the ball to leg—in exactly the same spot as when I equalled the record—it flew to the boundary, my score was 101, and I had beaten Jack Hobbs!

The first man to come up and shake me by the hand was Alan Melville, the South African captain. I mention this because there was quite a coincidence here. When first I appeared in the Middlesex side, against Sussex, Melville was in the Sussex team. I was a bowler—and one of the first wickets I ever got was Alan Melville's! That was eleven years ago. Alan, however, had not forgotten!

What did it feel like to have such a record "beneath my

belt"? Naturally I was elated, not so much because of myself, but it meant, so far as Middlesex C.C.C. was concerned, that, apart from winning the Championship, we had accomplished something else that will be remembered. As I have said before, however, records are made to be broken. I was just fortunate, in the 1947 season, to not only strike my best form, but also to "have the breaks". I have no illusions about the latter. Things worked out extremely well for me.

During my innings against Lancashire I was troubled by my right knee "locking", but after examination I was able to return to the field and finish my innings. When Middlesex, as Champions, played the Rest at Kennington Oval, however, I found the knee growing a little painful. The suspected piece of floating bone had previously settled in a "comfortable position", but now it was beginning to move again, and when, after scoring 55 against the Rest, my knee once more locked, I had to retire. R. W. V. Robins, my skipper, sensing that I was in some pain, had acted as runner to me for some time, but when it was too painful, advised me to return to the dressing-room.

Next morning, still in some pain, I called in to see Mr. Tom Whittaker, manager of my club, Arsenal F.C., at Highbury. At once that kindly and thoughtful expert got to work, and after a careful examination, came to the conclusion that an operation might be necessary to remove the fragment of bone.

Seeing how disappointed I was the genial Tom said: "Don't you worry, Denis, I'll fix that piece of bone in a comfortable position, strap it so that it cannot move into vulnerable joints, and you'll be able to resume batting to-morrow."

He was correct, too, and although my knee was anything but comfortable, it was nothing like so painful as when last I was at the wicket. As a matter of fact, having previously passed Tom Hayward's record aggregate figure at Hastings—I played for Sir Pelham Warner's XI against the South of England when accomplishing this—I felt that I could "let myself go" in this last match of the season. I did, and really think I played one of my best innings of the summer. I know, on one occasion, I rather shocked Frank Chester, who was umpiring at one end, for as I was about to sweep a delivery from Tom Goddard to leg I fell forward, but in falling managed to get in my shot, the ball flew to the boundary, and down went I onto my tummy.

"Well I'll be hanged!" exclaimed Frank Chester.

I was just as surprised as he—and, no doubt, Tom Goddard!—that my shot had come off. Eventually, after scoring 240 "on one leg", marching orders were given me, but on reflection I think I enjoyed that crack as much as any other I've had.

Naturally I was very happy that Mr. Tom Whittaker had been able to "fix" my injured knee until the cricket season had been concluded. Then, my bat, pads and flannels tucked away for another season, I entered the Great Northern Hospital for the removal of the fragment of bone. I say "fragment". Actually it measured one and a half inches by three-quarters of an inch, and the only way I can think it came about was a severe knock I received on my right knee when fielding in a match at Lord's. Whatever the cause, I was glad to have it removed, for, as you will appreciate, my big ambition was to again do well against the Australians when they visited this country in 1948.

But then, that should be the ambition of every Test cricketer. . . .

21

New Record for Brother Leslie and Myself—
Australians Impress—Tactical Talks for England—
Sydney Barnes, "Cricket Collector"—Strain of
Playing in England—"Smelling Salts" mean
Trent Bridge Century—My First Knock-out—Four-
leaf Clover for Hutton—What we Learnt from
the Australians.

THE PIECE of bone that had to be removed from my knee was the reason I missed so much of the 1947–48 season. Had not this been the case I should have been inside an Arsenal shirt in double-quick time, but, fortunately for me, during my forced stay in bed, I was constantly kept under observation by Arsenal F.C.

Nothing is too much trouble for Manager Tom Whittaker, and he, along with Trainer Billy Milne, did much to help put me once more on the left wing.

While in hospital, by the way, I broadcast over the radio to children throughout Great Britain. Believe me, that was one of the few pleasant experiences I had while cramped up in a hospital ward!

Returning to Arsenal, I had yet another of my schoolboy ambitions realised: the winning of a League Championship Medal. The previous summer my brother Leslie and I had been members of the Middlesex team which won the County Championship, so naturally were elated at this further success; it meant for the first time in sporting history two brothers have won, in following seasons, the games' honours at cricket and soccer.

This elation, however, was not allowed to remain for long, the arrival of the Australian cricketers in this country making me appreciate in full the great struggle that lay ahead of us during the summer of 1948.

Don Bradman and his Merry Men left Australia with the reputation of being the finest touring side for many years. It did not take me long after watching them, and then facing the Australians, to appreciate that they fully justified the confidence of their own folk.

Australian cricketers, as I have stressed so often before, take their game most seriously. Always they go into a match with a plan of campaign, and there is little doubt that this outlook has paid them rich dividends in the past.

When I toured Australia with the M.C.C. in 1946–47 it rather surprised me when we had but one tactical talk, this prior to the first Test match. In the spring of 1948 Norman Yardley, destined to lead us in the series against Australia, had most pronounced and accurate views on this subject. The outcome was a pre-Test discussion at which every player was invited to place before the skipper his personal opinion and any ideas he felt, if worked upon, would help improve us as a team.

Do not run away with the idea that only football or boxing matches can be won by following a plan. Cricket, to my mind, is a game that lends itself to planning for victory just as much. When you are faced by outstanding cricketers such as the Australians, too, it is essential you get down to discussing their strong and, if any, weak points. Don Bradman and his men discussed these things with us Englishmen under their spotlight. Norman Yardley followed suit. In fact, behind the scenes, Test Cricket is every season developing still more into a cold science, just as is football. I think, too, we all profited by these discussions, even if we were not destined to win the Ashes.

During my last visit to Australia I had become very friendly with a number of their leading cricketers, and when they arrived in England we resumed our friendship where it had left off "Down Under".

A man who appealed greatly to me was Sydney Barnes, the Australian's opening batsman. Sydney, who later in the season was to be in the news because of his "suicide" fielding position, is a grand chap with a rare sense of fun. He also happens to be an extremely shrewd business man, and, of course, like most Australians, a keen collector of cricketing trophies.

Shortly after Sydney arrived in this country he chanced to see my Middlesex sweater. "Say, Denis," said Barnes, "I rather care for that. Would you consider parting with it?"

"Yes," I replied, "providing you hand me your Australian cap for my personal collection."

"Sure," came the answer; so there and then we swopped. Now I have a South African cap which belonged to Dudley Nourse, their skipper, and many other Test trophies, including numerous stumps.

During the Australian tour of 1948 I was rather amused by the enthusiasm with which our visitors went about collecting as trophies stumps used in the Tests. At Nottingham, for instance, when Barnes once thought the England total had been passed he picked up some stumps and darted for the pavilion. Was his face red when it dawned upon him that an error had been made!

Returning to the crease Barnes eyed me as one of our bowlers got ready to open the attack again. "Play the game, Denis," said Sydney grimly; "if you get any of the stumps, save one for me. Remember Australia." I knew what he meant, for "Down Under", where I, too, became an avid collector, stumps—five in all—had been gathered for me by Barnes, Miller, Toshak and Morris. In due course I was able to repay Sydney in England. Incidentally, remember reading about the incident when wee Lindsay Hassett, in trying to get a stump, was hurt? It will probably interest you to hear that Hassett's efforts were on my behalf, and when, triumphant, he had gathered one of the "pegs", he was as pleased as punch when presenting it to me.

Hassett and I, when the M.C.C. visited Australia in 1946–47, also used to have a wager with each other as to who was going to win the toss. So far a £1 note has changed hands on several occasions, for we kept up this bet through-out the series in England.

To hear some folk talking in the course of a series of Tests one would imagine that the Englishmen and Australians were terrific rivals. Opponents we are, true, but the spirit of friendship, I'm delighted to report, has never been allowed to depart. This, after all, is how it should be.

At Lord's, for instance, when we met the Australians in the Test, they knew how interested I was in the Wimbledon Tennis Tournament, so, during the various breaks, invited me into their dressing-room to watch the various games on their television set. In many other ways, too, the Aussie cricketers and our own have stressed just how the spirit of friendship has grown during the past few years.

It may surprise many cricket enthusiasts to hear me say that a Test cricketer probably finds it a greater strain to play in front of his own folk than is the case overseas. There are two reasons for this. Firstly—and most important—so much is expected from him, especially if he has done well in county matches; the possibility of his occasionally failing is apt never to be considered. Secondly, the player, being anxious to do well, might because of this depart from his natural game. This, I might add, is the thing we all try to avoid. "Play your natural game, son," the stock phrase given to so many young cricketers when they are about to make their debut, applies just as much to a man appearing in a Test match.

When I went to the wicket for the first Test of the 1948 series my thoughts naturally went back to 1938 when, on making my debut in a Test against the Australians, I scored a century. Again good fortune proved to be with me at the famous Nottinghamshire ground, for I managed to score 184 runs, despite, I might add, a very bad headache in the early stages of my innings.

As I batted out there in the middle, knowing how much depended upon my holding on, my head fairly buzzed, but, thanks to Group Captain A. J. Holmes, chief of the selection committee, who loaned me a bottle of smelling salts, I was able to clear my head a little.

Playing for England

Believe me, I needed a clear head to face such bowlers as Ray Lindwall and Keith Miller. They were terrific; accurate and keeping a good length all the time.

The Australians, as you will recall, won that opening Test with plenty to spare, but, I know, we picked up a good deal in the cricketing sense. When I arrived home, too, I learnt something in an entirely different sphere. When falling over in making a shot I got my flannels covered in mud, and Mrs. Compton's remark, when she saw them, brought me back to realities. "It's all right for you, Denis Compton," she said, "to go falling around, and scoring centuries, but how are we going to get these clean again?"

I am afraid I did not have an answer. . . .

Doris, my wife, is, as you would expect, a great cricket enthusiast, but she has one superstition nothing, it seems, will change. When I am at the wicket about to take the first delivery she looks away until I have played it safely—or otherwise! This little fad is not, of course, unusual. I always buckle on my right pad first, put on my right glove before my left, and invariably, when going out to bat, want to have my partner on the right-hand side.

It was during the 1948 Tests that I experienced my first-ever knock-out on the cricket field: at Old Trafford. As I have remarked in an earlier chapter, the famous Manchester enclosure has always been a happy hunting ground for me, and even against the Australians I did not altogether fare too badly, but during one brilliant over by Ray Lindwall I well and truly "caught a packet". To some extent, too, it was my own fault, for I tried to hook a no-ball from Ray, did not quite connect properly, and the ball hit me on the forehead.

If Joe Louis had cracked me on the chin he could not have done a better job of sending me to sleep, but, again I would like to stress it was an accident that could have happened to anyone.

There never was anything vicious or unsportsmanlike about the way these fellows from Australia played their cricket.

Playing for England

When we played the fourth Test at Headingley, Leeds, I had a rather unusual experience. As I have so often said, it is my firm belief that if a cricketer finds a bat he likes it is a sound policy to use it and no other. Well, when my "favourite" was damaged, and needed repair, I at once sent it to a friend for the necessary "overhaul". When it arrived at Leeds, just in time for the Test, I felt very elated—until I went to the wicket. Then, instead of driving the ball, as I had hoped, to the boundary, the bat seemed to stop it and nothing more. In fact, to put it in a nutshell, my "favourite" had lost its "drive"! Fortunately I was able to hurry back to the pavilion and get another—but it might well have proved fatal had I not discovered the situation so early in my innings.

By the way, an admirer of Len Hutton sent the famous Yorkshire and England batsman a four-leafed clover for the Headingley Test. As Len cracked up a splendid 81 I suppose he has a belief in the clover's luck-bringing qualities.

Well, as you all know, Australia played brilliant cricket during their 1948 tour. Apart from dismissing us so cheaply in the last Test at Kennington Oval, all the time our visitors revealed skill far above the ordinary and even if we did not succeed in lowering their colours, there is little doubt, as a result of playing against them, we learnt a great deal.

"Well," I can hear some of you ask, "what was the paramount reason Australia won the Test series so easily?"

The answer can be summed up in two words: "Fast bowlers."

Before this series of Test matches we had faced Miller and Lindwall and appreciated their greatness. In England, to the surprise of many, these Australian speedsters were even more successful than back home. The fact, too, that we in England have no pace bowlers to compare with the Miller–Lindwall combine is another reason our batsmen did not fare at all well. Without wishing to make a case for our frequent failures against pace bowlers, there is no doubt that English batsmen, when they came across the Australian opening pair, faced something entirely new.

Playing for England

They are, believe me, great players, and the manner in which Lindwall and Miller can combine length and speed entitles them to rank among the best bowlers of their type for very many years.

We have, true, fast bowlers in England, but no one can come within a very long way of the Australians for sheer pace, and if a batsman has little experience of such bowlers it takes him a considerable time to get accustomed to them. In making this statement, I am speaking from experience.

Until we in England are able to find a fast bowler of the Miller–Lindwall calibre it stands out a mile that we cannot go into a Test match with the same confidence as when such bowling giants as Harold Larwood, Bill Voce, and Ken Farnes, were available. Fortunately this fact is generally appreciated, and a nation-wide hunt has commenced for young bowlers of pace.

I hope these talent-spotting efforts are a success, for to unearth a fast bowler who might develop into a Test player is a worthy ambition, and, I will add, a necessity if we are quickly to regain the Ashes.

22

*Herbert Chapman Makes Me an Offer—Nearly
"Sacked" in First Week as Ground-Boy—The
Stars Give Me Advice—I Turn Pro—Making My
Right Foot a "Winner"—My Friend "Wee Alex".*

I AM ONE of those chaps who believe that football
and cricket do mix. In fact, ever since I was little
taller than a pound's-worth of copper coins I have
done my utmost to play fairly well at both games. To some
extent I have had a certain amount of success.

The late Herbert Chapman, manager of Arsenal F.C.,
and one of the greatest soccer personalities of all time, was
the man who shaped my soccer career. I was playing for my
school at the time—left half-back was my position—when
he happened to see me and formed the impression that I
might well develop, with training, into a useful footballer.
As I was only fourteen years old at the time there was no
question of my becoming a professional, but, when Mr.
Chapman approached my father with an offer of a job on
the ground-staff for me, visions of playing before a 60,000
Arsenal "gate" were at once very much to the fore.

"Well, Denis," said my father, when we sat down to
discuss the Arsenal offer, "your ambition is to become a
sportsman for a living. Lord's are willing to take you on
their staff. Arsenal want you to learn the ropes at Highbury. What do you want to do now?"

At once I replied: "Accept their offers. It means all-
the-year-round employment, and I know that is what you
are anxious for me to be sure of."

And so it came about that I signed an amateur form for
Arsenal F.C. and went to work on their ground-staff.

My hours were a little different from those I had known
at school. Prompt at eight o'clock every morning, six

days a week, I had to report at Arsenal Stadium. My duties? Clearing and helping repair the terracing, rolling the pitch. On the surface this may not sound so very much, but you would be surprised at the terrific amount of work there is to be done "behind the scenes" on a football ground.

Naturally the thought of being so close to Alex James, David Jack, Joe Hulme, Bob John, and other great stars, meant a great deal to me—and might well have cost me my job in the first week. Instead of working, I'm afraid, I began to take more interest in the players at training. A short reminder that I would have to look around for another post if I wished to carry on in this way made me realise that I was being paid to do odd-jobs, not "study the stars" at Arsenal's expense!

A short time after I had arrived at Arsenal Stadium the great Herbert Chapman himself, while I was doing a spot of weeding, strolled up to me. "'Morning Compton," he said. "Settling down all right? Good. Now," he went on, "I want you to understand that we'll look after you here, try to bring you out and develop you into a useful footballer. The job is a nice healthy one, you're in the open air, and your physical welfare was in mind when this post was offered you. By the way," he added as an afterthought, "you can do your training here on Tuesday and Thursday evenings AFTER YOU HAVE FINISHED YOUR WORK."

Note that Mr. Chapman was quick to remind me that I was not a professional; only a member of the ground-staff, thus the "evenings only"—in your own time at that—training.

I started out with Hampstead Town, from whom my brother Leslie joined Arsenal, but as I was not deemed quite good enough for them, and wanted to make my way in the game, joined Nunhead, the Isthmian League side. In due course, after first assisting their reserve side, I became a regular in the Nunhead senior team, and I rank those days, when I was beginning to really appreciate the footballing art, among the most interesting I have ever had.

As part and parcel of the "Chapman Plan" to help me

progress, Arsenal occasionally gave me games in their "A" team. At first it quickly became obvious to me that I had a good deal to learn before a professional form could justly be passed my way. For all that, however, as now I was always keen to learn, and by talking with numerous professionals, began to find out my faults, and heeded their suggestions as to how I could rectify them. At sixteen years of age Mr. Chapman decided to give me an outing in the reserve team. No, my knees did not knock together when I trotted out with many distinguished players, for at Arsenal you are taught to have confidence in your colleagues. That afternoon I had plenty in mine, I understood them all well enough to know they would do everything possible to help me settle down. They did.

I have reason to think that Mr. Chapman was pleased with my progress, although it was not his habit to tell young players his inner thoughts, and it was to watch an "A" team match, in which I played, that he made the journey to Guildford, in Surrey. That was to be the last game our great chief saw, for a few days later he passed away, and to this day no one, in my opinion, has ever taken his place on the managerial side of the football world.

Although he said little, I had a feeling in my heart that he was behind every little plan that was moulded to help me improve, and without a doubt he was an ace among aces at getting the best out of a player.

It was bluff and cheerful George Allison who signed me as a professional for Arsenal when I had reached my seventeenth birthday, and I celebrated the occasion by going home and taking my mother out to the theatre. Putting pen to that form meant another step forward in my sporting life. Now I was able to use the reserve-team dressing-room, in which a peg had been placed with my name inscribed beneath it, and in general, what with full-time training, I began to feel that I was now "one of the boys".

What great names I began to find myself playing alongside in that Arsenal reserve side. Pat Beasley, destined to play for England, Tim Coleman, a grand centre-forward

from Grimsby, Jimmy Dunne, far-famed leader of the Irish
attack, and a host of others come to mind. Often, too,
following an injury, many of the stars would have an outing
with the reserve team to see if they were fit enough to resume
in the senior side. Joe Hulme, Cliff Bastin, Bobby Davidson,
Peter Dougal—greatest ball player I've ever met—Jackie
Milne, Norman Sidey, Reg Trim, and the grand Bob John,
were others with whom I found myself playing.

It is not until you have played with Arsenal that a full
appreciation of what it means to pull on their red and white
shirt can be understood. That shirt means something more
than a method of locating your colleagues on the field. More
than anything else, in my opinion, it draws footballers
together and makes them very good colleagues and friends.

As I was the youngest member of the team everyone
was most anxious to help me. Bob John, the Welsh international, especially, when he was at left-half behind me,
went right out of his way, even during a match, to explain
where I was right or wrong. Often, too, when my brother
Leslie and I were returning home from a game, he would
go right through the match with me, explain my faults
as he saw them, and offer suggestions as to how I could
overcome them. I noted everything and began to keep a
little book detailing the strong and weak points of opposing
defenders, and in general entered into the scientific approach
to the game that was the outlook of these grand men of
Arsenal.

Through playing consistently for Arsenal's reserve side
I began to develop into something of a goal-scoring left-
winger. My colleagues, appreciating that I could "crack
'em in" if the ball was placed to my liking, began to pick out
special passes for me—and I did the rest. At the time Cliff
Bastin was still playing like a champion, and I was wisely
not being rushed into the hurly-burly of top-class football,
but one Wednesday evening, during the course of the 1937
season, I was given my baptism in the first team. It was in
a friendly match against Glasgow Rangers played on Arsenal
Stadium, and well I remember a young auburn-haired

fellow playing at inside-right for the Scots. He was a brilliant ball player, made openings galore for his colleagues, and still found time to nip over and lend a hand in halting my progress. He created a great impression by the manner in which he went about his work.

Today that same player is a colleague and friend of mine with Arsenal. His name? Archie Macaulay, the distinguished Scottish international half-back.

The ambition of every young player is to do well when making his début. Apparently I satisfied at Arsenal Stadium, we won, 2—1, and every member of the side was presented with a golf-bag as a memento of the occasion. This came in useful, for I was just taking up the game. . . .

At Arsenal Stadium I have yet to find any player who is ever satisfied with himself. Everyone tries hard to improve his standard of play even when international rank has been reached, and after my début against Glasgow Rangers all I received was: "Well played, son, but . . ."

If I felt a little disappointed at that moment my spirits were raised a few hours later, for when the team chosen to meet Derby County was pinned on the notice-board, I ran cheerfully through it and felt my heart go pit-a-pat when the last name on the list came into view. It was "Compton D."

Another of my boyhood ambitions had come true. I was playing for the "Gunners'" League team!

On the Friday preceding the match, which was being staged on our own ground, there was a team-discussion under the chairmanship of Manager George Allison and, then, Trainer Tom Whittaker. The meeting was held in the board-room, we sat around a miniature football field, discs were placed upon it to represent players, and a plan of campaign was drawn up.

The strong points and weaknesses of every member in the Derby County side were summed up. We knew just how we were going to "take the game" to our opponents, and it did not take me long to understand that the seriousness displayed by Arsenal in such tactical talks provided the foundation upon which League Championships and Cup Finals were won.

When I was co-opted into the discussion—I admit feeling a little embarrassed at the time—the subject of my shooting powers was brought up, and it was decided to try to put the ball to me in the manner I could use it best, especially if we were near goal, and with this, together with other matters settled, we left the board-room, every man in the Arsenal side knowing what was expected from him, and his colleagues, when Derby County were faced the following afternoon.

"How did you feel when you took the field and found yourself surrounded by a sea of faces?" many folk have since asked me. To be quite honest I didn't notice the crowd so very much. My eyes were fixed on the opposition, and once the referee blew his whistle I didn't have time to think of anything else but the game!

We drew with Derby, 2—2, and on my début I managed to score our first goal. I shall never forget it. The ball was flashed across from the opposite wing by Pat Beasley, I allowed it to run on to my trusty left foot, and then let fly. It rocketed into the Derby net giving the goalkeeper no chance.

I kept my place in the side, and quickly learned to understand that every League match was an education for me. What artists with a ball are professional footballers! From the bankings or grandstand they may not look extraordinary chaps, but once you cross boots with them it is soon evident how talented they are when it comes to controlling a football.

When things were not going too well for Arsenal it was decided to bring back wee Alex James, now nearing the veteran stage, but still out on his own as a "master-mind" and tactician.

James was one of those rare soccer characters that come once in a generation. He had great talent, a keen sense of humour, and a human understanding that endeared him to young players, for he was always willing to give a piece of constructive advice.

Photo : Central Press

The author makes a shot through the covers. Note the full follow-through

"Well done!" Sir Pelham Warner (*left*), whom Denis describes as his cricket " Fairy Godfather ", congratulates his prodigy.

That record century—the author at Hastings 1947.

When I found that Alex James was going to partner me when we visited Charlton Athletic, my heart, once again, began to beat a little quicker. Alex, you see, had always been one of my boyhood soccer favourites. Now I was to have the benefit of his great experience!

Before we took the field at The Valley Alex James called me on one side in the dressing-room. "Sit down, Denis," he said, pointing to one of the benches, "and listen to what I have to say. You're a winger. Never forget that. Keep on the wing. If you do that things should work out quite well."

What a player was "Wee Alex!" That afternoon he "made" the Arsenal side, we won 4—2, and looking back I think he made things easier for me than any other partner I've had. A great believer in the long pass, he used this effectively, giving me the kind of ball every winger dreams about but so rarely receives. From one of his gem-like passes I cracked home a goal.

"Now you know why I want you to keep on the wing," James said to me, "for I know where you are."

Apart from his wonderful passes, Alex was constantly shouting instructions to me, and in the ninety-minutes I spent with him on the field at Charlton I probably learnt more than in nine years of schoolboy football! Yes, it was an education, in addition to a very great pleasure, to play alongside the Scottish wizard.

What a team we had in those days! It usually read something like this: Marks or Swindin; Male and Hapgood; Crayston, Bernard Joy, Copping; Kirchen, Davidson, Drake, James, and myself (at least, until I lost my form, and we're coming to that part!)

It was against Stoke City, on Boxing Day, that I had my worst-ever game. Nothing would go right for me, and when, to crown it all, I missed an open goal, and we only drew 0—0, I did not need to be intelligent to anticipate that I would be dropped. Sure enough, when the team-lists were put up in the dressing-rooms it was to find that my name was included in the reserve side. "Don't worry," said assistant-manager Joe Shaw, when he noticed me looking disappointingly at the team-sheet. "It comes to everyone. You'll be back."

But it was to be many months before I again took the field with Arsenal's League side, for Cliff Bastin moved once more on to the wing, showed all his old form, and when he did that I could not hope to even get an occasional look in.

Did I "give up the ghost"? Not on your life! I understood that the experience I was getting in the Arsenal reserve side was going to be worth a great deal to me in the years ahead. Anyway, the Arsenal reserve team in those days would most likely be among the leading sides in the First Division now. Yes, it was that good. In addition, I was able to put in a good deal of hard practice learning how to improve my ball control, shooting, and positional play.

One of my favourite methods, for dribbling, was to erect stakes at equal distances apart, and then dribble the ball round them, slowly working up speed. In due course I found that my ability in this direction had increased by fifty per cent.

As my right foot was nothing like so powerful as my left I decided that something had to be done about that as well. Some mornings, therefore, I went out wearing a rubber-soled shoe on my left foot, and an ordinary football boot on the other. By this way, hitting the ball as often as I could with my right, I was able to strengthen it a good deal.

Penalty-kicks, too, were another item I considered seriously. In every team there should be one man capable of taking them correctly. I decided that this was the job for me. It is no good, however, just walking up to the penalty-spot, cracking the ball hard, and hoping that it will go into the net. You must learn how to keep the ball low, and place it just where you want. That takes practice, I know, but it proves worth while if you study goalkeepers, notice the kind of shots they do not like, and use that type against them.

Corner-kicks were another thing I worked hard to perfect. It struck me that many wingers just lobbed the ball into the goal-mouth and hoped for the best. I reasoned that it would serve my team best if I could pick out the head of a particular player and try to "place" it so that he could nod the ball goalwards. For many hours I practised sending across low hard centres which came in about head-high, and just out of the goalkeeper's reach. Ted Drake, and my brother Leslie, I know, enjoyed this type of corner-kick, and both took full advantage of them.

Although I was now "established" in the Arsenal reserve side this did not prevent me being taken on some of the Continental trips. It was when we flew to Paris, where the Racing Club De Paris were met, that I had my first experience of travelling aboard a plane, but it was not, as it happened, when we were flying that I had one of my best laughs. Along with Ted Drake, my brother, and numerous other players, I had gone to the top of the famous Eiffel Tower. As we were aloft, and the Tower began to sway in the wind, one player, looking rather alarmed, exclaimed: "Lumme, it's going to fall over!"

We all laughed—but, if my memory serves me right, no one stayed very much longer!

23

*War is Declared so I Become a Policeman—My
Football Gains Me the England Team—The Finest
Side I've Played In—Personalities of Football—We
Meet the Barefooted Indian Stars—I Return to Play
for England In Borrowed Boots.*

THE SEPTEMBER of 1939 will never be forgotten
by my generation, for it was the month of destiny
when the Second World War began, and, like
millions of other folk all over the globe, I found the ambitions of Hitler had well and truly hit for six my personal hopes.

I was playing cricket when Hitler marched into Poland but it did not come as a surprise to me when every football club, just as did the county cricket clubs, decided to cancel all contracts, and when I returned home, in common with every other young fellow of my age, I asked myself the question: "What can I do to help finish the war quickly?"

My father left me in no doubt that I would soon be called for military service, but, while waiting for the necessary papers to reach me I joined the War Reserve Police. Yes, I became a "Copper", and thoroughly enjoyed the friendship of many "boys in blue" before being called for service.

In another chapter I have told in brief my Army experiences, and did not have any false ideas that sport would go my way in liberal doses. With a war on our hands I expected to have to work hard learning the job of being a good soldier. This was the case. Eventually, however, having satisfied those responsible that I would not go into action without knowing the correct way to defend myself, sports, as a means of helping keep me fighting fit, began once more to creep into my young life.

Whenever possible, especially when week-end leave was due, I was able to make the journey to assist Arsenal, and with Cliff Bastin getting no younger, and a general all-round shortage of players, the opportunity to establish myself in the League side went my way. This I did, finding the slower pace of war-time football, which was most noticeable, enabled me to play the kind of game it had always been my intention to try and develop. In fact, like so many other men, I was able to improve my ball play and as a result, I feel sure, proved more effective.

In that first wartime season I helped Arsenal win the League South title and found the experience among the élite of soccerdom of infinite value.

It was in 1941 that my first chance to prove myself in an England shirt was given me when we played Scotland, and on reflection I rank this moment, with my Test début in 1937, as among the most memorable in my life.

"How does playing in an international match at soccer compare with going out to bat in a Test!"

This is one of the stock questions I am often asked, and in answering it I often have to point out to my friends that they are seeking information of a type difficult to give, for at cricket you are for the most part an individual. When going on to the field at soccer you are first and foremost, a team-man.

On reflection, comparing my soccer and cricket "first-time ever" experience, I think my Test début at Kennington Oval in 1937 tested my nerve more than my initial appearance in England's wartime soccer team. It must be borne in mind, however, that I was four years older, and during those 48 months, had packed a good deal of sport experience into my life!

Wembley Stadium and Hampden Park, Glasgow, are the two major soccer stadiums in this country—but what a difference in the folk for whom they cater! Your Englishman, when he goes to an international match, is not very responsive and nationalistic, but the Scot will roar encouragement, shout like mad, sing, and, if the referee allowed him, even rush on to the field, and show his lads how he wanted a goal scored!

But on one thing these two different kinds of supporters are on common ground: their love of fair play and good football.

During the war years I had the honour to play for England in ten international matches, and might have nearly doubled this had not I been posted to serve with the Army in India, but there is one match during this period that will for ever be imprinted upon my brain.

It was when, during the 1943–44 season, we defeated Scotland, 8—0, at Maine Road, Manchester.

What grand teams were fielded on October 16, 1943, and every man, it was noticed, hailed from a service unit. The teams, as they lined up were: England: Swift (Manchester C.); Scott (Arsenal) and Hardwick (Middlesbrough); Britton (Everton), Cullis (Wolves), and Mercer (Everton); Matthews (Stoke), Carter (Sunderland), Lawton (Everton), Hagan (Sheffield United), and Compton, D. (Arsenal).

Scotland: Crozier (Brentford); Carabine (Third Lanark) and Miller (Hearts); Little (Rangers), Young (Rangers) and Campbell (Morton); Waddell (Rangers), Gillick (Everton), Linwood (St. Mirren), Walker (Hearts) and Deakin (St. Mirren).

Take a glance through the 21 names apart from my own and you will note some of the greatest personalities football has known in years. Big Frank Swift, for instance, the giant goalkeeper who can pick up a ball with one hand and toss it over the half-way line as if he were throwing a pea. Frank, who used to be a lifeboatman at Blackpool, is a great comedian, and when he shakes you by the hand . . . Well, you do at least know he is sincere.

The full-backs, George Hardwick (Middlesbrough), and my Arsenal colleague, Laurie Scott, have since been partners in many a stirring international. Hardwick, as it so happened, after this particular match was badly wounded by a flying bomb and there were some who feared he might never again play football. The handsome young man from the north-east, however, made a grand come-back and, as if for good measure, has since captained England and Great Britain.

They say a half-back line is the strength of any team. Well, we certainly had strength in Britton, Cullis and Mercer. Cliff Britton, of course, is now manager of Everton, after taking Burnley to the Cup Final in his first season in the managerial chair; Stan Cullis is manager of his old club, Wolves; Joe Mercer, still playing grandly, is skipper of my club, Arsenal.

I was the youngest member of that England team, and few players have been more fortunate in having so many grand colleagues. In the forward line that day were players I would willingly have paid money to be associated with in a game of this type! Jimmy Hagan, my partner, as it happened, was the young fellow who, during my schooldays, had played so well against me in an international trial game that I became a reserve, instead of a member of the England schoolboy team, and before we took the field in our first 'national together he and I chatted over old times.

In the middle, and ever-ready to take advantage of any centre I might send over, was the one and only Tommy Lawton. What a wonderful player is this dark-haired player from Bolton! Tom, believe it or not, can actually "steer" a ball with his head, and when you send over a "cross" you feel is worthy of a goal, it is more than likely, if it *is* any good, that Lawton will nod it into the back of the net.

What is the reason for Lawton's greatness? I should say perfect balance—as in cricket—anticipation, and above any and everything else, patient practice. No man could hope to become so talented as he without putting in a good deal of hard work.

Silver-haired, despite his youth, and looking more like a professor of music than one of the greatest inside-rights in the world, Raich Carter was the perfect partner to Stanley Matthews. Carter, who makes football look so easy—he never appears to run but glide about the field—is one of the deepest-thinking men I have ever played with or against. As he collects the ball, looks around, and then works out a plan, you can almost hear his icy-cool brain clicking. But then, to succeed for so many seasons, as he has done, a footballer must have ability above the ordinary.

Raich Carter most definitely has that!

In the past more was possibly written about Stanley Matthews than any other footballer. Without a doubt, in his quiet and unassuming manner, the Blackpool right-winger is the greatest draw in soccer to-day. It is not so much Stanley's personality that gets the crowds but the uncanny control he has over a football. Ask Matthews how he wriggles past defenders, sends a full-back running the wrong way, or diddles friend and foe with a deft flick, and he'll probably just smile and say it is one of those things. It is. Stanley Matthews happens to be one of those great footballers born once in a generation, and I feel honoured to think that I have had the opportunity to play in the same England team as he.

After all, when he is older it will be nice for me to say to my son, Brian: "Now, when I played with Stanley Matthews . . ."

What of the Scots? On paper they looked a powerful combination, and I was especially interested to see Willie Waddell in action. From my numerous Scottish colleagues and friends I had heard a good deal about "Scotland's Stanley Matthews". I was not disappointed, for Waddell is a brilliant ball-player and has, I am told, a little superstition; always prefers to have a new lace in his right boot!

At Maine Road that October afternoon, however, Willie had little chance to shine, for the England team, giving one of the greatest displays I've seen any side produce, completely swamped the Scots, running out winners by eight clear goals!

Tommy Lawton scored four goals, Jimmy Hagan a couple, and Matthews and Carter each cracked home a beauty. I was the only member of that England attack who failed to find the net, but although nothing would have pleased me more than to have scored, I was not disappointed. Team-work had been the essence of our success, and combination, I had always been taught, was the thing that wins cricket and football matches. This was the case at Maine Road in 1943.

It was in this match that Matthews did a thing that takes its place among my most cherished memories. The lean-faced young fellow from the Potteries, with fourteen minutes left for play, waltzed clean through the Scottish rearguard, took the ball right up to goalkeeper Joe Crozier, and then, as coolly as if it were a practice match, tapped the ball into the net.

Unashamedly we England players gave Stanley a "big hand". So, come to that, did several members of the Scottish team. Had I not seen such a cheeky performance, and a player having so much confidence in his own ability, I would not have believed anyone could have achieved such a feat in an international match.

Considering that Service duties did not allow us to get together for long periods before a match, the manner in which this wartime England side went about defeating all opposition was little short of amazing, but, as in the case of cricketers, the players, in odd moments, formulated plans, discussed their strong and weak points. So far as possible the side was kept intact, and by this method, and the talks we had, built up a good working knowledge of each other.

Cup Finals, League South matches, and Army representative games followed one on top of each other in a seemingly endless stream. Often the matches were held up by enemy air action, but the spirit of everyone associated with the game was never destroyed, and it is my belief that soccer, in its way, played a noble part in helping keep up public morale during those terrible years.

Early in 1944, before the end of the European War, I was posted to the Far East, and after I had been in India for some time, received a call to Delhi where the Army authorities were discussing the drawing up of two football teams to tour India and Burma. The idea was that I should captain and "manage" one of the teams—composed of Servicemen —and Tommy Walker, the famous Scottish international, now assistant-manager of Hearts, should take charge of the other.

Playing for England

One of the first things I was asked concerned the players in the area I could suggest as being worthy of a tour of this kind. I racked my brains for some time, wrote out a list—and then found that those in command had already issued instructions to the men I'd mentioned. But then, that's the Army!

Eventually, after some careful planning, two parties of fourteen players each were drawn up, I decided to tour Burma, Tommy Walker prepared to take his merry men around India, and off we moved, the idea being, at the end of the tour, both sides should meet in a big match to be staged at Madras.

The main point of this tour was to see that troops in camps and outposts in the Far East had an opportunity of watching some of their favourite soccer players from back home.

The first stage of our journey ended at Calcutta where we had an engagement against an Indian XI.

Now, do not get the impression that these Indian footballers did not know the game. As it happened they had shown extremely good form and it was essential from a prestige point of view that we did well against them. Because of the heat the kick-off was arranged for 6.30 in the evening, and, as if to suggest that luck might be with us on this occasion, it poured with rain just before the kick-off and our team felt delighted, for in India we had previously had to play on bone-hard grounds which not only interfered with our style but caused a number of minor injuries.

Our team on this occasion was: Ditchburn (Spurs); Milburn (Leeds), Trigg (Birmingham); Watson (Preston), Hayward (Blackpool), Ivor Powell (Q.P.R.); Stewart (Brentford), Compton (Arsenal), Potts (Burnley), Pearson (Manchester U.), and Ottewell (Chesterfield).

When we took the field, clad in white shirts, black shorts, and Army issue football boots, the 15,000 "Tommies" gave us a grand reception and the Indians, when they turned out, also received a big cheer. Although they did not wear boots, but just had their ankles bandaged, we all wore shin-pads. These Indians, you see, possess feet as tough as any boot, and if you collected an accidental kick from them you wouldn't have to be told about it!

That evening the Indians played well, but on this occasion they faced for the first time a team of professional footballers and from the kick-off stood but little chance against men who had made a very close study of the game, but I was pleased to hear that the soldiers who had travelled miles to see the game felt that their trouble was worth while.

We won 5—o, I scored three goals, and we all felt that this was a happy start to our tour.

By plane, train, and lorry, we footballers moved around Burma, and included in our party were the famous boxers, Freddie Mills and Al Robinson. What characters these "leather-pushers" proved to be! Apart from entertaining us with their jokes and banter, during the half-time period of our matches they used to go into the middle of the pitch and give an exhibition for the troops. How they loved the kidding of the boxers, and often when we were invited to the various officers' messes during our travels, these fistic stars showed their versatility by giving an entirely unexpected act.

I should explain that we always made it a rule that everyone gave a "turn" on an occasion such as this. Freddie Mills invariably gave us a one-man impression of the Mills Brothers; Ted Ditchburn, our goalkeeper, fancied himself as a crooner; I sang "Underneath the Arches", choosing this song because it happens to be the only one of which I am sure of the words. Our efforts, however, were nothing compared to Gracie Fields. Oh, yes, the famous Lancashire star crossed our path, in far-away Rangoon, where she sang to the service-men before our match against a Combined XI. A most gracious and kindly personality, Miss Fields did a great job of work out there in the Far East and those of us who saw her "in action", thousands of miles from the glittering lights, will never forget.

From Rangoon, by way of Pegu, we went through to Mandalay and up into the hill stations where our football team was almost as welcome as a letter from home. The height affected our breathing—we agreed that the altitude slowed us considerably—and were not altogether sorry when these fixtures "in the clouds" had been concluded.

It was during this stage of our Burma tour that I experienced one of the most exciting moments of my life, and, strange as it may seem, considering that a major part of my time is spent playing cricket or football, was in no way related to sport.

After we had concluded our last game in Mandalay all the gear was packed on to a lorry and, with me aboard to see that everything was in order and remained that way, the driver commenced the 140 miles journey to our next port of call: Meiktila. Soon after the commencement of the journey, however, misfortune went our way, for the driver was taken ill with malaria. At once I had to wrap him in blankets, make my colleague as comfortable as possible under the circumstances, take the wheel, and attempt to pick my way through the jungle, and across open country, to Meiktila.

It so happened, after the Japanese had been defeated, that there were a number of armed bands roaming the district, and, from what I had been told, they would not do me any good if we came face to face. Bearing this fact in mind, I put my foot down hard on the accelerator, made that lorry produce a turn of speed that would not have delighted our C.O., and as a result, reached my destination safely and in double-quick time. As we sped through the jungle, however, I often thought I saw strange things moving in the shadows; sometimes imagined that the "enemy" was hot on my tail. On reflection, however, I think it would have needed John Cobb to have caught me that day!

And so our tour went on until we arrived back in Calcutta, very tired, but for all that delighted at having been able to bring some cheer to the "Tommies" far away from the normal everyday enjoyments of life that we so often take for granted at home.

Earlier, you may recall, when the tour had been arranged,

it was decided that the teams captained by Tommy Walker and myself should meet in Madras after the round-trip had been completed, but, because of cricket calls, I was unable to go on with my team, but the match, which took place before a very excited crowd, ended in a draw.

And so concluded one of the strangest soccer tours I have ever experienced, but a tour, for all that, which did a great deal of good and, as I've said before, brought a little enjoyment to men who really did deserve something special.

It was in the February of 1946 that I arrived back in England. It was snowing hard at the time. Within a short time I was suffering from a bad cold, and on numerous occasions wished I was back in the warm sun that was one of the few delights, so far as I was concerned, in the Far East.

When I began to play football for Arsenal, however, these drawbacks in England were quickly forgotten, and although it was a much weightier and somewhat slower Denis Compton than had left these shores over two years before, some of the sports writers, after a few games, began to suggest that I might once again get a place in the England team to meet Scotland at Hampden Park, Glasgow, the following April.

Now I will let you into a secret. When I returned to England there were no football boots available for me. Apparently my foot had grown slightly, those in use before I went overseas were now beyond repair, and I wondered where I was going to get another size "9's". It was the son of Billy Milne, the Arsenal trainer, who had been only a nipper when last I saw him, who came to the "rescue". He loaned me a pair he wore in junior matches, they were comfortable, and good-naturedly he suggested I kept them.

Well, although I say this with modesty, I quickly settled down to English soccer again and when the international trial match was arranged for Wembley Stadium—it was an Army P.T. XI *v.* an F.A. XI—I was delighted to find that my name had been included in the Army attack. Among my front-line colleagues that day were Jimmy Hagan, Tommy Lawton, Don Welsh and George Wardle, all old friends of mine, and in that match those fellows did everything possible to help bring me into the game.

A special word, I feel, is due to the unselfishness of both Jimmy Hagan and Tommy Lawton. Some of the passes they sent out to me were of the copy-book variety; no player could but help do moderately well with such service. Apparently I must have satisfied the assembled selectors, for shortly after their meeting at half-time they announced the team to meet Scotland in the Victory International and to my delight I heard that I was included.

Believe it or not, as the news was released to the press while the second half of the game was in progress millions of people all over the country knew the Englishmen who were to appear in the game of the year even before the players themselves.

It was on April 13 that 138,000 excited soccer fans, a large percentage of them Scots, thronged into the mighty Hampden Park arena to see the great match. In the past Scotland had experienced several setbacks, and even the most ardent Scot was not keen to make a forecast, but for this game the home side had put in a course of special training at Aberfoyle which suggested they meant to produce something out of the ordinary.

As we neared Hampden Park the crowds welled around our coach; words of warning, and here and there a friendly cheer, came our way. Then, when outside the ground, a pipe band marched past us playing "Scotland The Brave". I may be wrong, but as that band strode by I'm willing to wager that the pipers blew a little harder; the drummers most certainly cracked their drums with more vim. In fact, if anything it occurred to me that they were telling us this game was going to be anything but a push-over.

In our dressing-room, despite the noise outside, everyone was extremely cool, and Joe Mercer, our captain, walked around giving the lads full benefit of his experience and ideal temperament.

"Well, fellows," said Joe, just before we were due to go out, "it's up to us to give of our best. I know you will."

Playing for England

Within a minute we were walking out with the Scottish side. After the usual formalities, during which we were introduced to several celebrities, the two teams lined up as follows:

Scotland: Brown (Queen's Park); Shaw, D. (Hibs.), Shaw, J. (Rangers) capt.; Campbell (Morton), Brennan (Airdrie), and Husband (Partick); Waddell (Rangers), Dougal (Birmingham C.), Delaney (Manchester U.), Hamilton (Aberdeen) and Liddell (Liverpool).

England: Swift (Manchester C.); Scott (Arsenal) and Hardwick (Middlesbrough); Wright (Wolves), Franklin (Stoke) and Mercer (Everton) capt.; Elliott (West Bromwich), Shackleton (Bradford), Lawton (Chelsea), Hagan (Sheffield U.) and Compton D. (Arsenal).

Referee: Mr. Peter Craigmyle (Aberdeen).

As Stanley Matthews was injured, Billy Elliott of West Bromwich Albion acted as deputy, while his partner, Len Shackleton, like myself, had once been a ground-boy at Arsenal Stadium. The rest of the side, however, was well-known to me, for we had either played with or against each other in various types of representative games. Personally, to have Jimmy Hagan by my side again, was wonderful. It seemed, when we began to find each other with the ball, that my months abroad had been nothing more than a dream. The Scots, however, had a most stubborn defence with the brothers Shaw at full-back, and a young fellow named Frank Brennan, who hailed from the same mining village, at centre-half. Brennan, who was celebrating his twenty-second birthday, and was a late substitute, played a most inspired game, and hard as Tommy Lawton struggled at centre-forward, "Big Frank" gave him little scope to show his wonderful skill. Three times, however, Tommy made the ball crack the woodwork, but luck, it seemed was against him. Once, too, following a run down the wing I was able to get across a centre which Tom, leaping like a stag into the air, managed to nod goalwards. To his chagrin it missed by inches. Meanwhile, in falling, I had broken one of the corner flags at the base—and before I quite knew what had happened one enthusiastic fan had run on to the field, grabbed the flag, and was swallowed up into the crowd before anyone could stop him!

Back and forth the play moved, neither side gave anything away. To hold on to the ball for any length of time courted trouble. The Scots, in fact, on their toes from the kick-off, played better than ever before since I had first appeared against them.

With but two minutes to go before final whistle, one of those things happened that can completely change the course of a game. At least, it did on this occasion. An England player was adjudged by Referee Craigmyle to have fouled a Scot near the corner-flag and Jackie Husband, Scotland's left-half, taking care to place the ball to his liking, then carefully lobbed it into our goalmouth.

There was a mighty roar that made the ground tremble beneath our feet as Frank Swift, our goalkeeper, and Willie Waddell, the Scottish right-winger, rose in the air together. Waddell reached the ball first, nodded it down to the feet of Jimmy Delaney, and Scotland's centre-forward, without hesitation, rammed it hard into the England net.

For two seconds there was silence—then the crowd let out a roar that might well have been heard in London! As for wee Delaney, he was lost to view, smothered by the congratulations of his colleagues.

Eventually both teams lined up once more, although the roar of the crowd had not subsided, Tommy Lawton kicked off, the referee glanced at his watch, pulled up dead, blew his whistle, and pointed to the centre of the field.

Scotland had won—and deservedly so—one of the most thrilling games in which I have ever taken part, and, even if for only a time, I had played my last game in England's soccer team, for cricket's call was just around the calendar, that match will for ever remain among my most memorable memories.

But then, I think that applies to the 138,000 folk fortunate enough to witness this, the last of the Victory Internationals.

24

I've Never Regretted a Sporting Life

IF EVER I had my life over again, and were faced with the same problems as when I left school, I'd without hesitation choose a sporting career. Maybe that is because fortune has been with me for a greater part of my life, but I have yet to meet any footballer or cricketer who really regretted making it their job.

The great thing in sport, amateur or professional, is to go into your game with a determination to enjoy it. I think it can safely be said that the majority of men whom I have played with, or against, have adopted this outlook. More than anything else, I have made it a rule to play the game in the best spirit.

If you cannot take a defeat, or setback, there is no place for you in sport.

As a means of "education" too, sport has provided me with endless opportunities of seeing, first of all, various parts of Britain. It has—in some instances allied with soldiering—taken me to India, Burma, Australia, New Zealand, South Africa, Belgium and France. Maybe, before I hang up my football boots for the last time, and hand over my cricket bat to son Brian, I shall have further travels beneath my "belt".

I have also found that sport is a great thing for giving a youngster self-confidence, but at the same time appreciate the true value of working together because of the part team-spirit plays in various games.

In short, apart from the enjoyment it brings to players and spectators, sport, I have always felt, has a moral uplift about it that is not always appreciated.

When I find time to sit back in my armchair and relax,

many pleasant thoughts come back to me of the various folk who have given me a helping hand along the road I hoped would lead to success.

Sir Pelham Warner, that great gentleman of cricket, will for ever hold a warm place in my heart. As I told early in this book, it was Sir Pelham who, when Denis Compton was thirteen years old, went out of his way to see that the boy had an opportunity to learn the business of being a cricketer. To Sir Pelham I was not just a passing interest; from the day I made my first appearance for an M.C.C. team, until I scored the seventeenth hundred last season that passed Jack Hobbs' record, Sir Pelham has either been on the spot to shake my hand if I did well, or send a telegram if business kept him away from his beloved cricket.

Like many other outstanding cricket personalities, Sir Pelham Warner has proved a great friend; as a student of cricket, too, I have learnt a great deal by heeding his words of advice. But then, from the day I began as a ground-boy at Lord's, I have never shut my ears to any advice that might have been given me, for you can always learn in sport, especially if the sport happens to be cricket.

In the ordinary daily life of a cricketer no one helped me more than Archie Fowler, our coach at Lord's. Archie is one of those men you often hear described as a "character". He believes in doing things the way he thinks best, and after many years of study under him, I am convinced he is right.

Certain am I that the hours of patience he exercised in coaching me have played a major part in helping me play cricket in the manner I always hoped would be possible.

Archie Fowler, too, in "taking me over" as a young cricketer, did something that I shall always deeply appreciate. He did not attempt to interfere with my natural style: he appreciated that providing I was able to make runs, even with strokes that might not be of the copy-book variety, it was not to my advantage for them to be "banned".

Playing for England

Mr. R. W. V. Robins and Mr. G. O. Allen, are two other gentlemen to whom I owe a great deal. Each, in his way, has guided me carefully along what I now appreciate was the right cricketing road, and in general made it his business to see that I avoided the pitfalls that might have gone the way of a youth who did not have their ever-helping hand.

There are others, too, among the cricketing fraternity to whom I owe a great debt. I hope they will take this "Thank you" as specially for them.

What of football?

Any young chap who has worked under the late Herbert Chapman, manager of Arsenal F.C., can look back and say: "What a fortunate fellow I was to have the interest of such a man." Mr. Chapman, it may be recalled, saw me as a promising footballer when I was only thirteen years old, and because he offered me a job on the Arsenal Stadium ground-staff my parents, when the Lord's appointment went my way, did not step in and say "No!" because the two jobs between them offered full-time employment.

I often wonder, though, what might have happened had I not taken that Lord's job. . . .

Seriously, friends in business—and sport *is* my business —can play a very important part in helping you to success or otherwise, and I have been most fortunate in this direction. In the cricket sphere I have mentioned several of those who have been close by my side since I left school. At football, Tom Whittaker, Arsenal's great secretary-manager, who has been almost a father to me, kindly Joe Shaw, his assistant, the ever-youthful Alex James, Sir Stanley Rous, F.A. secretary, and, of course, my brother, Leslie, have all done everything possible to assist me.

To them all I say "Thank you" most sincerely, and if I again had to make the decision whether or not to make my career in sport, I still insist I'd say "Yes".

Cricket-and-football, you see, is not only my business but my life. . . .

INDEX

Index

Index

Index

Index

238

Index